TABLE OF

ILLUSTRATION CREDITS

ACKNOWLEDGEMENTS

The publisher and the author would like to thank the many authors of former Lone Pine texts who have created such a great library of background information. Special thanks to Lisa Priestley and Patsy Cotterill for their suggestions for the Alberta species lists. And a heartfelt thanks to illustrator Frank Burman, editor Nicholle Carrière and the Lone Pine production staff for their patience, dedication and attention to detail.

burrowing owl

MAMMALS

Bison
p. 50

Mountain Goat
p. 50

Bighorn Sheep
p. 51

North American Elk
p. 51

White-tailed Deer
p. 52

Mule Deer
p. 52

Moose
p. 53

Woodland Caribou
p. 53

Pronghorn
p. 54

Cougar
p. 54

Canada Lynx
p. 55

Bobcat
p. 55

Striped Skunk
p. 56

American Marten
p. 56

Fisher
p. 56

Least Weasel
p. 57

Short-tailed Weasel
p. 57

Long-tailed Weasel
p. 57

Mink
p. 58

Black-footed Ferret
p. 58

Wolverine
p. 58

Badger
p. 59

Northern River Otter
p. 59

Raccoon
p. 59

Black Bear
p. 60

Grizzly Bear
p. 60

Coyote
p. 61

Grey Wolf
p. 61

Arctic Fox
p. 62

Swift Fox
p. 62

Red Fox
p. 63

Porcupine
p. 63

Beaver
p. 64

Muskrat
p. 64

Meadow Jumping Mouse
p. 65

House Mouse
p. 65

Deer Mouse
p. 65

Bushy-tailed Woodrat
p. 66

Southern Red-backed Vole
p. 66

Meadow Vole
p. 66

Northern Bog Lemming
p. 67

Ord's Kangaroo Rat
p. 67

Olive-backed Pocket Mouse
p. 67

Northern Pocket Gopher
p. 68

Woodchuck
p. 68

MAMMALS

Hoary Marmot
p. 68

Yellow-bellied Marmot
p. 69

Columbian Ground Squirrel
p. 69

Thirteen-lined Ground Squirrel
p. 69

Richardson's Ground Squirrel
p. 70

Golden-mantled Ground Squirrel
p. 70

Least Chipmunk
p. 70

Red Squirrel
p. 71

Northern Flying Squirrel
p. 71

Pika
p. 71

Snowshoe Hare
p. 72

White-tailed Jackrabbit
p. 72

Nuttall's Cottontail
p. 72

Northern Bat
p. 73

Long-eared Bat
p. 73

Little Brown Bat
p. 73

Hoary Bat
p. 74

Silver-haired Bat
p. 74

Big Brown Bat
p. 74

Masked Shrew
p. 75

Northern Water Shrew
p. 75

Pygmy Shrew
p. 75

Snow Goose
p. 78

Canada Goose
p. 78

Tundra Swan
p. 78

American Wigeon
p. 79

Mallard
p. 79

Blue-winged Teal
p. 79

Northern Shoveler
p. 80

Northern Pintail
p. 80

Lesser Scaup
p. 80

Common Goldeneye
p. 81

Common Merganser
p. 81

Ruddy Duck
p. 81

Gray Partridge
p. 82

Ring-necked Pheasant
p. 82

Ruffed Grouse
p. 82

Spruce Grouse
p. 83

Wild Turkey
p. 83

Common Loon
p. 83

Red-necked Grebe
p. 84

American White Pelican
p. 84

BIRDS

Double-crested Cormorant
p. 84

American Bittern
p. 85

Great Blue Heron
p. 85

Turkey Vulture
p. 85

Bald Eagle
p. 86

Northern Harrier
p. 86

Swainson's Hawk
p. 86

Red-tailed Hawk
p. 87

Rough-legged Hawk
p. 87

American Kestrel
p. 87

Merlin
p. 88

Peregrine Falcon
p. 88

Sora
p. 88

American Coot
p. 89

Sandhill Crane
p. 89

Killdeer
p. 89

Spotted Sandpiper
p. 90

Lesser Yellowlegs
p. 90

Marbled Godwit
p. 90

Wilson's Snipe
p. 91

Wilson's Phalarope
p. 91

Franklin's Gull
p. 91

Ring-billed Gull
p. 92

Black Tern
p. 92

Common Tern
p. 92

Rock Pigeon
p. 93

Mourning Dove
p. 93

Great Horned Owl
p. 93

Snowy Owl
p. 94

Burrowing Owl
p. 94

Great Gray Owl
p. 94

Short-eared Owl
p. 95

Northern Saw-whet Owl
p. 95

Common Nighthawk
p. 95

Ruby-throated Hummingbird
p. 96

Rufous Hummingbird
p. 96

Belted Kingfisher
p. 96

11

BIRDS

Yellow-bellied Sapsucker
p. 97

Downy Woodpecker
p. 97

Northern Flicker
p. 97

Pileated Woodpecker
p. 98

Least Flycatcher
p. 98

Eastern Phoebe
p. 98

Eastern Kingbird
p. 99

Northern Shrike
p. 99

Red-eyed Vireo
p. 99

Gray Jay
p. 100

Blue Jay
p. 100

Black-billed Magpie
p. 100

Common Raven
p. 101

Horned Lark
p. 101

Tree Swallow
p. 101

Barn Swallow
p. 102

Black-capped Chickadee
p. 102

Red-breasted Nuthatch
p. 102

House Wren
p. 103

Ruby-crowned Kinglet
p. 103

Mountain Bluebird
p. 103

American Robin
p. 104

Varied Thrush
p. 104

Gray Catbird
p. 104

Brown Thrasher
p. 105

European Starling
p. 105

Bohemian Waxwing
p. 105

Yellow Warbler
p. 106

Yellow-rumped Warbler
p. 106

American Redstart
p. 106

Common Yellowthroat
p. 107

Chipping Sparrow
p. 107

Savannah Sparrow
p. 107

Song Sparrow
p. 108

White-throated Sparrow
p. 108

Dark-eyed Junco
p. 108

Western Tanager
p. 109

Rose-breasted Grosbeak
p. 109

Red-winged Blackbird
p. 109

Western Meadowlark
p. 110

Yellow-headed Blackbird
p. 110

Brown-headed Cowbird
p. 110

Baltimore Oriole
p. 111

Pine Grosbeak
p. 111

House Finch
p. 111

Common Redpoll
p. 112

American Goldfinch
p. 112

House Sparrow
p. 112

13

AMPHIBIANS & REPTILES

Tiger Salamander
p. 114

Long-toed Salamander
p. 114

Plains Spadefoot Toad
p. 114

Western Toad
p. 115

Canadian Toad
p. 115

Great Plains Toad
p. 115

Boreal Chorus Frog
p. 116

Spotted Frog
p. 116

Northern Leopard Frog
p. 116

Wood Frog
p. 117

Western Painted Turtle
p. 117

Short-horned Lizard
p. 117

Western Hog-nosed Snake
p. 118

Bullsnake
p. 118

Wandering Gartersnake
p. 118

Plains Gartersnake
p. 119

Red-sided Gartersnake
p. 119

Prairie Rattlesnake
p. 119

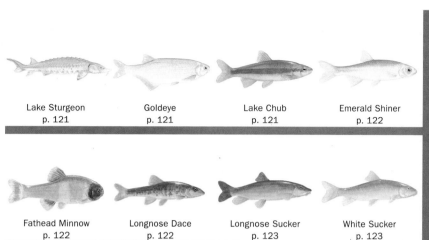

Lake Sturgeon	Goldeye	Lake Chub	Emerald Shiner
p. 121	p. 121	p. 121	p. 122

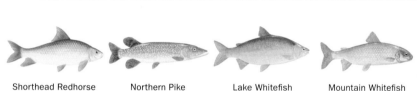

Fathead Minnow	Longnose Dace	Longnose Sucker	White Sucker
p. 122	p. 122	p. 123	p. 123

Shorthead Redhorse	Northern Pike	Lake Whitefish	Mountain Whitefish
p. 123	p. 124	p. 124	p. 124

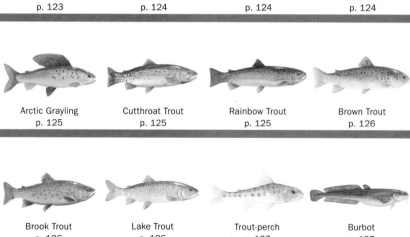

Arctic Grayling	Cutthroat Trout	Rainbow Trout	Brown Trout
p. 125	p. 125	p. 125	p. 126

Brook Trout	Lake Trout	Trout-perch	Burbot
p. 126	p. 126	p. 127	p. 127

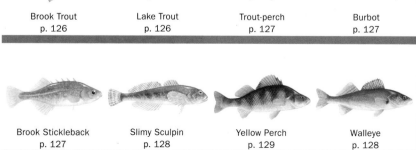

Brook Stickleback	Slimy Sculpin	Yellow Perch	Walleye
p. 127	p. 128	p. 129	p. 128

INVERTEBRATES

Cabbage White
p. 130

Canadian Tiger Swallowtail
p. 130

Spring Azure
p. 130

Mourning Cloak
p. 131

Monarch
p. 131

Polyphemus Moth
p. 131

Woolly Bear Caterpillar
p. 132

Two-spot Ladybug
p. 132

Spruce Sawyer
p. 132

Carpenter Ant
p. 133

Bumblebee
p. 133

Yellow Jacket
p. 133

Giant Crane Fly
p. 134

Green Lacewing
p. 134

Stinkbug
p. 134

Road Duster Grasshopper
p. 135

Variable Darner
p. 135

Cherry-faced Meadowhawk
p. 135

INVERTEBRATES

Water Strider
p. 136

Giant Diving Beetle
p. 136

Caddisfly Larvae
p. 136

Orbweaver
p. 137

Harvestman
p. 137

Garden Centipede
p. 137

TREES

Subalpine Fir
p. 141

Balsam Fir
p. 141

White Spruce
p. 142

Black Spruce
p. 142

Engelmann Spruce
p. 143

Tamarack
p. 143

Jack Pine
p. 144

Lodgepole Pine
p. 144

Limber Pine
p. 145

Whitebark Pine
p. 145

Paper Birch
p. 146

Water Birch
p. 146

Speckled Alder
p. 147

Trembling Aspen
p. 147

REFERENCE GUIDE

TREES

Western Cottonwood
p. 148

Balsam Poplar
p. 148

Manitoba Maple
p. 149

SHRUBS & VINES

Common Juniper
p. 151

Creeping Juniper
p. 151

Crowberry
p. 151

Dwarf Birch
p. 152

Beaked Hazelnut
p. 152

Sweet Gale
p. 152

Bebb's Willow
p. 153

Red-osier Dogwood
p. 153

Pin Cherry
p. 153

Chokecherry
p. 154

Western Mountain-ash
p. 154

Round-leaved Hawthorn
p. 154

Saskatoon
p. 155

Wild Red Raspberry
p. 155

Prickly Wild Rose
p. 155

Prairie Rose
p. 156

White Mountain-avens
p. 156

Shrubby Cinquefoil
p. 156

Narrow-leaved Meadowsweet
p. 157

Wild Black Currant
p. 157

Skunk Currant
p. 157

Wild Gooseberry
p. 158

Wild Red Currant
p. 158

Canada Buffaloberry
p. 158

Wolf Willow, Silverberry
p. 159

Silver Sagebrush
p. 159

Greasewood
p. 159

Pink Mountain-heather
p. 160

White Mountain-heather
p. 160

Labrador Tea
p. 160

Bearberry, Kinnikinnick
p. 161

Velvetleaf Blueberry
p. 161

Bog Cranberry
p. 161

Leatherleaf
p. 162

Bog Rosemary
p. 162

Common Snowberry
p. 162

Buckbrush
p. 163

Highbush Cranberry
p. 163

Twining Honeysuckle
p. 163

Bracted Honeysuckle
p. 164

Purple Clematis
p. 164

Caragana
p. 164

FORBS, FERNS & GRASSES

Water Arum
p. 168

Western Wood Lily
p. 168

Wild Lily-of-the-Valley
p. 168

Star-flowered Solomon's-seal
p. 169

Prairie Onion
p. 169

White Death-camas
p. 169

Common Blue-eyed Grass
p. 170

Yellow Lady's-slipper
p. 170

Rattlesnake-plantain
p. 170

Northern Green Orchid
p. 171

Stinging Nettle
p. 171

Bastard Toadflax
p. 171

Yellow Umbrellaplant
p. 172

Western Dock
p. 172

Water Smartweed
p. 172

Strawberry Blite
p. 173

Sea-blite
p. 173

Field Chickweed
p. 173

Yellow Pond-lily
p. 174

Prairie Crocus
p. 174

Canada Anemone
p. 174

Marsh-marigold
p. 175

Red and White Baneberry
p. 175

Blue Columbine
p. 175

Veiny Meadowrue
p. 176

Meadow Buttercup
p. 176

White Water Crowfoot
p. 176

White Globe-flower
p. 177

Wormseed Mustard
p. 177

Marsh Yellow Cress
p. 177

Round-leaved Sundew
p. 178

Pitcher-plant
p. 178

Lance-leaved Stonecrop
p. 178

Marsh Grass-of-Parnassus
p. 179

Bishop's-cap
p. 179

Purple Saxifrage
p. 179

Spotted Saxifrage
p. 180

Common Wild Strawberry
p. 180

Three-flowered Avens
p. 180

Common Silverweed
p. 181

Ground-plum
p. 181

Purple Prairie-clover
p. 181

Alfalfa
p. 182

Yellow Sweet-clover
p. 182

Showy Locoweed
p. 182

FORBS, FERNS & GRASSES

Early Yellow Locoweed
p. 183

Wild Licorice
p. 183

Golden-bean
p. 183

American Vetch
p. 184

Alsike Clover
p. 184

Northern Crane's-bill
p. 184

Sticky Purple Geranium
p. 185

Wild Blue Flax
p. 185

Spotted Touch-me-not
p. 185

Scarlet Globemallow
p. 186

Early Blue Violet
p. 186

Canada Violet
p. 186

Prickly-pear Cactus
p. 187

Common Fireweed
p. 187

Scarlet Butterfly-weed
p. 187

Common Evening-primrose
p. 188

Wild Sarsaparilla
p. 188

Spotted Water-hemlock
p. 188

Common Cow-parsnip
p. 189

Common Pink Wintergreen
p. 189

Bunchberry
p. 189

Saline Shootingstar
p. 190

Fringed Loosestrife
p. 190

Sweet-flowered Androsace
p. 190

FORBS, FERNS & GRASSES

Felwort
p. 191

Buck-bean
p. 191

Spreading Dogbane
p. 191

Showy Milkweed
p. 192

Tall Jacob's-ladder
p. 192

Alpine Forget-me-not
p. 192

Narrow-leaved Puccoon
p. 193

Tall Lungwort
p. 193

Blue Giant-hyssop
p. 193

Wild Mint
p. 194

Wild Bergamot
p. 194

Common Red Paintbrush
p. 194

Butter-and-eggs
p. 195

Bracted Lousewort
p. 195

Twinflower
p. 195

Common Bladderwort
p. 196

Northern Bedstraw
p. 196

Harebell
p. 196

Common Yarrow
p. 197

Pussytoes, Everlasting
p. 197

Heart-leaved Arnica
p. 197

Canada Thistle
p. 198

Subalpine Fleabane
p. 198

Great Blanketflower
p. 198

FORBS, FERNS & GRASSES

Curly-cup Gumweed
p. 199

Rhombic-leaved Sunflower
p. 199

Narrow-leaved Hawkweed
p. 199

Common Blue Lettuce
p. 200

Oxeye Daisy
p. 200

Pineapple-weed
p. 200

Arrow-leaved Coltsfoot
p. 201

Prairie Coneflower
p. 201

Marsh Ragwort
p. 201

Canada Goldenrod
p. 202

Perennial Sow-thistle
p. 202

Lindley's Aster
p. 202

Common Dandelion
p. 203

Common Goat's-beard
p. 203

Ostrich Fern
p. 203

Common Horsetail
p. 204

Common Cattail
p. 204

Marsh Reedgrass, Bluejoint
p. 204

Foxtail Barley
p. 205

Wire Rush
p. 205

Water Sedge
p. 205

INTRODUCTION

Alberta is one of the most biologically diverse provinces in Canada. Encompassing an area of more than 660,000 km², it is Canada's fourth-largest province and exhibits dramatic variation in landscape. Snow-capped mountains, expansive boreal forest and associated lakes, central parklands and vast expanses of arid grasslands all contribute to our province's scenic beauty and ecological uniqueness.

monarch

Alberta's ecosystems are internationally significant, linking the province to the rest of the world. The headwaters of most of our major rivers begin in the Rocky Mountains and flow for thousands of kilometres, emptying into the Arctic Ocean, Hudson Bay or the Gulf of Mexico. Many of Alberta's wildlife species regularly travel across provincial and international borders. Migratory birds are perhaps the best known, but bats, monarch butterflies and dragonflies also migrate south of the border. Alberta is an important link in the Yellowstone to Yukon Conservation Initiative (Y2Y), one of the world's leading mountain conservation projects, which seeks to preserve and maintain a connected wilderness region. The Y2Y mountain corridor allows wide-ranging animals such as wolves and bears to travel safely between protected areas.

In addition to diverse wildlife, thousands of native plant species paint Alberta habitats in showy palettes of every hue and include some very rare and local species to excite botanists. The diverse plant communities in turn provide the vegetative bedrock that supports myriad insect species, which then provide fodder for higher animals.

Scenery in Alberta is always interesting, often awesome and never disappointing. Whether it is a white mountain goat framed by a turquoise lake, a delicate pink prairie rose or a rattlesnake camouflaged in the sage flats, a visit to Alberta is always memorable.

This guide provides an overview to the incredible diversity of the province, but it is just a beginning. Although it would take many volumes to do justice to the thousands of animals and plants that occur in Alberta, we hope this book helps you to discover the rich natural history of our province.

prairie rattlesnake

ECOREGIONS

Alberta harbours biodiversity on a grand scale, and a nature enthusiast could spend a lifetime exploring its varied habitats. The diversity of flora and fauna is fantastic. Several thousand native plant species occur in the province and form the habitats that support rich animal life. Alberta is home to 85 native mammals, from the hefty bison to the tiny pygmy shrew. Almost

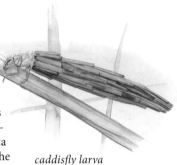

caddisfly larva

400 species of birds overwinter, breed, migrate through or have occurred here at least on rare occasions. Lakes and rivers draw thousands of anglers. In total, 51 native and 14 introduced species of fishes are found in Alberta drainages, ranging from the ancient lake sturgeon to tiny minnows. Insects? There are many thousands of species, including 75 different species of ladybugs! Some insects can't be missed, such as the beautiful swallowtail butterfly. Others, such as the caddisfly larva, are intriguing but easily overlooked, but all have their place in Alberta's ecology.

woodland caribou

Although many animals and plants, such as the ones featured in this guide, are easily observed, others are far rarer. There are several globally significant habitats in Alberta, and they are home to equally significant animals and plants. Examples of federally endangered or threatened species include the Ord's kangaroo rat of the southern sandhills, the woodland caribou of the old-growth coniferous forests, the bull trout found in the East Slope streams of the Rockies and the western blue flag of southern Alberta.

Alberta is commonly divided into six natural regions or ecoregions—Rocky Mountains, Foothills, Boreal Forest, Parkland, Grassland and Canadian Shield. Looking at these natural regions in detail can lead to a better understanding of Alberta's mammals and how they live and interact with each other.

Ord's kangaroo rat

limber pine

Rocky Mountains

Unsurpassed in their magnificence, the Rocky Mountains make up the most rugged natural region in Alberta. Major glaciation events recently carved the Rockies into deep, U-shaped valleys and jagged, steep slopes. Sinuous rivers line the valley bottoms, and sapphire lakes dot the gullies between the rugged peaks.

The Rockies occupy about eight percent of the province. They were thrust upward about 140 to 145 million years ago and are young compared to the world's other mountain ranges. Two major mountain series occur in the province: the easterly Front Ranges and the westerly Main Ranges (shared with British Columbia). Both ranges are composed of thrust-faulted sedimentary rock underlain by folded bedrock.

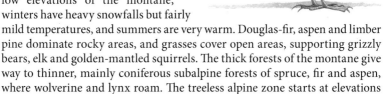

The Rocky Mountains ecoregion is divided into three subregions—montane, subalpine and alpine—whose boundaries primarily reflect differences in climate that are linked to changes in elevation. At the low elevations of the montane, winters have heavy snowfalls but fairly

horned lark

mild temperatures, and summers are very warm. Douglas-fir, aspen and limber pine dominate rocky areas, and grasses cover open areas, supporting grizzly bears, elk and golden-mantled squirrels. The thick forests of the montane give way to thinner, mainly coniferous subalpine forests of spruce, fir and aspen, where wolverine and lynx roam. The treeless alpine zone starts at elevations of about 2000 to 2300 metres and is dominated by hardy, ground-hugging plants such as crowberry and purple saxifrage. Animals include the mountain goat, hoary marmot, horned lark and pika.

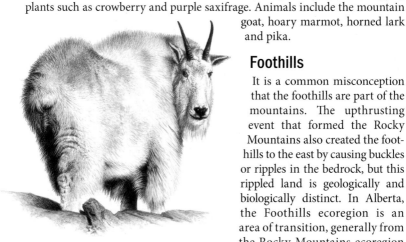

Foothills

It is a common misconception that the foothills are part of the mountains. The upthrusting event that formed the Rocky Mountains also created the foot-hills to the east by causing buckles or ripples in the bedrock, but this rippled land is geologically and biologically distinct. In Alberta, the Foothills ecoregion is an area of transition, generally from the Rocky Mountains ecoregion

mountain goat

to the Boreal Forest natural region. In a few small areas in southwestern Alberta, however, the Foothills ecoregion links the Rocky Mountains to the Parkland.

In this landscape of rolling hills and long ridges, small streams meander through valley bottoms of dwarf birch, willows and grasses, and the hills are cloaked in mixedwood forests of spruce, birch and aspen. Fens and bogs occur in some parts of the region. The climate of the Foothills region is quite mild, being generally cooler than the Boreal Forest in summer and warmer in winter.

long-eared bat

Numerous animals inhabit the Foothills region, including American mink, grey wolves, black bears, cougars, deer, grouse, long-eared bats, rufous hummingbirds and pine grosbeaks. The foothills include many fast-flowing streams and cold, clear lakes that are home to lake and bull trout. Amphibians include western toads and wood frogs.

western toad

Boreal Forest

The expansive Boreal Forest ecoregion is a broad, circumpolar belt that circles the earth, and it also forms the largest natural region in Alberta, covering almost half the province. Its underlying geology is very similar to that of the prairies—a rolling landscape covered in glacial till—but the Boreal Forest region has more rainfall, longer winters and less intense summer heat. As a result, the

yellow-rumped warbler

land is covered in thick forests and muskegs, bogs and fens. Coniferous trees, mainly pine, spruce and tamarack, dominate this northern forest. Broadleaf trees, such as aspen, become increasingly common toward the south of the region. This natural area is important both climatically and biologically; the nutrient cycling and gas exchange of the boreal forest have far-reaching effects, not only in Alberta, but around the globe.

moose

Great rivers, such as the Peace and the Athabasca, have carved routes through this land, carrying water from the Rocky Mountains to the Arctic Ocean. Many of Alberta's boreal lakes are shallow and algae-covered; creeks are often slow moving and muddy. Fish such as lake whitefish and white suckers are adapted to low oxygen levels, heavy silt and large fluctuations in water temperature. Walleye, northern pike and Arctic grayling provide great sport fishing opportunities.

Scattered throughout and becoming more frequent in northern reaches of Alberta's boreal forest are bogs and fens. These wetlands are botanical treasure troves, filled with odd and often rare plants such as orchids or the carnivorous round-leaved sundew. Bogs tend to be dormant with regard to water movement, acidic and dominated by *Sphagnum* mosses and plants in the heath family (Ericaceae). Fens are fed by artesian springs, have an alkaline substrate and are dominated by sedges and other plants specialized for these harsh growing conditions.

round-leaved sundew

lodgepole pine

No other natural area defines Canada as well as the Boreal Forest ecoregion, and many the animals that live there have inspired our country's defining images. This northern forest is home to Canada lynx, grey wolves, black bears, moose, caribou, northern flying and red squirrels, owls, woodpeckers, flycatchers, gray jays and a myriad of wood-warblers, to name just a few.

northern flying squirrel

Parkland

Alberta's aspen parkland is a patchy mosaic of deciduous forests, ponds, marshes, prairies and brushy grasslands. Comprising about 12 percent of the province, the Parkland ecoregion is primarily a transition between the colder coniferous forests of the northern and upland regions and the drier grasslands of the plains. Geologically, the rolling terrain and hummocky landscape are the result of post-glacial deposits. The Parkland ecoregion's mild, moist climate

tiger salamander

29

and its extremely rich, black soil support deciduous forests and extensive wetlands with bounteous vegetation and high biological diversity. Aspen trees dominate, mixed with willows and balsam poplar. Large, shallow lakes support northern pike, burbot and suckers. Several reptile and amphibian species are found in the Parkland ecoregion, including red-sided gartersnakes, tiger salamanders and several kinds of frogs and toads.

northern saw-whet owl

Only isolated pockets of natural parkland vegetation remain in this region; humans have altered the rest into a patchwork of croplands and pastures. The wildlife of this region has, in some cases, adapted to the human alterations. Common mammals of the Parkland ecoregion include coyotes, northern pocket gophers, porcupines, weasels, ground squirrels and red foxes. Common birds include red-tailed hawks, northern saw-whet owls, ruffed grouse, ruby-throated hummingbirds, woodpeckers, swallows, yellow warblers and sparrows.

trembling aspen

burbot

Grassland

No one who has walked Alberta's grasslands would describe them as flat; rather, the landscape is a series of gently rolling, shallow hills set in a sea of grass. A few major rivers, destined for either the Hudson Bay or the Gulf of Mexico, cut through the Grassland ecoregion, sometimes carving deep valleys and creating the haunting beauty of the badlands. In some areas, large cottonwood trees line the rivers, providing a ribbon of shelter for deer, bats, fish and birds such as mourning doves and common nighthawks. Slow-moving rivers, warm pothole lakes and irrigation canals are home to small fishes, painted turtles and a variety of amphibians.

The Grassland ecoregion is well suited for field crops, and more than 80 percent of the native grasslands have been converted to agriculture. Many of the mammals that historically

pronghorn

roamed this landscape, such as bison, wolves and grizzly bears, no longer occur on Alberta's grasslands. Because of habitat loss or degradation, more than half the animals on Canada's endangered species list are grassland species, including the burrowing owl, swift fox and Ord's kangaroo rat.

prickly wild rose

You can still experience wildness in the lives of the pronghorn, coyote, badger, mule deer or western meadowlark. Huge irrigation reservoirs such as Newell, McGregor and Tilley now support large commercial lake whitefish fisheries. The grasslands are also home to unique animals typical to warmer, southern climates, such as the turkey vulture, the short-horned lizard (Alberta's only lizard), many of our snakes, the northern scorpion and the western black widow spider.

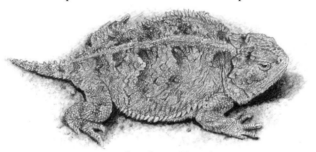

short-horned lizard

Canadian Shield

One of the harshest environments in the province, the Canadian Shield is a spectacular landscape of granite cliffs, great sand dunes and pristine waters. The rocky outcroppings of the underlying bedrock produce a terrain of dry, soil-impoverished highlands and wet, sparsely forested lowlands. Although it is a dominant eco-region in much of Canada, the Canadian Shield covers just a sliver of the far northeastern corner of Alberta.

The strange, wind-blown pines and sand dunes of this remote area create a mysterious feeling of true wilderness. It is home to many animals such as moose, fishers, northern bog lemmings and snowy owls. In winter, this corner of Alberta may also attract typically Arctic animals, such as the Arctic fox and the woodland caribou.

Arctic fox

31

TOP WILDLIFE-WATCHING SITES

There are hundreds of areas in Alberta where you can go for rewarding wildlife watching and nature experiences. The province's varied landscapes and habitats make it a mecca for nature lovers. The following areas have been selected because they offer a broad range of habitats, with an emphasis on diversity and accessibility.

NATIONAL PARKS
1 Banff NP
2 Elk Island NP
3 Jasper NP
4 Waterton Lakes NP
5 Wood Buffalo NP

PROVINCIAL PARKS
6 Aspen Beach PP
7 Beauvais Lake PP
8 Big Hill Springs PP
9 Bow Valley PP
10 Brown-Lowery PP
11 Calling Lake PP
12 Carson-Pegasus PP

13 Chain Lakes PP
14 Cold Lake PP
15 Crimson Lake PP
16 Cross Lake PP
17 Cypress Hills PP
18 Dinosaur PP
19 Dry Island Buffalo Jump PP
20 Fish Creek PP
21 Gooseberry Lake PP
22 Kinbrook Island PP
23 Lesser Slave Lake PP
24 Long Lake PP
25 Midland PP
26 Miquelon Lake PP
27 Notikewin PP

28 Peter Lougheed PP
29 Rochon Sands PP
30 Saskatoon Island PP
31 Sir Winston Churchill PP
32 Taber PP
33 Thunder Lake PP
34 Vermilion PP
35 Wabumun Lake PP
36 William A. Switzer PP
37 Writing-on-Stone PP
38 Wyndham-Carseland PP

OTHER RECREATIONAL AREAS
39 Kananaskis Country
40 Lakeland Provincial Recreation Area

LAKES & RESERVOIRS
1 Beaverhill Lake
2 Big Lake
3 Birch Lake
4 Bittern Lake
5 Brazeau Reservoir
6 Cavan Lake
7 Chappice Lake
8 Chip Lake
9 Coleman Lake
10 Crow Indian Lake
11 Dickson Dam
12 Dowling Lake
13 Eagle Lake
14 Fincastle Lake
15 Frank Lake

16 Ghost Dam
17 Handhills Lake
18 Hastings Lake
19 Kimiwan Lake
20 Kitsim Reservoir
21 Lake Athabasca
22 Langdon Reservoir
23 Lost Lake
24 Margaret Lake
25 Muriel Lake
26 Namaka Lake
27 Pakowki Lake
28 Scope Lake
29 Seebe Dam
30 Slack Slough
31 Stirling Lake

32 Tilley Reservoir
33 Travers Reservoir
34 Verdigris Lake
35 Whitford Lake

OTHER SITES
36 Clifford E. Lee Nature Sanctuary
37 Kininvie Marsh
38 Kootenay Plains
39 Porcupine Hills
40 Sheep River Wildlife Sanctuary
41 Wagner Natural Area
42 Wildcat Hills

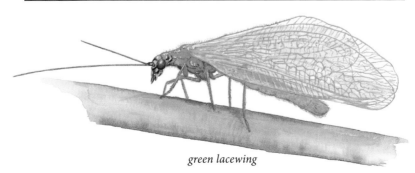

green lacewing

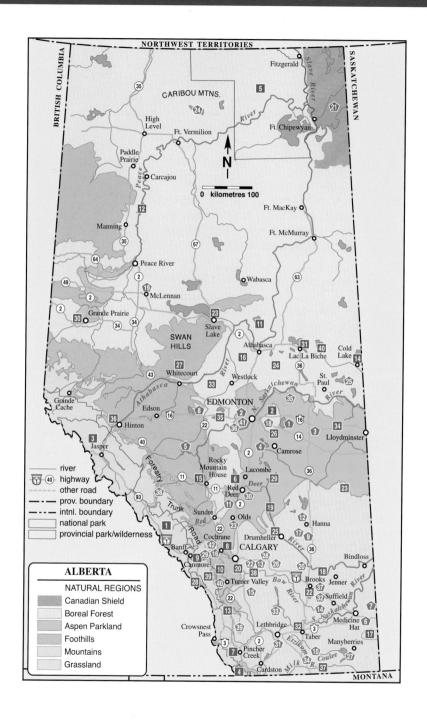

NORTHWEST TERRITORIES

BRITISH COLUMBIA

SASKATCHEWAN

Fitzgerald

35

CARIBOU MTNS.

5

24

High Level

Ft. Vermilion

River

21

Ft. Chipewyan

Paddle Prairie

Peace

Carcajou

N

0 kilometres 100

12

Manning

35

Ft. MacKay

67

64

Ft. McMurray

49

2

Peace River

2

19

McLennan

Wabasca

63

2

30

Grande Prairie

34

34

23

Slave Lake

11

SWAN HILLS

2

16

Athabasca

31

40

Cold Lake

14

27

43

Whitecourt

River

Westlock

24

36

Lac La Biche

25

33

Grande Cache

Athabasca

Edson

16

8

EDMONTON

35

N. Saskatchewan

35

River

St. Paul

3

36

Hinton

22

6

41

2

2

16

34

Lloydminster

3

Jasper

40

26

1

14

5

4

2

Camrose

Forestry

Rocky Mountain House

Lacombe

29

36

11

15

11

Red Deer

Deer

23

93

38

2

30

Trunk

Sundre

19

12

Hanna

1

Red

22

23

Olds

Cochrane

25

17

9

Banff

42

8

Drumheller

36

CALGARY

River

Bindloss

9

16

28

Canmore

10

20

13

26

20

18

29

39

40

Turner Valley

38

Bow

1

Brooks

37

Jenner

River

22

Suffield

22

15

River

7

13

33

14

Medicine Hat

6

39

Lethbridge

32

S. Saskatchewan

17

Crowsnest Pass

3

2

31

Taber

Etzikom

Manyberries

7

Pincher Creek

Coulee

10

27

Milk

R.

37

4

Cardston

MONTANA

river

highway

1   40

other road

prov. boundary

intnl. boundary

national park

provincial park/wilderness

ALBERTA

NATURAL REGIONS

Canadian Shield

Boreal Forest

Aspen Parkland

Foothills

Mountains

Grassland

Wood Buffalo National Park

Nature rules in this massive park, which extends into the Northwest Territories and includes the impressive Peace-Athabasca Delta. Wood Buffalo National Park is Canada's largest park and the world's second largest protected area, encompassing a whopping 44,807 km^2. Bison and caribou continue their ancient dance with grey wolves, while some 44 other mammal species including lynx, moose, bears, beavers and martens play their own roles in the boreal food web. Wood Buffalo National Park is home to the world's largest beaver dam, which measures 850 metres in length and is visible from space.

The internationally significant wetlands of the Peace-Athabasca Delta host 226 species of birds, including nesting whooping cranes, a variety of shorebirds and the largest concentra-

bison

tions of waterfowl in Alberta. There are two red-sided gartersnake hibernacula in the park, five amphibian species and 33 fish species. Vegetation includes drier sites with jack pine, buffaloberry and bearberry, wetter areas with aspen, alder and red-osier dogwood, and nutrient-poor sites that feature black spruce, larch and Labrador tea.

Notikewin Provincial Park

North of Manning in the Peace Country, Notikewin Provincial Park is one of the largest provincial parks in Alberta. Located where the Peace and Notikewin rivers converge, the park is primarily a mixture of old-growth white spruce forests, young aspen forests and balsam poplar forests with ostrich ferns in the undergrowth. Arctic grayling, northern pike, walleye, rainbow trout and yellow perch are some of the better-known fish species that inhabit the rivers, with boaters and shoreline wanderers catching occasional glimpses into their underwater lives. The valley is composed of eroded Cretaceous sandstone, so a walk along the river occasionally reveals fossils such as ammonite and petrified wood. Sandhill cranes and Canada geese stage here during migration, and woodpeckers nest in the forests. Moose, elk, white-tailed and mule deer, and black and grizzly bears all inhabit the forests of Notikewin Provincial Park.

sandhill crane

Lakeland Country

Undoubtedly, Lakeland Provincial Park and Recreation Area and the provincial parks of Cold Lake, Sir Winston Churchill and Lesser Slave Lake are the best places in the province to be at the end of May if you're a birder. The mature trees come alive with hundreds of species of migratory birds, including 20 species of colourful wood-warblers, some of which are difficult to find elsewhere in Alberta. This northern frontier of lake-dotted forests remains wild enough to support populations of black bears, moose, white-tailed deer, red foxes, river otters, muskrats, snowshoe hares and grey wolves. Grebes, common loons, cormorants and American white pelicans can be seen fishing on the larger lakes, which are home to species such as walleye, whitefish, northern pike and burbot.

black bear

Saskatoon Island Provincial Park

This provincial park and federal migratory bird sanctuary is located 15 minutes west of Grande Prairie. Named after the berries that are so abundant in the shrublands in July, Saskatoon

grey wolf

Island Provincial Park is home to diverse plant and animal species within its wetlands, grasslands, aspen forest and shrubland. Northern harriers hunt over the wetlands, where muskrats and beavers busily tend their territories. Weasels, woodchucks, deer and snowshoe hares are some of the animals that you may encounter on terrestrial adventures. Saskatoon Lake is a nesting site for rare trumpeter swans, and in spring and autumn, tundra swans visit for a few weeks as well. In April, the park celebrates the swans in its annual Swan Festival.

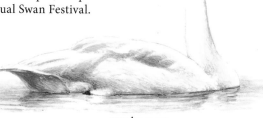

tundra swan

Carson-Pegasus Provincial Park

Just a short drive from Whitecourt on Highway 32, Carson-Pegasus Provincial Park offers a diversity of habitats and wildlife viewing. The mixedwood forests, bogs, marshes, fens and shrubby meadows provide homes for many mammals, including red squirrels, northern flying squirrels, beavers, muskrats, porcupines, Canada lynx, deer, moose and several weasel species. The park also hosts a colony of nesting great blue herons. Other notable bird species include Canada loons, trumpeter swans, bald and golden eagles, several owl species, belted kingfishers, black-backed woodpeckers and an abundance of wood-warblers. A walk along one of the trails in the park may reveal saskatoon and raspberry bushes, twinflowers, harebells and feather moss.

beaver

Elk Island National Park

Just an hour's drive from Edmonton, Elk Island National Park is a paradise for nature lovers. The park has a very high concentration of hoofed mammals, and a stroll at dawn or dusk may reveal good numbers of bison, moose, elk and deer. The fenced park is home to free-roaming plains bison and wood bison, with the two subspecies separated by a highway that runs through the park. Elk Island has an extensive trail system through the Parkland ecoregion, allowing visitors to explore both forests and wetlands. The park boasts 250 bird species, including the largest waterfowl in North America, the trumpeter swan, whose population in the park has been growing thanks to a reintroduction program. Other notable bird species include American white pelicans, red-necked grebes, black-crowned night herons, great gray owls and black-backed woodpeckers. Western gartersnakes slither through the grasses, and wood frogs, boreal chorus frogs and tiger salamanders inhabit the wetter areas. Trails are maintained year-round for hiking or cross-country skiing.

boreal chorus frog

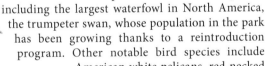

North American elk

Edmonton River Valley

Whether you are driving or walking through Edmonton's ribbon of green, be on the lookout for wildlife. White-tailed deer, coyotes, northern flying squirrels, porcupines, snowshoe hares, beavers, foxes and many more mammals all live in the capital city. A single birding trip in the river valley may turn up dozens of species, from bald eagles to pileated woodpeckers. The North Saskatchewan River is home to many species of

porcupine

fish, including lake sturgeon, goldeye, northern pike, suckers and many kinds of minnows. Gartersnakes den in the riverbanks and wood frogs croak in spring. The Edmonton Nature Club offers field trips and events throughout the year that take place both in the river valley and in the areas surrounding the city.

red-sided gartersnake

Beaverhill Lake

Located about 45 minutes southeast of Edmonton near the town of Tofield, Beaverhill Lake is not suitable for swimming, fishing or boating, so the recreational opportunities here are almost entirely for the birds. A designated Ramsar site (a wetland of international significance), Beaverhill Lake boasts some of the most concentrated migrations of birds in our province. Visitors to the

cherry-faced meadowhawk

lake and the surrounding area witness tens of thousands of birds, including snow, Canada, Ross's and greater white-fronted geese, sandhill cranes, most of Alberta's duck species and almost 40 species of shorebirds. Many of the over 250 species of birds recorded in the area are rarities, and the lake always has the potential to produce more unusual sightings. The Beaverhill Bird Observatory and the Francis Point viewing blind provide convenient access to birding sites, but the entire area is worth exploring for its surprising diversity. Wood frogs and boreal chorus frogs are also present and monitored through

snow goose

37

RANA (Researching Amphibian Numbers in Alberta). Bring your butterfly net along to check out the over 20 species of butterflies and 18 or more species of dragonflies and damselflies present in this natural area.

Slack Slough

Just south of Red Deer, on the east side of Highway 2, lies Slack Slough, a 66-hectare wetland preserve with an elevated viewing platform that is ideal for trying to spot the 90 bird species that have been recorded in this bulrush marsh. A great variety of waterfowl can be seen from spring through fall. Shorebirds congregate on the low islands during migration, and hawks can sometimes be seen circling overhead. Marsh wrens, yellow-headed blackbirds and tree swallows all add to the sense of avian abundance. Foxes, muskrats, beavers and the occasional moose can

yellow-headed blackbird

sometimes be observed, and, in spring and summer, a plethora of wildflowers colours the landscape. A trip between Edmonton and Calgary just isn't complete without a stop at "the slough."

Banff National Park and Jasper National Park

Alberta's premier tourist destinations continue to be a naturalist's paradise. There is a good chance that visitors will encounter elk, moose, bears, bighorn sheep or mountain goats during backcountry explorations, or even without leaving their vehicles. Pikas frequent the rockslides at Lake Louise in Banff National Park and Mount Edith Cavell in Jasper National Park, and hoary marmots can be seen

bighorn sheep

perched on alpine rocks on the numerous day-hiking trails that can be found in both parks. Day hikes also reveal characteristic mountain wildflowers such as Indian paintbrush, fireweed and wild strawberries. The subalpine zone is home to bronze bells, twinflower, Labrador tea and fleabanes, whereas the alpine zone is bejewelled with moss campion, alpine forget-me-not, glacier lily and purple saxifrage. Gray jays and Clark's nutcrackers frequent day-use areas and campgrounds, and ptarmigans, mountain chickadees and golden eagles are at home in alpine regions.

Labrador tea

In Banff, a hike along the Johnson Canyon trail will reveal black swift nests. Colourful harlequin ducks nest on the Bow River in Banff National Park and along the Maligne River in Jasper National Park. The Cave and Basin Marsh at the Banff hotsprings will reveal the weirdest fish in Alberta, the African jewelfish (*Hemichromis bimaculatus*), a beautiful but unwanted introduction from an illegal aquarium release. Mountain rivers also offer opportunities to watch the breeding antics of fishes more typical of the Rockies. For example, in June, rainbow trout spawn in the Maligne River in Jasper National Park where it leaves Maligne Lake, and northern pike spawn in Talbot Lake in Jasper National Park in early spring.

Kananaskis Country

Kananaskis Country is located in the front ranges of the Rocky Mountains. Habitats range from wetlands to subalpine forests and alpine meadows. Lodgepole pine, heart-leaved arnica and bunchberry are common in the shaded forests, and carpets of bearberry cover open slopes. Moist meadows have bracted lousewort and elephant's-head, and alpine meadows boast forget-me-nots and Indian paintbrush. The internationally recognized trail system of this provincial recreation area gives you easy entry into the world of elk, moose, bears, cougars, bighorn sheep, pikas, Columbian and golden-mantled ground squirrels and 130 bird species. Brown, bull, cutthroat and brook trout, as well as whitefish, are found in the lakes and streams of the Kananaskis.

cougar

Canmore

The town of Canmore offers much for a visiting naturalist. Along the river, many species can be seen both on the water and at feeders in riverside yards. Osprey nesting platforms west of the old railway bridge provide superb opportunities to observe these magnificent

brown trout

fish eagles close at hand, and the open waters of Policeman's Creek, right downtown, are the year-round home of hundreds of mallards, as well as the occasional belted kingfisher. With its proximity to the Rocky Mountains, Canmore visits can also yield viewings of moose, elk, bears and cougars, and you are almost guaranteed to see a member of Canmore's feral domestic rabbit population. In late October and November, you can take a short drive out of town to watch the waters come alive as brown trout spawn at Bill Griffith's Creek on the Bow River. A fish-viewing site has been set up, so you can watch from shore as female brown trout dig their redds (nests) and lay their eggs.

Calgary Parks

Beautifully protected and enhanced parks line the Bow and the Elbow rivers as they wind through Calgary. Rainbow trout, brown trout and whitefish are found in the river. A lunchtime or after-dinner walk may yield encounters with white-tailed and mule deer, coyotes, beavers, weasels and badgers. The diverse birdlife ranges from large raptors to tiny hummingbirds. On sunny summer days, there are many colourful butterflies to enjoy. The Inglewood Bird Sanctuary and Fish Creek Provincial Park provide year-round opportunities to observe both familiar and unusual species. Nature Calgary organizes field trips, outings and species counts year-round.

mule deer

Dinosaur Provincial Park

The wildlife of the Triassic Period is celebrated at this World Heritage Site, but the modern-day wildlife of the badlands is equally fascinating. Mule deer and Nuttall's cottontails drift through the park's campsite and common nighthawks fly overhead, ushering in spring visitors with their nasal *peent* calls. Interpretive trails guide visitors through the cottonwood, sage flat, coulee and grassland ecosystems. A variety of wildflowers adorn the landscape, with such species as wild strawberry, saskatoon, wild licorice, wild bergamot, prairie crocus, yellow flax, wild rose and cocklebur. Birding opportunities abound, and visitors can expect a rainbow of colourful birds, including yellow meadowlarks, bluebirds, orange orioles and red-breasted robins. Visitors are encouraged to stay on the paths to avoid surprise encounters with rattlesnakes!

wild bergamot

Waterton Lakes National Park

From rolling grasslands to alpine peaks, this small national park has it all. Several ecological regions meet here, and the many habitats include plants from the Great Plains, Rocky Mountains and the Pacific Coast. Water from this mountain park flows into three separate river systems—a triple divide. Waterton Lakes National Park boasts 970 vascular plant species and another 400 bryophyte and lichen species. Two-thirds of Alberta's mammal species occur in the park, including mountain goats, bighorn sheep, bison and a famous "international" elk herd that migrates between Waterton and neighbouring Glacier National Park

bald eagle

in the United States. There are over 250 bird species, including nesting sandhill cranes and bald eagles, boreal chickadees, three-toed woodpeckers and over 60 songbird species. Twenty-four fish species and 10 amphibian and reptile species are found here as well. Elk and deer browse the grasslands, the marshes are important for migrating waterfowl, and the forests provide cover for wolves, bears and other wildlife.

Cypress Hills

The lodgepole pine forests of Cypress Hills rise out of the floodplains in southeastern Alberta like a displaced boreal foothill lost in a sea of grass. Wildlife typically found in the Rocky Mountains or boreal forests such as moose, elk, deer and cougars find themselves isolated in these hills. Birders will enjoy more than 200 species, including mountain species such as the pink-sided subspecies of the dark-eyed junco and the "Audubon's" yellow-rumped warbler and boreal species such as the ruffed

northern leopard frog

grouse. Grassland animals include mule deer, northern leopard frogs and wild turkeys. Plant life not found elsewhere in the prairies abounds here, including the yellow lady's-slipper and 13 other orchid species. Nearby Pakowki Lake occasionally attracts a few rare bird species, such as the Clark's grebe and the white-faced ibis, and it is home to many kinds of waterfowl.

Writing-on-Stone Provincial Park

prickly-pear cactus

The finest example of native grasslands remaining in Alberta can be found near Writing-on-Stone Provincial Park. This World Heritage Site is an important spiritual site for the Blackfoot people. The Milk River has cut an emerald valley of balsam poplar and cottonwoods in the landscape. Mammals such as mule deer, bushy-tailed woodrats, Nuttall's cottontails, striped skunks, pronghorns, yellow-bellied marmots and bats are found here. Bird species include mourning doves, American kestrels and ring-necked pheasants. Reptiles and amphibians include prairie rattlesnakes, bullsnakes, tiger salamanders, leopard frogs and plains spadefoot toads. Look for prickly-pear and pincushion cacti flowering in spring.

bullsnake

CHALLENGES

Conserving Alberta and protecting its biodiversity are tasks fraught with challenges. Human development and other activities of people have obliterated or degraded many habitats. Rivers and streams carry unwanted pollutants. Invasive nonnative species such as European starlings, house sparrows, mountain pine beetles and Dutch elm disease take hold and reduce native biodiversity. Much has changed in Alberta since the last of the great bison herds roamed freely a century ago, but our province remains an internationally recognized destination for visitors seeking rewarding natural experiences. We hope that this guide helps to introduce more people to Alberta's incredibly diverse regions and creates more supporters of our amazing province.

house sparrow

HUMANS AND WILDLIFE

Each year, many Alberta residents and tourists from outside the province enjoy the scenic vistas, fresh air and wilderness that the province's natural areas provide. Although people have become more conscious of the need to respect and protect wildlife and wild places, the pressures of increased human visitation can have a negative effect on our natural areas. Practising minimum-impact techniques such as those listed below will help keep Alberta clean, beautiful and wild for people, plants and animals:

western wood lily

Do not feed wildlife. Wildlife that learns to associate people with food can become aggressive and dangerous once the animals stop foraging for natural foods.

Never chase or flush animals from cover or try to touch them. Use binoculars and keep your distance, for the animals' sake and for your own.

Pets that chase or kill wildlife are best left at home. Dogs should always be kept on leash. Cats are responsible for the deaths of many songbirds and other small animals each year, so are best kept indoors or on a leash.

Stay on designated trails and camping sites. These sites have been hardened to bear the impact of repeated human use. There is minimal

Richardson's ground squirrel

American white pelican

impact on vegetation and fewer animal conflicts when people stay on the trails.

Bring your eyes to the flower, not the flower to your eyes. Picking flowers and removing them can damage or kill the plant and prevent others from enjoying its beauty. Similar respect should be shown toward fossils, artifacts, antlers and other sources of natural history.

Keep your food secure from animals, keep your cooking materials clean and dispose of your garbage in designated animal-proof containers.

Resist littering! Backcountry campers should pack out all of their garbage rather than burying it or leaving it in the backcountry.

Respect the rights of landowners and other wildlife viewers. Ask permission to access private lands and respect the rules of public lands.

NATURE ORGANIZATIONS IN ALBERTA

Alberta is home to many nature-lovers, from casual observers to wildlife enthusiasts and professional researchers. As a result, there is an abundance of nature organizations, from nature clubs that organize wildlife observation outings to conservation societies that work hard to make sure that important wildlife areas in Alberta are protected from harm. Here are just a few of the organizations that are actively involved in Alberta's wild world.

Alberta Birds of Prey Foundation

Swainson's hawk

Located two hours south of Calgary in Coaldale, this is Canada's largest birds of prey facility. The main goal of the organization is to rescue and rehabilitate injured hawks, falcons, eagles and owls, and to release the birds into the wild when they are ready. In addition to rehabilitating wildlife, the birds of prey centre is also an educational facility that is open to the public from May to September. For more information, visit their website at www.burrowingowl.com.

Alberta Native Plant Council

The purpose of this group is to educate people and organizations about Alberta's botanical heritage and to help conserve habitats important to our native plant species. Membership is open to everyone, and activities include plant studies, field trips and May species counts. The Alberta Native Plant Council is also involved in the Adopt-A-Plant program, in which a volunteer can "adopt" one to three rare plant species. Each volunteer is then trained in identifying, locating and surveying that species to assist in its assessment as rare or threatened and thus aid in its conservation. Find the ANPC online at www.anpc.ab.ca. More information about the Adopt-A-Plant program can be found at www.ab.adoptaplant.ca.

Canada violet

ruby-crowned kinglet

Boreal Centre for Bird Conservation

Located within Lesser Slave Lake Provincial Park, this centre, formerly called the Lesser Slave Lake Bird Observatory, is dedicated to researching and educating people about boreal forest birds. The interpretive centre includes a range of indoor and outdoor programs and exhibits. It is a great place to be in spring and fall, when migratory birds are present in large numbers, and in the summer, when the forest is alive with the activities of breeding birds. The centre is open year-round, and more information can be found at www.borealbirdcentre.ca.

Canadian Parks and Wilderness Society

This nonprofit organization promotes the establishment of new parks, aims to protect the integrity of existing parks and promotes responsible land-use practices. They also run various educational programs. You can find more information at cpaws.org.

Polyphemus moth

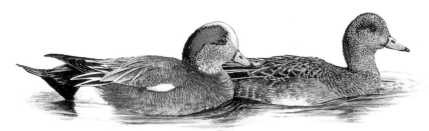

American wigeon

Ducks Unlimited Canada

Alberta is naturally rich in wetlands, with eight million waterfowl and 20 million shorebirds using its wetlands and associated habitats every year. This long-time organization is devoted to conserving and protecting wetland habitats for waterfowl and other species. Some important wetland sites in Alberta as recognized by Ducks Unlimited include Saskatoon Island Provincial Park near Grande Prairie, Kimiwan Lake south of Peace River, Lois Hole Centennial Park and Clifford E. Lee Nature Sanctuary near Edmonton, Inglewood Bird Sanctuary and Bow Habitat Station in Calgary, Frank Lake near High River and the Elizabeth Hall Wetlands in Lethbridge. Find Ducks Unlimited online at www.ducks.ca.

Nature Alberta: Federation of Alberta Naturalists

This Alberta-wide organization, which includes over 40 clubs across the province, produces *Nature Alberta* magazine, and runs several programs, including the Young Naturalists' Club, Alberta Plant Watch and the Alberta Bird Atlas Project. Find their website at naturealberta.ca.

northern river otter

NatureWatch

Do you feel that you missed your true calling as a scientist, or do you just wonder if your observations about the natural world around you could be meaningful or relevant? Run by Nature Canada and Environment Canada's Ecological Monitoring and Assessment Network, the NatureWatch program allows you to be a "citizen scientist" and submit your natural history observations to help scientists monitor and protect the natural world. To find out more, visit www.naturewatch.ca.

marsh-marigold

Wildlife Rehabilitation Organizations

There are many wildlife rehabilitation centres across Alberta, including Edmonton and Calgary. If you come across an injured animal and are wondering what to do, there now is a province-wide, toll-free Wildlife Help Line at 1-888-924-2444.

rufous hummingbird

ABOUT THIS GUIDE

Each section begins with a quick reference guide that lists the animals or plants by family name.

Identification measurements are listed at the beginning of each species account.

Dimensions given for fauna are for length, meaning "total length including tail," and for larger mammals, height is also given, which is measured from the ground to shoulder level. Wingspans are provided for birds, bats and butterflies.

Dimensions given for flora are for total height as well as for additional features diagnostic to that plant.

Canada buffaloberry

Canada lynx

ANIMALS

Animals are mammals, birds, reptiles, amphibians, fish and invertebrates, all of which belong to the Kingdom Animalia. They obtain energy by ingesting food that they hunt or gather. Mammals and birds are endothermic, meaning that their body temperature is internally regulated and will stay nearly constant despite the surrounding environmental temperature, unless the external temperature is extreme and persistent. Reptiles, amphibians, fish and invertebrates are ectothermic, meaning that they do not

bison

yellow perch

have the ability to regulate their own internal body temperature and tend to be the same temperature as their surroundings. Animals reproduce sexually, and they have a limited growth that is reached at sexual maturity. They also have diverse and complicated behaviours displayed in courtship,

woolly bear caterpillar

defence, parenting, playing, fighting, eating, hunting, their social hierarchy and how they deal with environmental stresses such as weather, change of season or availability of food and water. We have included Alberta's most common, wide-ranging, charismatic or historically significant animals and have chosen a few representatives for diverse families such as rodents.

wood frog

tundra swan

MAMMALS

Mammals are the group to which human beings belong. In general, mammals are endothermic, bear live young (with the exception of the platypus), nurse their young and have hair or fur on their bodies. Typically, all mammals larger than rodents are sexually dimorphic, meaning that the male and the female differ in appearance, either by size or by other diagnostics such as antlers. Males are usually larger than females. Different groups of mammals include herbivores, carnivores, omnivores and insectivores. People often associate large mammals with wilderness, making these animals prominent symbols in Native legends and stirring emotional connections with people in modern times.

Bison
p. 50

Hoofed Mammals
pp. 50–53

Pronghorn
p. 54

Cats
pp. 54–55

Skunks & Weasels
pp. 56–59

Raccoon
p. 59

Bears
p. 60

Dogs
pp. 61–63

Porcupine
p. 63

Beaver & Muskrat
p. 64

Mice, Voles & Kin
pp. 65–68

Marmots & Squirrels
pp. 68–71

Pikas & Hares
pp. 71–72

Bats
pp. 73–74

Shrews
p. 75

Bison

Bison bison

Length: 2.4–3.9 m
Shoulder height: 1.62–1.82 m
Weight: *Male:* 642–910 kg; *Female:* 493–567 kg

North America's largest native land mammal, the bison literally weighs a tonne! Before the arrival of Europeans, great herds totalling millions of bison roamed parts of western North America. By the early 1900s, overhunting, disease, severe winters and interbreeding had devastated their numbers and extirpated these noble beasts from much of their range. Today, the vast majority of bison are raised in private herds. Free-ranging or semi-wild herds are almost exclusively restricted to protected areas over a patchy range. • Two subspecies exist: the wood bison (*B. b. athabascae*) and the plains bison (*B. b. bison*). **Where found:** prairies or forested areas; Elk Island NP; Wood Buffalo NP; Waterton Lakes NP.

Mountain Goat

Oreamnos americanus

Length: 1.2–1.5 m
Shoulder height: 90–120 cm
Weight: 45–135 kg

Watching a mountain goat climbing or descending the steep rocky slopes of its high alpine home can leave observers feeling on edge, but this animal is more than comfortable on precarious cliffs and high precipices. A mountain goat can place and manoeuvre all four hooves on a ledge as small as 15 cm long by 5 cm wide. • Within hours of being born, playful mountain goat kids are able to run, jump and climb. **Where found:** steep slopes and rocky cliffs in alpine and subalpine areas.

Bighorn Sheep

Ovis canadensis

Length: 1.5–1.8 m
Shoulder height: 75–115 cm
Weight: 55–155 kg

Male bighorn sheep have spectacular horns and use them in head-butting clashes during autumn rut. Both sexes have brown horns, but the female's are short and do not curve around as impressively as those of the male. • Mountain meadows provide feeding grounds, and rocky outcroppings provide protection from predators, namely eagles, mountain lions and bobcats, which prey on the lambs. **Where found:** rugged mountain slopes, cliffs and alpine meadows.

North American Elk

Cervus canadensis

Length: 1.8–2.7 m
Shoulder height: 1.7–2.1 m
Weight: 180–500 kg

The impressive bugle of the male North American elk once resounded throughout much of the continent, but the advance of civilization pushed these animals west. Today, elk are common in the Rocky Mountains and are scattered locally in the western plains. • During the autumn mating season, rival males use their majestic antlers to win and protect a harem of females. An especially vigorous bull might command over 50 females. After the rut, bull elk can put on as much as a kilogram every 2 to 3 days if conditions are good. The extra weight helps them survive the winter. **Where found:** grasslands and open woodlands; throughout the western half of Alberta; Elk Island NP; scattered locally in central and extreme southern areas. **Also known as:** *C. elaphus*; wapiti.

White-tailed Deer

Odocoileus virginianus

Length: 1.4–2.1 m
Shoulder height: 70–115 cm
Weight: 30–115 kg

Easily our most abundant hoofed mammal, white-tailed deer populations have boomed in many areas. These animals are even found in urban and suburban areas, often near forested tracts, wooded ravines or river valleys. • When startled, white-tails bound away, flashing their conspicuous white tails. • Feeding does (females) leave their speckled, scentless fawns in dense vegetation to hide them from predators. • Bucks (males) regrow their racks, or antlers, each year, and can develop massive racks with age. **Where found:** most habitats except the densest forests; throughout.

Mule Deer

Odocoileus hemionus

Length: 1.3–1.9 m
Shoulder height: 90–105 cm
Weight: 31–215 kg

These gentle and often approachable deer frequent open areas and parks, where they are wonderful to watch. They travel with a characteristic, bouncing gait, launching off and landing on all fours at the same time. • As its name suggests, the mule deer has very large ears. Its white rump patch and black-tipped tail distinguish it from the white-tailed deer. **Where found:** open coniferous woodlands, grasslands and river valleys; throughout. **Also known as:** black-tailed deer.

Moose

Alces alces

Length: 2.5–3.0 m
Shoulder height: 1.7–2.1 m
Weight: 230–540 kg

Moose are world's largest deer. These impressive beasts have long legs that help them navigate bogs and deep snow. They can run as fast as 55 km/h, swim continuously for several hours, dive to depths of 6 m and remain submerged for up to a minute. • Saplings with the tops snapped off and other damaged plants are an indication that a moose stopped by for lunch. Voracious eaters, an individual might consume 7250 kg of vegetation annually. **Where found:** coniferous forests, young poplar stands and willows; throughout except southeastern grasslands.

Woodland Caribou

Rangifer tarandus

Length: 1.4–2.3 m
Shoulder height: 90–170 cm
Weight: 90–110 kg

The seasonal movements of woodland caribou hardly compare to the incredible migrations of their Arctic kin, but they do travel widely between summer and winter feeding grounds. Mountain populations generally spend the summer at high elevations to avoid the heat and flies, descending to lower foraging areas for winter. Caribou feed by digging through the snow with their broad hooves to expose lichens, their favourite winter food. In summer, they add grasses, mosses, sedges and mushrooms to their diet. • There are two caribou populations in Alberta. One population is found in the mountains and foothills, and another is found in the boreal forests of northern Alberta. Both populations are threatened and declining because of habitat loss or degradation, harassment and increased predation. **Where found:** mature coniferous forests and muskeg; some may move to alpine and sub-alpine areas in summer; foothills, mountains and northern parts of Alberta.

Pronghorn

Antilocapra americana

Length: 1.7–2.5 m
Shoulder height: 88–103 cm
Weight: 32–63 kg

Capable of reaching speeds of up to 90 km/h, the pronghorn is the fastest land mammal in North American and the second fastest in the world, after the cheetah. A large heart and lungs relative to its body size, an efficient metabolism and lack of a dewclaw are all adaptations for speed. Although swift, the pronghorn is a poor jumper, and the fencing of the prairies in the early 1900s resulted in population declines. Today, fences are built with enough space for pronghorns to slip underneath. • Pronghorns are sometime called antelope, but they, in fact, have no close living relatives. • The male's pronged horns are unique; each year, only the outer keratin sheath is shed but not the bony core. **Where found:** grasslands of southeastern Alberta.

Cougar

Puma concolor

Length: 1.5–2.7 m
Shoulder height: 65–80 cm
Weight: 30–90 kg

The cougar is a skilled hunter with specialized teeth and claws for capturing prey; its sharp canines can kill a moose or deer in one lethal bite. This nocturnal hunter can travel an average of 10 km per night. • Historically, cougars were found throughout most of southern Canada, with a range overlapping that of deer, their favourite prey. With the arrival of settlers, cougars were pushed westward to the foothills and mountains. **Where found:** variety of habitats that provide cover, especially remote, wooded areas; western half of Alberta. **Also known as:** mountain lion.

Canada Lynx

Lynx canadensis

Length: 80–100 cm
Shoulder height: 45–60 cm
Weight: 7–18 kg

Elusive, elegant and gener-ally secretive, the Canada lynx is a well-equipped hunt-ing machine. It has bristle-tipped ears that can detect the slightest sound, large paws that function as snowshoes and swim-ming paddles, and dense pelage to protect against the bitterest cold. Lynx are excellent climbers and often crouch on tree branches, ready to pounce on passing prey. • Lynx populations fluctuate every 7 to 10 years along with snowshoe hare numbers. When hares are plentiful, lynx kittens are more likely to survive to adulthood and reproduce; when there are fewer hares, more kittens starve and the lynx population declines. **Where found:** coniferous forests and mountains; central and northern Alberta.

Bobcat

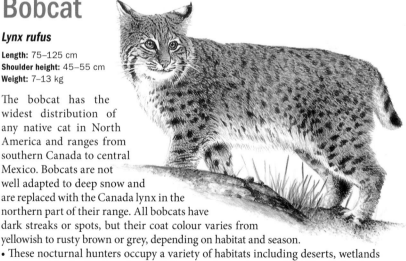

Lynx rufus

Length: 75–125 cm
Shoulder height: 45–55 cm
Weight: 7–13 kg

The bobcat has the widest distribution of any native cat in North America and ranges from southern Canada to central Mexico. Bobcats are not well adapted to deep snow and are replaced with the Canada lynx in the northern part of their range. All bobcats have dark streaks or spots, but their coat colour varies from yellowish to rusty brown or grey, depending on habitat and season.
• These nocturnal hunters occupy a variety of habitats including deserts, wetlands and, surprisingly, developed areas. Feline speedsters, they can hit 50 km/h for short bursts. • The similar-looking Canada lynx has longer ear tufts and a longer, black-tipped tail. **Where found:** forested areas, brushy coulees and mountain forests where lynx are absent; southern Alberta.

Striped Skunk

Mephitis mephitis

Length: 53–76 cm
Weight: 1.9–4.2 kg

Equipped with a noxious spray that can be accurately fired over distances up to 6 m, the striped skunk gives both humans and animals alike an overpowering reason to avoid it. But come spring, when the mother skunk emerges with her fluffy, two-toned babies trotting behind her, you may find yourself enjoying her company—from a distance. • Skunk families typically den in hollow logs or rock piles in summer, then switch to old woodchuck or badger burrows for winter. **Where found:** moist, urban and rural habitats, including streamside woodlands and agricultural areas; throughout.

American Marten

Martes americana

Length: 56–66 cm
Weight: 0.5–1.2 kg

Much smaller than the similar fisher and the mink, the American marten's relatively diminutive size allows it to den in woodpecker cavities, which it often does. The marten is active during the day, so it is more likely to be seen than other weasels. It feeds mainly on small rodents, but also consumes fish, snakes, small birds or eggs, carrion and sometimes berries. • Prized for its soft, luxurious fur, trapping combined with habitat loss has contributed to the American marten's decline. **Where found:** mature coniferous forests and mountains; central and northern Alberta.

Fisher

Martes pennanti

Length: 79–107 cm
Weight: 2–5.5 kg

Like all members of the weasel family, the fisher is an aggressive, capable predator. But this animal is misnamed—though it can swim well, it rarely eats fish, preferring snowshoe hares and other small mammals. The fisher is one of the only animals that regularly kills porcupines, adeptly flipping them over to gain access to the soft, unprotected belly region. • Fishers have specially adapted ankle bones that allow them to rotate their feet and climb down trees headfirst. • These reclusive animals prefer intact wilderness and disappear once development begins. **Where found:** dense coniferous and mixed forests; mountains; central and northern Alberta.

Least Weasel

Mustela nivalis

Length: 15–23 cm
Weight: 28–70 g

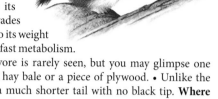

Woe to the hiding vole when one of these miniscule barbarians charges into its burrow. The least weasel regularly invades holes in search of prey, and it eats up to its weight in food each day to fuel its incredibly fast metabolism.
This small, mainly nocturnal carnivore is rarely seen, but you may glimpse one dashing for cover when you move a hay bale or a piece of plywood. • Unlike the larger weasels, the least weasel has a much shorter tail with no black tip. **Where found:** open fields, forest edges, rock piles and abandoned buildings; throughout.

Short-tailed Weasel

Mustela erminea

Length: 25–33 cm
Weight: 45–105 g

If the short-tailed weasel were the size of a black bear, we'd all be dead. These voracious, mainly nocturnal predators kill anything they can take down, especially mice and voles. A typical glimpse is of a small, eel-like mammal bounding along and then vanishing before a positive identifiacation can be made. • The short-tailed weasel's coat becomes white in winter, but the tail is black-tipped year-round. **Where found:** dense coniferous and mixed forests, shrublands, meadows and riparian areas; throughout except the extreme southeast. **Also known as:** ermine, stoat.

Long-tailed Weasel

Mustela frenata

Length: 30–46 cm
Weight: 85–400 g

Like other mustelids, long-tailed weasels exhibit serial-killer tendencies, killing more than they can consume. Excess prey is sometimes cached for later use. Capable hunters, these hyperactive beasts can bring down animals twice their size, though normal fare consists of small vertebrates, insects and occasionally fruit. • Like other true weasels, the long-tailed weasel turns white in winter, but the tip of the tail remains black. **Where found:** open, grassy meadows, brushland, woodlots, forest edges and fencerows; central and southern Alberta.

Mink

Mustela vison

Length: 47–70 cm
Weight: 0.6–1.4 kg

Once coveted for their silky fur, over-trapping led to localized declines of mink populations. Today, most mink coats come from ranch-raised animals. • Rarely found far from water, the mink's webbed feet make it an excellent swimmer and diver, and it often hunts for prey underwater. Its thick, oily, dark brown to blackish fur insulates its body from extremely cold water. • Mink move with graceful, fluid motions, resembling ribbons as they wind along shorelines. They travel along established hunting routes, sometimes resting in a muskrat lodge after eating the original inhabitant. **Where found:** shorelines of lakes, marshes, streams and in nearby forests; throughout.

Black-footed Ferret

Mustela nigripes

Length: 45 cm
Weight: 1.0 kg

Our only native ferret is also one of the most endangered mammals in North America. Black-footed ferrets live in grasslands, where they coexist with prairie dogs, their main prey. Once believed to be globally extinct, a small ferret population was found in Wyoming in 1981. Some of these ferrets have been captive bred and reintroduced to suitable habitat in the United States and, beginning in October 2009, to Saskatchewan's Grasslands National Park. • Historically, black-footed ferrets reached the northern edge of their range in the extreme southeastern corner of the province. **Where found:** grasslands with prairie dogs; extirpated from Alberta.

Wolverine

Gulo gulo

Length: 70–110 cm
Weight: 7–16 kg

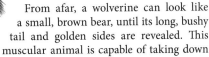

From afar, a wolverine can look like a small, brown bear, until its long, bushy tail and golden sides are revealed. This muscular animal is capable of taking down a caribou or moose but usually scavenges carrion left behind by larger predators. With its powerful jaws, the wolverine can crunch through bone to access the nourishing marrow, leaving little trace of a carcass. It also eats small animals, fish, bird eggs and berries. With a fondness for plastic and for marking its territory with musk and urine, a wolverine can wreak havoc on unoccupied camps. • Chances of seeing this elusive animal are slim, even in the most remote areas. **Where found:** remote alpine areas; boreal forest and tundra of northern Alberta.

Badger

Taxidea taxus

Length: 64–89 cm
Weight: 5–11 kg

These burly, burrowing beasts are like mammalian augers. A badger at full whirl sends a continuous plume of sediment skyward, quickly disappearing underground. Equipped with huge claws, strong forelimbs, powerful jaws and a pointed snout, badgers pursue subterranean prey such as ground squirrels, mice and snakes. • Badger holes are essential in providing den sites, shelters and hibernacula for many creatures, from coyotes to black widow spiders. **Where found:** low-elevation fields, meadows, grasslands, fence lines and ditches; central and southern Alberta.

Northern River Otter

Lontra canadensis

Length: 90–140 cm
Weight: 5–11 kg

Playful otters are extremely entertaining, whether you are watching them at the zoo or are lucky enough to see them in the wild. Their fully webbed feet, long, streamlined bodies and muscular tails make them swift, effortless swimmers with incredible fishing ability. • River otters are highly social animals, usually travelling in small groups. Good clues to their presence are "slides" on the shores of water bodies or troughs in the snow created by tobogganing otters. **Where found:** near wooded lakes, ponds and streams; central and northern Alberta.

Raccoon

Procyon lotor

Length: 65–100 cm
Weight: 5–14 kg

These black-masked bandits are common in many habitats, including suburbia, and are often found near water. When on the move, raccoons present a hunchbacked appearance and run with a comical, mincing gait. While not a true hibernator, they become sluggish during colder weather and may hole up for extended periods. These agile climbers are often seen high in trees or peeking from arboreal cavities. • Raccoons are known for wetting their food before eating, a behaviour that allows them to feel for and discard any inedible matter. **Where found:** wooded areas near water; southern Alberta.

Black Bear

Ursus americanus

Length: 1.4–1.8 m
Shoulder height: 90–110 cm
Weight: 40–270 kg

Don't be fooled by the clumsy, lumbering gait of a black bear. Deceptively speedy, it can run at 50 km/h for short bursts. This bear is also an excellent swimmer and can climb trees. • Black bears are omnivorous, eating an incredibly varied diet and exploiting whatever food sources are at hand. During much of the year, up to three-quarters of their diet may be vegetable matter. • One of the few North American mammals that truly hibernates, black bears pack on fat, then retire to a sheltered den for the winter. Vegetable matter in their pre-hibernation diet forms an anal plug, preventing expulsion during their long slumber. **Where found:** forests, open, marshy woodlands and mountains; central and northern Alberta.

Grizzly Bear

Ursus arctos

Length: 1.8–2.6 m
Shoulder height: 90–120 cm
Weight: 110–530 kg

Knowing that grizzly bears are around, though they are rarely seen, makes camping in the woods a truly wild experience. A mother grizzly with cubs can be very dangerous, and hikers are advised to practice bear-avoidance techniques. • Grizzlies have a prominent shoulder hump, a dished face, pale yellow to dark brown pelage and long front claws that are always visible. Plants and carrion make up most of their omnivorous diet. **Where found:** forests and riparian areas in valley bottoms to high-alpine tundra and mountains; Rocky Mountains and boreal forest areas of north-central and northwestern Alberta. **Also known as:** brown bear.

Coyote

Canis latrans

Length: 1–1.3 m
Height: 58–66 cm
Weight: 10–22 kg

Occasionally forming loose packs and joining in spirited yipping choruses, coyotes are clever and versatile hunter-scavengers. They often range into suburbia, and some even live in densely urban areas. This doglike mammal has benefited from large-scale, human-induced habitat changes, booming in numbers and greatly expanding its range. Also, widespread eradication of predators such as grey wolves has helped coyotes to prosper. • The coyote has a smaller, thinner muzzle than the wolf, and its tail drags behind its legs when it runs. **Where found:** open woodlands, agricultural lands and near urban areas; throughout.

Grey Wolf

Canis lupus

Length: 1.5–2.0 m
Height: 66–97 cm
Weight: 38–54 kg

Wolves have been persecuted since the first Europeans arrived in North America and eradicated these animals from vast areas of their former range, including Banff National Park, in the 1970s. Their large size, fierce predatory nature, pack-forming habits and role in fables caused people to fear them, and some still do. Today, wolves are once again established in the mountain parks. They are a valued symbol of the wilderness and crucial to a healthy, balanced food chain. Wolves require expansive wild lands, such as the connected mountain ecosystem that the Yellowstone to Yukon (Y2Y) conservation initiative aims to preserve and maintain. • Wolf packs cooperate within a strong social structure that is dominated by an alpha pair (dominant male and female). **Where found:** boreal forests, tundra and mountains; central and northern Alberta. **Also known as:** timber wolf.

Arctic Fox

Alopex lagopus

Length: 75–91 cm
Height: 25–30 cm
Weight: 1.8–4.1 kg

White in winter and bluish grey in summer, the Arctic fox is the only member of the dog family that changes fur colour with the seasons. Uniquely adapted to the Arctic, this small fox has a dense, insulating coat, furry feet and acute hearing for tracking small animals under the snow. • The Arctic fox feeds on polar bear or grey wolf kills, rodents, bird eggs and occasionally seal pups. During the summer months, when prey is plentiful, this resourceful fox stores food for the winter by digging a hole into the permafrost layer. **Where found:** tundra; extreme northeastern Alberta.

Swift Fox

Vulpes velox

Length: 80 cm
Height: 30 cm
Weight: *Male:* 2.45 kg;
Female: 2.25 kg

About the size of a house cat, the swift fox is North America's smallest wild dog. These little foxes disappeared from Canada in the 1930s as a result of drought, habitat loss and trapping, and from eating poisoned bait meant for rodents and coyotes. In the 1970s, an Alberta couple began a captive-breeding program and, with the cooperation of prairie ranchers, swift foxes were reintroduced to their former grassland habitat. About 300 swift foxes live on the Canadian prairies today. • These opportunistic hunters feed mainly on small rodents and carrion and are in turn preyed upon by coyotes, eagles and hawks. • Unlike other foxes, swift foxes use their dens year-round for protection and birthing. **Where found:** dry grasslands of extreme southeastern Alberta; endangered.

Red Fox

Vulpes vulpes

Length: 91–107 cm
Height: 38 cm
Weight: 3.6–6.8 kg

Most red foxes are rusty reddish brown, but rare variations include blackish forms and even a silvery type. These small animals look like dogs but often act like cats, stalking mice and other small prey, and making energetic pounces to capture victims. • Red foxes typically den in old woodchuck burrows or similar holes. Unlike grey foxes, this species ranges into open landscapes and even suburbia. Tracks are often the best sign that foxes are present—their small, oval prints form a nearly straight line. **Where found:** open habitats with brushy shelter, riparian areas and edge habitats; throughout.

Porcupine

Erethizon dorsatum

Length: 66–104 cm
Weight: 3.5–18 kg

Prickly porcupines are best left alone. Contrary to popular myth, a porcupine cannot shoot its 30,000 or so quills, but with a lightning-fast flick of the tail, it will readily impale a persistent attacker with some of its spikes. • Slow but excellent climbers, porcupines clamber about in trees, stripping off the bark and feeding on the sugary cambium layer. Although sure-footed, they aren't infallible; about one-third of museum specimen skeletons examined in one study had old fractures, presumably from arboreal mishaps. • Porcupines crave salt and will gnaw on rubber tires, wooden axe handles, toilet seats and even hiking boots! **Where found:** coniferous and mixed deciduous-coniferous forests up to the subalpine; throughout.

63

Beaver
Castor canadensis
Length: 91–122 cm
Weight: 16–30 kg

No mammal influences its environment to the degree that this jumbo rodent—North America's largest—does. Its complex dams are engineering marvels that create ponds and wetlands that are then occupied by a diverse array of flora and fauna. In fact, the world's largest beaver dam, found in Wood Buffalo National Park, is 850 m long and is visible from space. Conical, gnawed stubs of tree trunks are a sure sign that beavers are present. With a loud warning slap of its tail on water, a beaver will often disappear before it is detected. **Where found:** lakes, ponds, marshes and slow-flowing rivers and streams; throughout.

Muskrat
Ondatra zibethicus
Length: 14–61 cm
Weight: 0.8–1.6 kg

More comfortable in water than on land, the muskrat has a laterally compressed tail that allows it to swim like a fish. Its occurrence in wetlands is easily detected by the presence of cone-shaped lodges made from cattails and other vegetation. • Muskrats play an important role in marsh management by thinning out dense stands of cattails. They also vex marsh managers by digging burrows in dikes. In general, muskrats are quite valuable in wetland ecosystems, creating diversified habitats that benefit many other species. **Where found:** lakes, marshes, ponds, rivers, reservoirs, dugouts and canals; throughout.

Meadow Jumping Mouse

Zapus hudsonius

Length: 19–22 cm
Weight: 15–25 g

Like a tiny kangaroo, the meadow jumping mouse can leap almost a metre when startled. It has large hind feet, powerful rear legs and a long tail to help it balance as it jumps. Mostly found in damp meadows, it can be identified by its distinctive mode of locomotion. • Meadow jumping mice hibernate for 6 to 7 months in underground burrows, one of the longest hibernation periods of any North American mammal. Their metabolism slows, and they survive on stored fat deposits. • The similar-looking western jumping mouse (*Z. princeps*) is common in the mountains, as well as in central and southern Alberta. **Where found:** prefers fields; also forest edges, marshes and streambanks; central and northern Alberta.

House Mouse

Mus musculus

Length: 14–19 cm
Weight: 14–25 g

If you have a mouse in your house, chances are it is a house mouse. This mouse has been fraternizing with humans for several thousand years. Like the brown rat, it stowed away on ships from Europe, quickly spreading across North America with settlers. • House mice are gregarious and social, even grooming one another. They are destructive in dwellings, however, shredding insulation for nests, leaving droppings and raiding pantries. • These tiny beasts have brownish to blackish grey backs and grey undersides. **Where found:** usually associated with humans, including houses, garages, farms, landfills and granaries; throughout.

Deer Mouse

Peromyscus maniculatus

Length: 12–18 cm
Weight: 18–35 g

This abundant mouse often occupies cavities in trees, stumps and logs, old buildings and bluebird nest boxes, where it builds a dense nest of plant matter. Strong swimmers, these little critters often brave the water to colonize islands. They primarily eat nuts, berries, seeds, vegetation and insects, but will also raid your pantry. • The deer mouse is pale to dark reddish brown above and white below, with protruding ears and a bicoloured tail. • The northern grasshopper mouse (*Onychomys leucogaster*) of southern Alberta is similar in colouration but is stockier and has thicker legs. **Where found:** varied habitats including woodlands, riparian areas, shrubby areas and some farmlands; throughout.

Bushy-tailed Woodrat

Neotoma cinerea

Length: 29–45 cm
Weight: 80–520 g

Woodrats are infamous for collecting objects, whether natural or human-made and whether useful or merely decorative, for their large, messy nests. Twigs, bones, pine cones, bottle caps, rings, pens and coins are picked up as this rodent scouts for treasures, often trading an object in its mouth for the next, more attractive item it encounters. A woodrat's nest is often more easily found than the woodrat itself. **Where found:** rocky outcroppings, shrublands, caves and mine shafts; from the grasslands of southern Alberta to alpine zones in the mountains. **Also known as:** packrat, trade rat.

Southern Red-backed Vole

Clethrionomys gapperi

Length: 12–16 cm
Weight: 12–43 g

Active day and night in spruce-fir forests and bogs, this abundant vole is easily recognized by its reddish brown back on an otherwise greyish body. As with other voles, the southern red-backed vole does not hibernate during winter; instead, it tunnels through the subnivean layer—along the ground, under the snow—in search of seeds, nuts and leaves. • Populations of these prolific voles vary according to predators and food supplies. They are probably the primary prey of the northern saw-whet owl. **Where found:** mixed and coniferous forests, bogs and riparian areas; throughout except the extreme southeast.

Meadow Vole

Microtus pennsylvanicus

Length: 14–20 cm
Weight: 18–64 g

Little furry sausages with legs, meadow voles are an important food for raptors, especially in winter. This rodent's populations have cyclical highs and lows, and in boom years, impressive numbers of hawks and owls will congregate in good vole fields. • Primarily active at night, this common vole can be seen during the day as well, especially when populations are high. • Meadow voles rank high among the world's most prolific breeders. If left unchecked by predators, they would practically rule the earth. • The heather vole (*Phenacomys intermedius*) is also common throughout Alberta except in southeastern grasslands. **Where found:** open woodlands, meadows, fields, fencelines and marshes; throughout.

Northern Bog Lemming

Synaptomys borealis

Length: 11–14 cm
Weight: 27–35 g

Lemmings look rather like voles but have larger, rounded heads. They live primarily in extensive systems of subsurface tunnels and feed mainly on grasses and sedges. Neatly clipped piles of grass along paths and their curious green scat indicate this animal's presence. • Lemmings remain active during winter, tunnelling through the subnivean layer—along the ground, under the snow. • Lemming populations vary from year to year, and in boom years especially, they are a major prey item for predators. **Where found:** among sedges and grasses; moist spruce forests and sphagnum bogs; throughout mountains; also central and northern Alberta.

Ord's Kangaroo Rat

Dipodomys ordii

Length: 26 cm
Weight: 68–71 g

With the aid of its extra-long tail, the Ord's kangaroo rat can leap 1.8 metres to avoid predators. These nocturnal mammals have acute hearing, tuned to detect an owl's near-silent wingbeats. • Ord's kangaroo rats live among sand dunes, surviving on seeds that they collect in their fur-lined cheek pouches. In Canada, they occupy only about 50 km^2 of open, arid sand dunes on the southern Alberta-Saskatchewan border, a habitat that is rapidly shrinking because of climate change and human encroachment. **Where found:** sparsely vegetated grassland and sandhills near Bindloss, Empress and Suffield in southeastern Alberta; endangered.

Olive-backed Pocket Mouse

Perognathus fasciatus

Length: 10–15 cm
Weight: 8–14 g

The tiny olive-backed pocket mouse explodes into motion when threatened, sometimes leaping 60 cm vertically. This specialized rodent inhabits open, sandy, thinly vegetated grasslands. Considered the slowest of all rodents, it spends much of the day grooming itself in an underground burrow but becomes active at dusk. • The olive-backed pocket mouse has large hind legs and small forelegs, and moves in an unusual hop, using all four limbs. **Where found:** open sandhills near Bindloss, Empress and Suffield in southeastern Alberta; military reserve roads on dark nights.

67

Northern Pocket Gopher

Thomomys talpoides

Length: 19–26 cm
Weight: 75–210 g

Supremely adapted for underground living, this burrowing mammal—incorrectly called a "mole"—has naked feet equipped with long front claws for digging. Other adaptations to tunnelling include furred lips that extend over the long incisor teeth to prevent dirt from entering the pocket gopher's mouth while it eats and digs, and fur-lined cheek pouches for temporary storage of roots, tubers and green plants. • A pocket gopher's incisor teeth grow as much as 1 mm per day. If unchecked by constant gnawing, the lower incisors could grow 36 cm in a year! • Pocket gophers leave fresh mounds of dirt on fields, lawns and gardens. **Where found:** various habitats including agricultural fields, grasslands and suburban lots; central and southern Alberta.

Woodchuck

Marmota monax

Length: 46–66 cm
Weight: 1.8–5.4 kg

Burly woodchucks have powerful claws for digging burrows up to 15 m long. Most people are used to seeing woodchucks scuttling along the ground, so it is a surprise to find them high up a tree, but they are squirrels, after all. More typically, they graze along forest edges and clearings, using their sharp incisors to rapidly cut plants, bark and berries. • Woodchucks are true hibernators and spend much of the year tucked away underground. Groundhog Day (February 2) celebrates their emergence. **Where found:** meadows, pastures and open woodlands; central and northern Alberta. **Also known as:** groundhog.

Hoary Marmot

Marmota caligata

Length: 70–80 cm
Weight: 5.0–7.0 kg

High up in alpine environments, hoary marmots excavate burrows in rocky terrain to hide from the elements and from predators such as eagles and foxes. They greet hikers with shrill whistles, from which the marmot's old nickname "whistler" is derived. • Hoary marmots spend their lazy days eating, sleeping and raising young, basking in the summer sun or hibernating in winter. **Where found:** rocky alpine tundra and subalpine areas near abundant vegetation; throughout the mountains.

Yellow-bellied Marmot

Marmota flaventris

Length: 47–67 cm
Weight: 1.6–5.2 kg

Yellow-bellied marmots may be seen basking in the morning sun or foraging in late afternoon, but they disappear into their burrows during the heat of midday. In Alberta, these stocky marmots are found south of the Milk River, at Head-Smashed-In Buffalo Jump or Writing-on-Stone Provincial Park. The Alberta-U.S. border marks the northern edge of their range, which extends from central BC south to central California and northern New Mexico. **Where found:** along rock piles and cou... from valley bottoms to alpine tundra; extreme southern Alberta.

Columbian Ground Squirrel

Spermophilus columbianus

Length: 33–41 cm
Weight: 8–12 cm

This vocal mammal is sometimes heard before it is seen. Robust Columbian ground squirrels chirp loudly, often at the first sight of anything unusual, and issue loud trills. These common ground squirrels are found everywhere from montane valleys to alpine meadows. • Columbian ground squirrels have been known to hibernate up to 220 days of the year. Some authorities believe they spend up to 90 percent of their lives underground. **Where found:** varied habitats including intermontane valleys, woodlands and alpine tundra; also mountains of western Alberta.

Thirteen-lined Ground Squirrel

Spermophilus tridecemlineatus

Length: 18–30 cm
Weight: 110–270 g

Highly social, these ground squirrels live in colonies and construct complex underground labyrinths to retreat to when threatened. From October to March, they retire into their burrows, singly or communally, spending winter curled up into tight balls. During hibernation, their respiration decreases from 100 to 200 breaths per minute to one breath every 5 minutes. **Where found:** prairies, abandoned fields, mowed lawns and agricultural areas; central and southern Alberta.

Richardson's Ground Squirrel

Spermophilus richardsonii

Length: 25–36 cm
Weight: 370–480 g

Familiar prairie inhabitants, Richardson's ground squirrels—more commonly known as "gophers"—issue shrill whistles and habitually flick their tails. They are often seen sitting upright at the entrance to a burrow or scampering through roadside ditches. • Burrows are hidden in the dense grass of open prairies and fields. Some authorities believe that these mammals spend up to 90 percent of their lives underground. • The Franklin's ground squirrel (*S. franklinii*) has a noticeably bushy tail and occurs in east-central Alberta's tall- and mid-grass prairies. **Where found:** prairies, meadows and pastures; central and southern Alberta; absent from mountains.

Golden-mantled Ground Squirrel

Spermophilus lateralis

Length: 28–33 cm
Weight: 170–340 g

A familiar campground resident, this ground squirrel is frequently misidentified as a large chipmunk because of its somewhat similar striping. Closer inspection reveals a distinct difference—the stripes stop short of this ground squirrel's neck (all chipmunks have stripes running through their cheeks). • The golden-mantled ground squirrel often has its cheek pouches crammed with seeds. **Where found:** montane and subalpine forests with rocky outcroppings or talus slopes; mountains of western Alberta.

Least Chipmunk

Neotamias minimus

Length: 17–23 cm
Weight: 35–71 g

Scampering along forest paths between hollowed-out logs, this cute, curious rodent has the widest distribution of the 22 North American chipmunk species. Its habitat ranges from sagebrush deserts to alpine tundra. • These incurable seed gatherers play an important role in forest ecology. In addition to hoarding food in their burrows, they often "lose" acorns and other fruit, helping to distribute plants. • Although chipmunks hibernate more or less from fall until spring, they wake every few weeks to feed, even coming above ground in mild weather. • The tawny to cinnamon-coloured yellow-pine chipmunk (*N. amoenus*) occurs in the mountains. **Where found:** campgrounds, coniferous forests, pastures and rocky outcroppings; throughout except the extreme south.

Red Squirrel

Tamiasciurus hudsonicus

Length: 28–34 cm
Weight: 140–250 g

This pugnacious and vocal squirrel often drives larger squirrels and birds from feeders, and sometimes takes bird eggs and nestlings. It can even eat highly poisonous *Amanita* mushrooms. Large piles of discarded pinecone scales are evidence of its buried food bounty. • During the short spring courtship, squirrels engage in incredibly acrobatic chases. • Introduced from the east, the black-coloured form of the eastern grey squirrel (*S. carolinensis*) is found in the Calgary area. **Where found:** coniferous and mixed forests; throughout.

Northern Flying Squirrel

Glaucomys sabrinus

Length: 24–36 cm
Weight: 75–180 g

Long flaps of skin (called the "patagium") stretched between the fore and hind limbs and a broad, flattened tail allow this nocturnal flying squirrel to glide swiftly from tree to tree. After landing, the squirrel inevitably hustles around to the opposite side of the trunk, in case a predator such as an owl has followed. • Flying squirrels play an important role in forest ecology because they dig up and eat truffles, the fruiting bodies of an ectomycorrhizal fungus that grows underground. Through its stool, the squirrel spreads the beneficial fungus, helping both the fungus and the forest plants. **Where found:** primarily old-growth coniferous and mixed forests; throughout except southern areas east of the mountains.

Pika

Ochotona princeps

Length: 16–21 cm
Weight: 150–300 g

The busy pika scurries in and out of rocky crevices issuing its warning *peeek!* call and gathering large bundles of succulent grasses to dry on sun-drenched rocks. It will store the dried grasses for consumption during winter, when the pika rarely leaves its shelter under the snow. In summer, it makes grassy nests within the rocks to have its young. • Although tail-less and with rounded ears, the pika is a close relative of rabbits and hares. **Where found:** rocky talus slopes and rocky fields at higher elevations; mountains.

Snowshoe Hare

Lepus americanus

Length: 38–53 cm
Weight: 1.0–1.5 kg

The snowshoe hare is completely adapted for life in snowy conditions. Large, snowshoe-like feet enable it to traverse powdery snow without sinking. Primarily nocturnal, this hare blends in perfectly with its surroundings regardless of the season. It is greyish, reddish or blackish brown in summer and white in winter. • If detected, the hare explodes into a running zigzag pattern in its flight for cover and can reach speeds of up to 50 km/h on hard-packed snow trails. **Where found:** brushy or forested areas; throughout except extreme southern grasslands.

White-tailed Jackrabbit

Lepus townsendii

Length: 54–64 cm
Weight: 3.0–5.4 kg

The speedy white-tailed jackrabbit is capable of 70 km/h sprints to outrun potential predators. Before taking flight, it sits motionless with its ears laid flat over its back. • Unlike rabbits, which give birth to altricial young and hide from danger, hares give birth to precocial young capable of running nearly from birth. Recent clearing of forests has created new habitat for this species. • The jackrabbit's buffy to brownish grey pelage turns white in winter. Its undersides, hind feet and tail remain white all year, and the long ears remain black-tipped. **Where found:** grasslands, shrublands and sagebrush; central and southern Alberta.

Nuttall's Cottontail

Sylvilagus nuttallii

Length: 34–40 cm
Weight: 0.7–1.0 kg

The Nuttall's cottontail is the smallest of our lagomorphs. Adapted to the arid prairie grasslands, cottontails avoid daytime predators by hiding in shallow depressions under thorny buffaloberry or similar shrubs, or under other cover such as rocks or machinery. They emerge at dusk to graze on grasses, forbs and sagebrush or juniper berries, but cottontails never stray far from cover. Areas such as Dinosaur Provincial Park or the Oldman River valley in southern Alberta offer intimate viewing opportunities. **Where found:** variety of habitats near shrubby cover; southern Alberta. **Also known as:** mountain cottontail.

Northern Bat

Myotis septentrionalis

Length: 8.3–10 cm
Forearm length: 3.3–4.0 mm
Weight: 3.5–8.9 g

With Spock-like ears, the northern bat presents an outrageous visage—if you are lucky enough to be able to admire one close up. • Most bats forage by catching insects while in flight, pursuing them with incredible aerial acrobatics. Instead, the northern bat picks an insect victim from the foliage of a tree, and then hangs from a branch to consume it. • With almost 1000 species found worldwide, bats are the most successful mammals after rodents. **Where found:** coniferous and deciduous forests, often close to water; roosts in tree cavities, under peeling bark and in rock crevices; hibernates in caves and abandoned mines; central and northern Alberta.

Long-eared Bat

Myotis evotis

Length: 9–10 cm
Forearm length: 2.7 cm
Weight: 4.2–10.0 g

Like all other bats, the long-eared bat uses echolocation to navigate and to find prey in complete darkness. By producing short bursts of high-frequency sound and then listening for the echo bouncing off objects in the distance, bats can determine the direction, distance, size and texture of objects to avoid or eat. This bat's black ears are 2 cm long with a long, sharp tragus.
Where found: roosts in buildings, under tree bark and occasionally in caves; hibernates in caves and mines; southern Alberta including the mountains.

Little Brown Bat

Myotis lucifugus

Length: 7–10 cm
Forearm length: 3.5–4.1 cm
Weight: 5.3–8.9 g

Each spring, little brown bats form maternal roosting colonies that can number thousands of individuals—one colony had nearly 7000 members. • Virtually helpless at birth, the single offspring clings to its mother's chest until it is strong enough to remain on its own at the roost site. • A single little brown bat can consume 900 insects per hour. A typical bat colony will eat 50 kg of insects per year. **Where found:** roosts in buildings, barns, caves, crevices, hollow trees and under tree bark; hibernates in buildings, caves and old mines; throughout.

Hoary Bat

Lasiurus cinereus

Length: 11–15 cm
Forearm length: 4.5–5.7 cm
Weight: 19–35 g

The hoary bat is the most widely distributed—and arguably the most beautiful—bat in North America. Its large size and frosty-silver fur make it quite distinctive. • These bats roost in trees, not caves or buildings, and wrap their wings around themselves for protection against the elements. They often roost in orchards, but they are insectivores and do no damage to fruit crops. You can identify them at night by their large size and slow wingbeats over open terrain. **Where found:** roosts in coniferous and deciduous trees, occasionally in tree cavities; migrates south for the winter; throughout.

Silver-haired Bat

Lasionycteris noctivagans

Length: 9–11 cm
Forearm length: 3.5–5.0 cm
Weight: 7–18 g

The silver-haired bat is most likely to be found roosting under a loose piece of bark. It sometimes occurs in small, loosely associated groups. • These bats mate in the fall, but actual fertilization doesn't occur until spring. This odd strategy ensures that plenty of food will be available when the young are born. • To conserve energy on cold days, bats can lower their body temperature and slow their metabolism—a state known as "torpor." **Where found:** roosts in cavities and crevices of old-growth trees; migrates south for the winter; throughout except extreme northern Alberta.

Big Brown Bat

Eptesicus fuscus

Length: 9–14 cm
Forearm length: 4.6–5.4 mm
Weight: 12–28 g

This bat's ultrasonic echolocation (20,000 to 110,000 Hz) can detect flying beetles and moths up to 5 m away. It flies above water or around streetlights searching for prey, which it scoops up with its wing and tail membranes. • Few animals rest as much as bats, and they can live for many decades owing to the low stress on their physiological systems. After 2 or 3 hours on the wing each evening, they perch, and their body functions slow down for the rest of the day. **Where found:** in and around artificial structures; occasionally roosts in hollow trees and rock crevices; hibernates in caves, mines and old buildings; throughout except the extreme northeast.

Masked Shrew

Sorex cinereus

Length: 7–11 cm
Weight: 2–7 g

This mammal is one of our most
abundant—but good luck seeing one.
Mostly nocturnal, this voracious shrew scurries about in dense cover, consuming
its body weight or more in food daily. • To balance high late-winter mortality
rates and year-round predation, females may have 2 to 3 litters per year, giving
birth to as many as 8 blind, toothless and naked young per litter. • The brown
or cinnamon-coloured prairie shrew (*S. haydeni*) inhabits prairie regions in
southeastern Alberta. **Where found:** forests and occasionally tall-grass prairies;
throughout except the southeast.

Northern Water Shrew

Sorex palustris

Length: 13–17 cm
Weight: 9–19 g

The water shrew has large feet fitted with
stiff, bristly hairs that allow it to run across the water's
surface for a surprising distance. Thick, insulating body fur traps
air bubbles between the hairs and allows this shrew to hunt aquatic invertebrates
in cold ponds and streams. Robust for a shrew, it catches small fish and tadpoles
that other shrews cannot. • The smaller, greyish dusky shrew (*S. monticolus*)
inhabits moist habitats over a similar range. **Where found:** fast-flowing
streams; also lakes, ponds and marshes with vegetated shorelines; throughout
except the southeast.

Pygmy Shrew

Sorex hoyi

Length: 11–13 cm
Weight: 2–7 g

The pygmy shrew is our smallest mammal and weighs no
more than a penny. • Shrews have an incredibly high metabolic rate, with heart
rates often reaching 1200 beats per minute. Most of the heat energy the pygmy
shrew produces is quickly lost, so it routinely eats 3 times its body weight in a day,
taking down and consuming any prey that can be overpowered. • These secretive,
pennyweight shrews stand up on their hind legs, curiously like bears. **Where
found:** various habitats from forests to open fields and sphagnum bogs; throughout except the southeast.

BIRDS

Birds are the most diverse class of vertebrates. All birds are feathered but not all fly. Traits common to all birds are that they are two-legged, warm-blooded and lay hard-shelled eggs. Some migrate south in the colder winter months and return north in spring. For this reason, the diversity of Alberta birds varies with the seasons. Some of our well-known winter birds include chickadees, downy woodpeckers, waxwings, nuthatches and snowy owls. Spring brings scores of migrant waterfowl and colourful songbirds that breed in our region and other birds such as shorebirds that continue on to Arctic breeding grounds. Even more migratory birds pass through in autumn, their numbers bolstered by the young of the year. Many are in duller plumage at this time, and they are largely silent. Scores of migrating birds fly as far south as Central and South America. These neotropical migrants are of concern to biologists and conservationists because of habitat degradation and loss, collisions with human-made towers, pesticide use and other factors that threaten their survival. Education and an increasing appreciation for wildlife may encourage solutions to these problems.

Waterfowl
pp. 78–81

Grouse & Allies
pp. 82–83

Diving Birds
pp. 83–84

Herons & Vultures
p. 85

Birds of Prey
pp. 86–88

Rails & Coots
pp. 88–89

Cranes
p. 89

Shorebirds
pp. 89–91

Gulls & Allies
pp. 91–92

Pigeons & Doves
p. 92

Owls
pp. 93–95

Nighthawks
p. 95

Hummingbirds & Kingfishers
p. 96

Woodpeckers
pp. 97–98

Flycatchers
pp. 98–99

Shrikes & Vireos
p. 99

Jays, Magpies & Ravens
pp. 100–101

Larks & Swallows
pp. 101–102

Chickadees & Nuthatches
p. 102

Wrens
p. 103

Kinglets & Thrushes
pp. 103–104

Mimics, Starlings & Waxwings
pp. 104–105

Wood-warblers
pp. 106–107

Sparrows
pp. 107–108

Tanagers & Grosbeaks
p. 109

Blackbirds & Allies
pp. 109–111

Finch-like Birds
pp. 111–112

Snow Goose

Chen caerulescens

Length: 71–84 cm
Wingspan: 1.4–1.5 m

Noisy flocks of snow geese fly in wavy, disorganized lines, giving loud, nasal *houk-houk* calls in flight, higher pitched and more constant than the calls of Canada geese. • Snow geese breed in the Arctic, some travelling as far as northeastern Siberia and crossing the Bering Strait twice a year. These common geese have all-white bodies and black wing tips. An equally common colour morph known as the "blue goose" has a dark body and a white head, and was considered a distinct species until 1983. **Where found:** croplands, fields and marshes; locally common migrant in eastern Alberta, Mar–Apr and Sept–Oct.

Canada Goose

Branta canadensis

Length: 92–122 cm
Wingspan: up to 1.8 m

Few avian spectacles rival that of immense flocks of migrating Canada geese. The collective honking of airborne groups can be heard for 2 km or more. • This goose varies throughout its range and was split into 2 species in 2004. The large subspecies are called Canada geese, and the smaller, mallard-sized birds are now known as cackling geese. The latter is scarcer in our region. Canada geese are probably the most instantly recognizable species of waterfowl in North America. **Where found:** lakeshores, riverbanks, ponds, farmlands and city parks; common throughout, Mar–Oct; a few may overwinter.

Tundra Swan

Cygnus columbianus

Length: 1.2–1.5 m
Wingspan: 1.8–2.1 m

As waters begin to thaw in early April, noisy tundra swans arrive on the prairies to feed in flooded fields and pastures. Swans have all-white wings, unlike snow geese, which have black wing tips. • Other than the rare trumpeter swan (*Cygnus buccinator*), this species is the largest native bird in our region, and adults can weigh up to 7 kg. It would take about 2075 ruby-throated hummingbirds to equal the weight of a tundra swan, illustrating the dramatic diversity of the bird world. **Where found:** shallow areas of lakes and wetlands; flooded agricultural fields and pastures; common migrant throughout, Apr and Oct.

American Wigeon

Anas americana

Length: 46–58 cm
Wingspan: 65 cm

The American wigeon
may dabble for aquatic plants or steal the succulent stems or leaves of pond-bottom plants from more accomplished divers such as redheads (*Aythya americana*) or American coots. Wigeons also commonly graze on shore, uprooting young shoots in fields. They are good walkers compared to other ducks. This species occurs in wetlands with abundant surface vegetation, but city parks, golf courses and airports also provide opportunities for grazing. **Where found:** shallow wetlands and pond or lake edges east of the mountains; common, Mar–Oct.

Mallard

Anas platyrhynchos

Length: 51–71 cm
Wingspan: 76 cm

The male mallard, with his shiny green head, chestnut brown breast and stereotypical quack, is one of the best-known and most commonly seen ducks. • Mallards are extremely adaptable and can become semi-tame fixtures on suburban ponds. They will remain year-round wherever open water is available. • After breeding, male ducks lose their elaborate plumage, helping them stay camouflaged during their flightless period. In early fall, they moult back into breeding colours. **Where found:** lakes, wetlands, rivers, city parks, agricultural areas and sewage lagoons; very common throughout, Mar–Nov; may overwinter where open water persists.

Blue-winged Teal

Anas discors

Length: 36–41 cm
Wingspan: 58 cm

Blue-winged teals are speedy on the wing, able to execute sharp twists and turns, often just above the water's surface. These dabbling ducks lurk in dense marsh vegetation and can be easily overlooked. Look for the white, crescent-shaped patch next to the male's bill, visible in all plumages. As is typical with waterfowl, the female is much plainer, her dull plumage providing camouflage as she incubates her eggs on a ground nest. **Where found:** lake edges, shallow wetlands and flooded fields; common throughout, Apr–Oct.

Northern Shoveler

Anas clypeata

Length: 46–50 cm
Wingspan: 76 cm

The northern shoveler has a green, mallard-like head but is distinguished by its much-larger bill. • A shoveler dabbles on the surface for food, stirring up shallow water with its feet, then submerging its head to feed. It pumps water into and out of its bill with its tongue, using long, comb-like structures (called "lamellae") that line the sides of its bill to filter out food. **Where found:** wetlands, sloughs and lakes with muddy bottoms and emergent vegetation; uncommon to common throughout, Apr–Oct.

Northern Pintail

Anas acuta

Length: *Male:* 64–76 cm; *Female:* 51–56 cm
Wingspan: 86 cm

Elegant and graceful both on water and in air, the northern pintail is a beautiful bird. The male's 2 long, pointed tail feathers are easily seen in flight and point skyward when the bird tips up to dabble. • Northern pintails are the most widely distributed duck in the world. Despite impressive numbers in our region, drought, wetland drainage and changing agricultural practices are the most serious threats to this species and are contributing to a slow population decline. **Where found:** shallow wetlands, flooded fields and lake edges; common throughout, Mar–Oct.

Lesser Scaup

Aythya affinis

Length: 38–45 cm
Wingspan: 63 cm

Like an Oreo cookie, scaups are white in the middle and dark at both ends. Two similar-looking species occur in our region, the lesser scaup and greater scaup (*A. marila*), but it takes a lot of experience to reliably separate them in the field. • Lesser scaups are the most abundant diving duck in North America. They make up nearly 90 percent of the total scaup population, but for unknown reasons, the combined numbers of the 2 species are decreasing by over 150,000 birds per year. **Where found:** lakes, open marshes and slow-moving rivers; common throughout, Apr–Oct.

Common Goldeneye

Bucephala clangula

Length: 41–51 cm
Wingspan: 66 cm

Common goldeneyes are sometimes called "whistlers" because the drake's wings create a loud, distinctive hum in flight • In mid-April, testosterone-flooded males arrive and begin their crazy courtship dances, emitting low buzzes, lunging across the water and kicking their brilliant orange feet forward like aquatic break-dancers. • The Barrow's goldeneye (*B. islandica*) is a characteristic diving duck of the mountains and foothills. The male has a dark purple head and white cheek crescent; the female has a chocolate brown head. **Where found:** lakes and rivers near mature forests; common throughout except southern grasslands, Apr–Oct.

Common Merganser

Mergus merganser

Length: 56–69 cm
Wingspan: 86 cm

Like gleaming white submarines, merganser drakes ride low in the water. Noticeably larger than most other duck species, these jumbos can tip the scales at 1.6 kg, making them one of our heaviest ducks. • Mergansers have bills that are sharply serrated like carving knives, designed to catch and hold their fishy prey. • Outside the breeding season, mergansers are highly social, forming large flocks. Three merganser species occur in our province: the common, the red-breasted (*M. serrator*) and the hooded (*Lophodytes cucullatus*). **Where found:** large, forest-lined rivers, deep lakes and reservoirs; common in boreal forests and mountains, uncommon migrant on the prairies, Mar–Oct.

Ruddy Duck

Oxyura jamaicensis

Length: 38–41 cm
Wingspan: 56–62 cm

This unusual little duck often holds its stiff tail upright. The drake is resplendent in breeding plumage, with a bright azure bill, a large, white cheek patch and a rusty brown body. During courtship, the male puts on a vigorous bill-pumping display accompanied by staccato grunts and a stream of bubbles. • Although the ruddy is one of our smallest ducks, the female lays enormous eggs, larger than those of a mallard, even though a mallard is twice the size of a ruddy duck. **Where found:** prairie wetlands with emergent vegetation; common east of the mountains, Apr–Sept.

Gray Partridge

Perdix perdix

Length: 28–36 cm
Wingspan: 20 cm

Watch for the grey partridge at dawn, "gravelling up" along quiet country roads. Like other seed-eating birds, it regularly swallows small bits of gravel. The gravel accumulates in the bird's gizzard, a muscular pouch of the digestive system, and helps crush the hard seeds the partridge feeds on. • During cold weather, gray partridges huddle together in a circle with the birds all facing outward, ready to burst into flight at the first sign of danger. These Eurasian game birds are relatively hardy, but many perish during harsh winters. **Where found:** weedy fields and agricultural lands, often near hedgerows; uncommon year-round in the southern half of Alberta, east of the mountains.

Ring-necked Pheasant

Phasianus colchicus

Length: *Male:* 76–91 cm; *Female:* 51–66 cm
Wingspan: *Male:* 71–84 cm; *Female:* 49–63 cm

The spectacular Asian ring-necked pheasant was introduced to North America in the mid-1800s, mainly for hunting purposes. Unlike most other introduced species, ring-necks became established in southern areas and thrived almost everywhere they were released. The loud, distinctive *krahh-krawk* of the male pheasant is often heard, but the birds themselves are less frequently observed. • Like other game birds, pheasants have poorly developed flight muscles and rarely fly far. **Where found:** farmlands, brushy hedgerows, forest edges and marshes; uncommon to common year-round in the southern half of Alberta, east of the mountains.

Ruffed Grouse

Bonasa umbellus

Length: 38–48 cm
Wingspan: 56 cm

A displaying male ruffed grouse makes a sound that is felt more than heard. Each spring, the male grouse proclaims his territory by strutting along a fallen log with his tail fanned wide and his neck feathers ruffed, beating the air with accelerating wing strokes. Drumming is usually restricted to spring, but ruffed grouse may also drum for a few weeks in autumn. • This grouse is well adapted to its northern environment. In autumn and early winter, scales on the sides of its toes grow out, creating temporary snowshoes. **Where found:** deciduous and mixed forests, and riparian woodlands; undergoes cyclical population fluctuations; common year-round throughout except southern grasslands.

Spruce Grouse

Falcipennis canadensis

Length: 33–41 cm
Wingspan: 57 cm

The forest-dwelling spruce grouse trusts its cryptic plumage to conceal it from view in its dark, damp, year-round home. Despite its many predators, this grouse often allows people to approach to within a few metres, which is the reason it is sometimes called "fool hen." • In spring, strutting male spruce grouse are seen in open areas along trails and roads. A displaying male transforms from his usual dull camouflage to a red-eyebrowed, puff-necked, fan-tailed splendour. • In Alberta, there are 2 distinct forms of the spruce grouse: the "Franklin's grouse" in the mountains and the "Boreal grouse" in the boreal forest. **Where found:** conifer-dominated forests; sometimes disperses into deciduous forests; uncommon to common year-round throughout except southern grasslands.

Wild Turkey

Meleagris gallopavo

Length: *Male:* 1.2–1.3 m; *Female:* 89–94 cm
Wingspan: *Male:* 1.6 m; *Female:* 1.2 m

This charismatic bird is the only widely domesticated native North American animal—the wild ancestors of most other domestic animals came from Europe. • More common in eastern Canada, wild turkeys were introduced into the Cypress Hills in 1962, and this bird's loud, distinctive voice is a reliable wake-up call in the park campgrounds. The species was also introduced into the Porcupine Hills, and birds are seen regularly in the foothills near Turner Valley. • Wild turkeys prefer to stay on the ground and can run faster than 30 km/h. However, they are able to fly short distances and roost in trees at night. **Where found:** deciduous, mixed and riparian woodlands; uncommon year-round in Cypress Hills PP and the Porcupine Hills.

Common Loon

Gavia immer

Length: 71–89 cm
Wingspan: 1.2–1.5 m

The wild, yodelling cries of loons are a symbol of our northern wilderness and evoke images of remote lakes. • These excellent underwater hunters have nearly solid bones that decrease their buoyancy (most birds have hollow bones), and their feet are placed well back on their bodies to aid in underwater propulsion. Small bass, perch and sunfish are all fair game for these birds, and they will chase fish to depths of up to 55 m. **Where found:** large lakes and rivers; uncommon to common throughout but rare in grasslands, May–Oct.

Red-necked Grebe

Podiceps grisegena

Length: 43–56 cm
Wingspan: 76–84 cm

The whinnying of red-necked grebes can heard around lake margins throughout Alberta. Although these grebes aren't as vocally refined as loons, few loons can match the energy of a pair of grebes. • Grebes carry their newly hatched, striped young on their backs. The young can stay aboard even when the parents dive underwater. • Grebes have individually webbed, or "lobed," feet. The three forward-facing toes have special flanges that are not connected to the other toes. **Where found:** lakes and ponds; breeds in the emergent vegetation zone; uncommon to locally common throughout, May–Oct.

American White Pelican

Pelecanus erythrorhynchos

Length: 1.3–1.7 m
Wingspan: 3 m

Majestic American white pelicans breed in colonies on the Canadian prairies and in the western United States, and they winter from the southern U.S. to Guatemala, travelling between breeding and wintering areas in flocks of dozens of individuals. • American white pelicans feed cooperatively, swimming in flocks and herding fish into shallow water. As a pelican lifts its bill from the water, fish are held within the flexible pouch while the water drains, then the fish are swallowed whole. The pelican's pouch can hold up to 12 litres! **Where found:** rivers and freshwater lakes; uncommon to locally common in the eastern half of Alberta, Apr–Sept.

Double-crested Cormorant

Phalacrocorax auritus

Length: 66–81 cm
Wingspan: 1.3 m

Double-crested cormorants can outswim fish, which they capture in underwater dives. Most waterbirds have water-proof feathers, but the cormorant's feathers allow water in. "Wettable" feathers make this bird less buoyant and a better diver. It has sealed nostrils for diving and therefore must occasionally open its bill while in flight. Cormorants feed mainly on shallow-water, non-commercial fish such as suckers. **Where found:** large lakes; uncommon to locally common east of the mountains in the southern two-thirds of Alberta, Apr–Sept.

American Bittern

Botaurus lentiginosus

Length: 58–70 cm
Wingspan: 1.1 m

Cryptic American bitterns inhabit marshes throughout our region. Their deep, resonate calls can be heard on spring nights, but these well-camouflaged birds tend to remain hidden. A threatened bittern will freeze with its bill pointed skyward—its vertically streaked, brown plumage blends in perfectly with the surrounding marsh. In most cases, intruders simply pass by without ever noticing the bird. • American bitterns are sensitive to human disturbance. Populations are declining across North America because of wetland habitat loss or degradation. **Where found:** marshes, wetlands and lake edges with tall, emergent vegetation; uncommon east of the mountains, Apr–Oct.

Great Blue Heron

Ardea herodias

Length: 1.3–1.4 m
Wingspan: 1.8 m

The stealthy great blue heron waits motionlessly for a fish or frog to approach, spears the prey with its bill, and then swallows it whole. Herons usually hunt near water, but they also stalk fields and meadows in search of rodents. • Great blue herons settle in communal treetop nests called rookeries. Nesting herons are sensitive to human disturbance, so observe this bird's behaviour from a distance. **Where found:** along the edges of rivers, lakes, marshes, fields and wet meadows; common in the southern two-thirds of Alberta east of the mountains, Mar–Oct; a few may overwinter.

Turkey Vulture

Cathartes aura

Length: 66–81 cm
Wingspan: 1.7–1.8 m

Turkey vultures rock slightly from side to side as they soar, rarely flapping their wings. They hold their wings in a dihedral, or V-shaped position. Endowed with incredible vision and olfactory senses, turkey vultures can detect carrion, their only food source, at great distances. • Vultures often form communal roosts in trees, atop buildings, in barn lofts or on power line towers and will use the same roosting sites for decades. • Do not approach a turkey vulture nest; these birds will vomit a decidedly unpleasant goop on invaders. **Where found:** habitat generalist; uncommon in southeastern Alberta, May–Sept.

Bald Eagle

Haliaeetus leucocephalus

Length: 79–109 cm
Wingspan: 1.7–2.4 m

The majestic bald eagle is usually found near water. It preys on fish but is also an inveterate scavenger. • Bald eagles do not mature until their fourth or fifth year, when they develop the characteristic white head and tail plumage. • These birds mate for life and reuse nests year after year, adding to them each season. Their aeries can grow to mammoth proportions and are the largest of any North American bird. **Where found:** large lakes and rivers; uncommon throughout except grasslands, Mar–Nov; may overwinter near open water.

Northern Harrier

Circus cyaneus

Length: 41–61 cm
Wingspan: 1.1–1.2 m

In flight, this graceful raptor is unmistakable. Harriers have a distinctive white rump patch and fly low over the ground with their wings raised in a slight dihedral, or "V" shape. Their sudden appearance startles small prey such as voles, which are quickly pounced on. • A perched northern harrier looks astonishingly like an owl—it has prominent facial discs to better detect and focus sounds. • Britain's Royal Air Force was so impressed by the northern harrier's manoeuvrability that it named the Harrier aircraft after this bird. **Where found:** open country including fields, wet meadows and marshes; common on the prairies, uncommon elsewhere, Mar–Oct.

Swainson's Hawk

Buteo swainsoni

Length: 48–51 cm
Wingspan: 1.3 m

The common buteo of the prairies, the Swainson's hawk dominates the skies wherever ground squirrels are abundant. Pointed wing tips, slightly upturned wings and dark flight feathers differentiate the Swainson's hawk from all other raptors in flight. • Every year, these hawks undertake long migrations, from the tip of South America as far north as Alaska and back again. Travelling up to 20,000 km in a single year, the Swainson's hawk is second only to the Arctic-breeding peregrine falcon for long-distance travel among birds of prey. **Where found:** open fields and grasslands with scattered trees; common on the prairies, Apr–Sept.

Red-tailed Hawk

Buteo jamaicensis

Length: *Male:* 46–58 cm; *Female:* 51–64 cm
Wingspan: 1.2–1.5 m

Common and widespread, red-tailed hawks are often seen along country roads, perched on fences or trees, especially in the aspen parkland ecoregion. Their white breasts render them conspicuous. Red-tails belong to a group of hawks known as buteos, which typically soar in lazy circles or perch prominently, searching for prey. • The red-tailed hawk's impressive, piercing call is often paired with the image of an eagle in TV commercials and movies. **Where found:** open country with some trees; also roadsides or woodlots; very common in central and southern Alberta, becoming uncommon northward, Mar–Oct.

Rough-legged Hawk

Buteo lagopus

Length: 48–61 cm
Wingspan: 1.2–1.4 m

When lemming and vole numbers are high on their Arctic breeding grounds, these hawks can produce up to 7 young, resulting in many sightings in our area. In lean years, a pair is fortunate to raise a single chick, and sightings here are rarer. • Rough-legged hawks show great variety in colouration, from a whitish light morph to an almost entirely dark morph, both with contrasting patterning. • This buteo often hovers in a stationary position, an adaptation to hunting in open-country habitat that often lacks high perches. **Where found:** fields, wet meadows, open bogs and croplands; uncommon to common migrant throughout, Mar and Sept–Oct; overwinters south of Calgary.

American Kestrel

Falco sparverius

Length: 23–30 cm
Wingspan: 50–62 cm

The colourful American kestrel frequently perches on roadside wires or hovers over fields like an avian helicopter. This little falcon feeds on small rodents but switches to a diet heavy in grasshoppers in warmer months. • Most evidence suggests that kestrel populations are declining significantly in many areas, partly because of a lack of nesting holes. You can help these cavity-nesting falcons by erecting appropriate nest boxes in suitable habitat. **Where found:** open fields, grassy roadsides and agricultural areas; common throughout, Apr–Oct.

Merlin

Falco columbarius

Length: 25–35 cm
Wingspan: 60–68 cm

Using speed, surprise and sharp talons, the merlin often snatches songbirds in midair. This aerodynamic falcon, with its pointed wings and narrow, banded tail, is often seen flying low and fast over treed urban areas. Its noisy, cackling *kek-kek-kek-kek* call is heard in spring. • Most merlins migrate south each autumn, but some remain on the prairies for the winter, enticed by milder urban climates and an abundance of songbirds at backyard feeders. **Where found:** treed areas next to open hunting grounds; also suburban areas and lakeshores; uncommon year-round; fairly common, mainly in cities, in winter.

Peregrine Falcon

Falco peregrinus

Length: *Male:* 38–43 cm; *Female:* 43–48 cm
Wingspan: 1.0–1.1 m

Nothing causes more panic in a flock of ducks or shorebirds than a hunting peregrine falcon. This agile raptor matches every twist and turn the flock makes, then dives to strike a lethal blow. • The peregrine falcon is the world's fastest bird. In a headfirst dive, it can reach speeds of up to 350 km/h. • The peregrine falcon represents a successful conservation effort since the banning of DDT in North America in 1972. In 1999, it was removed from the Endangered Species list. **Where found:** open marine areas, rivers, lakeshores, open fields and urban areas; nests on rocky cliffs or skyscraper ledges; uncommon migrant and local breeder throughout, Apr–Oct.

Sora

Porzana carolina

Length: 20–25 cm
Wingspan: 30–36 cm

Two loud, plaintive whistles followed by a descending whinny announce the presence of the sora. Although you have probably never seen this bird, it can be surprisingly abundant. A stone tossed into the dense, inaccessible marshes that the sora inhabits during summer might elicit a sharp *keek* alarm call. • Soras and other rails have large, chicken-like feet for walking on aquatic vegetation, and they swim quite well over short distances. They can laterally compress their bodies to slip effortlessly through thick cattail stands. **Where found:** marshes and sloughs with abundant emergent vegetation; fairly common in the north, common elsewhere, May–Sept.

American Coot

Fulica americana

Length: 33–40 cm
Wingspan: 58–70 cm

Sometimes called "mudhens," coots are the extroverts of the rail world. While the rest of the clan remains hidden in wetland vegetation, coots swim in open water like ducks. Their individually webbed toes make them efficient swimmers and good divers, but they aren't above snatching a meal from another skilled diver. • In marshes where they breed, American coots give loud, maniacal, laughing calls. Newly hatched young have distinct, reddish orange down and bald, red crowns. **Where found:** shallow, open wetlands with emergent vegetation; common to abundant on the prairies, becoming rare northward, Apr–Oct.

Sandhill Crane

Grus canadensis

Length: 1.1–1.2 m
Wingspan: 1.8–2.1 m

The sandhill crane has a deep, rattling call that resonates from its coiled trachea to carry great distances. Migrating flocks sail on thermal updrafts, circling and gliding at such great heights that they can scarcely be seen. In spring, cranes occasionally touch down on open fields to perform spectacular courtship dances, calling, bowing and leaping with partially raised wings. • The larger, white whooping crane (*G. americana*) migrates through eastern Alberta and breeds in Wood Buffalo National Park, which straddles the Alberta-NWT border. **Where found:** uncommon migrant in agricultural fields and on shorelines; uncommon breeder in isolated, northern boreal bogs, May–Oct.

Killdeer

Charadrius vociferus

Length: 23–28 cm
Wingspan: 61 cm

When an intruder wanders too close to its nest, the killdeer puts on its "broken wing" display. It greets the interloper with piteous *kill-dee kill-dee* cries while dragging a wing and stumbling about as if injured. Most predators take the bait and follow, and once the intruder has been lured far away from the nest, the killdeer flies off with a loud call. • This species' population has grown tremendously in modern times because human activities have increased suitable habitat. **Where found:** open fields, lakeshores, gravel streambeds, parking lots and large lawns; very common throughout, Apr–Oct.

Spotted Sandpiper

Actitis macularius

Length: 18–20 cm
Wingspan: 38 cm

In a rare case of sexual role reversal, the female spotted sandpiper is the aggressor. She diligently defends her territory and may mate with several males, an unusual breeding strategy known as "polyandry." Each summer, the female can lay up to 4 clutches and is capable of producing 20 eggs. She lays the eggs but does little else, leaving the males to tend the clutches. • The solitary sandpiper (*Tringa solitaria*), found in central and northern Alberta's forested wetlands from May to September, has a grey-brown, spotted back and unmarked white underparts. **Where found:** shorelines, gravel beaches, swamps and sewage lagoons; common throughout, May–Sept.

Lesser Yellowlegs

Tringa flavipes

Length: 25–28 cm
Wingspan: 71 cm

The lesser yellowlegs and the greater yellowlegs (*T. melanoleuca*) are very similar, medium to large sandpipers. The lesser has a much finer, shorter bill (about as long as its head is wide), longer, thinner legs and normally delivers a pair of whistles, whereas the greater yellowlegs utters a louder, more strident series of 3 or more whistles. The overall body mass of a lesser is only half that of a greater, a trait that is very apparent when the species are seen together. • Yellowlegs are sometimes called "telltales" because they alert all the shorebirds on a mudflat to invaders such as birders. **Where found:** shallow wetlands, shorelines and flooded fields; common migrant on the prairies, common breeder in the boreal forest and northward, Apr–Oct.

Marbled Godwit

Limosa fedoa

Length: 41–51 cm
Wingspan: 76 cm

Marbled godwits, with their distinctive, large, upturned bills, are the most common large shorebird throughout the southern half of Alberta. They draw attention to themselves with their loud vocalizations. • The dark tip on a godwit's bill may give it extra strength, because the dark pigment, melanin, hardens the structures of both bills and feathers. **Where found:** muddy shorelines of lakes, reservoirs, wet meadows, moist grasslands and open areas; common in the southern half of Alberta east of the mountains, Apr–Oct.

Wilson's Snipe

Gallinago delicata

Length: 27–29 cm
Wingspan: 46 cm

The winnowing of the Wilson's snipe is synonymous with spring evenings at a wetland. Snipes engage in spectacular aerial courtship displays, swooping and diving at great heights with their tails spread—the winnowing sound is made by air rushing past the outer tail feathers. • Well-camouflaged snipes are often concealed by vegetation. When flushed from cover, the snipe utters a harsh *skape* note, and then flies in a low, rapid, zigzag pattern to confuse any would-be predators. **Where found:** marshes, meadows and wetlands; common throughout except dry grasslands, Apr–Sept.

Wilson's Phalarope

Phalaropus tricolor

Length: 21–24 cm
Wingspan: 36–40 cm

Phalaropes are the windup toys of the bird world—when feeding, they spin and whirl about in tight circles, stirring up the water, then, with needlelike bills, they pick out the aquatic insects and small crustaceans that funnel toward the surface. • With all phalaropes, sexual roles are reversed. The larger, more colourful female may mate with several males, an unusual strategy known as "polyandry." The female lays the eggs, but the male incubates them and tends the young. **Where found:** marshes, wet meadows, sewage lagoons and lakeshores during migration; uncommon to common throughout but absent from the mountains, May–Sept.

Franklin's Gull

Leucophaeus pipixcan

Length: 33–38 cm
Wingspan: 90 cm

Small and buoyant on the wing, Franklin's gulls are very different from their larger, cruder cousins. This common prairie gull nests on inland lakes but winters on the coast. • Feeding Franklin's gulls often follow tractors across agricultural fields, snatching up insects from the tractor's path in much the same way other gulls follow fishing boats. • Spring migrants are resplendent with their black heads, as if the birds had been dunked in dark paint. **Where found:** agricultural fields, marshy lakes, landfills, riverbanks and lake shorelines; common in the eastern half of Alberta, Apr–Sept.

Ring-billed Gull

Larus delawarensis

Length: 46–51 cm
Wingspan: 1.2 m

Few people can claim that they have never seen this common and widespread gull. Highly tolerant of humans, ring-billed gulls eat almost anything and will swarm parks, beaches, golf courses and fast-food restaurant parking lots looking for food handouts. • The ring-bill is a three-year gull, acquiring adult plumage in its third calendar year of life after going through a series of subadult moults. **Where found:** lakes, rivers, landfills, parking lots, fields and parks in migration; breeds on small, barren islands; abundant in the eastern half of Alberta, Mar–Oct.

Black Tern

Chlidonias niger

Length: 23–25 cm
Wingspan: 61 cm

Graceful black terns dip, swoop and dive above cattail marshes and over adjacent fields, catching insects in midair or picking them from the water's surface. • Wetland habitat loss and degradation have caused black tern populations to decline. These birds are sensitive nesters and will not return to a nesting area if the water level or plant density changes. Wetland conservation efforts may eventually help them recover to their former numbers. **Where found:** shallow marshes, wet meadows and sewage ponds with emergent vegetation; locally common east of the mountains, May–Sept.

Common Tern

Sterna hirundo

Length: 33–40 cm
Wingspan: 76 cm

Common terns capture shiners and other small fish in spectacular aerial dives, plunging into the water from heights of 30 metres or more. Groups of terns sometimes follow feeding schools of large fish, snatching the smaller fish that are flushed to the surface. • A courting male tern will offer a small fish to a female. If she accepts the gift, they pair up and nest. • In some places, tern colonies have been detrimentally affected by large gulls, which prey on the eggs and chicks. **Where found:** large lakes, wetlands and slow-moving rivers; common east of the mountains, May–Sept.

Rock Pigeon

Columba livia

Length: 31–33 cm
Wingspan: 71 cm

Formerly known as rock dove, this Old World pigeon
is one of the world's most recognized birds and has
been domesticated for about 6500 years. Because of their ability
to return to far-flung locales, these birds are often bred as "homing pigeons."
• In the wild, rock pigeons breed on cliffs; their urban counterparts nest on building
ledges or under bridges. • All pigeons and doves feed their young a nutritious liquid
called "pigeon milk" that is produced in the birds' crop (it's not real milk). • Rock
pigeons display a staggering array of colour variations, but the most commonly
encountered is the wild phenotype "blue-bar" pigeon, which is mostly grey with
2 black wing bars. **Where found:** urban areas, railways and agricultural areas;
abundant year-round throughout but absent from mountains and the northeast.

Mourning Dove

Zenaida macroura

Length: 28–33 cm
Wingspan: 46 cm

The mourning dove is the leading game bird in North America,
with hunters taking up to 70 million annually, but the species
remains one of the most abundant and widespread native
birds on the continent. • An average clutch usually consists of only 2 eggs, but doves raise multiple broods and
breed nearly year-round in warmer climates. • When a mourning dove bursts into
flight, its wings often create a whistling sound. • This dove's softly repeated *coo*
sounds much like a hooting owl. **Where found:** open woodlands and agricultural
and suburban areas; common on the prairies, Apr–Oct.

Great Horned Owl

Bubo virginianus

Length: 46–64 cm
Wingspan: 91–152 cm

Our most common large owl, the great horned owl occurs in all
manner of habitats. This powerful predator can take mammals the size
of a small house cat and is one of the few predators of skunks. • Great
horned owls begin their courtship as early as January, and by February
and March, the females are incubating eggs. Most great horned owls use
old crow or hawk stick nests and may be spotted by their "ears" projecting
above the nest. • The long-eared owl (*Asio otus*), found in central and southern Alberta's mixed forests and shrublands, has a thinner, compressed body and ear
tufts set closer together. **Where found:** everywhere from open agricultural landscapes
to marshes with scattered woodlots; also suburban areas; common year-round.

Snowy Owl

Bubo scandiacus

Length: 51–69 cm (female is noticeably larger)
Wingspan: 1.4–1.7 m

Feathered to the toes, the ghostly white snowy owl is well adapted to frigid winter temperatures. Its transparent feathers trap heat like a greenhouse, especially when they are ruffled out. • Male snowy owls stockpile lemmings at nest sites for foggy or rainy days when hunting is poor. Nests have been found in the Arctic with up to 56 lemmings piled nearby. When lemming and vole populations crash in the Arctic, more snowy owls venture south in search of food. **Where found:** open country including forest clearings, agricultural areas and lakeshores; uncommon to common throughout, Nov–Apr.

Burrowing Owl

Athene cunicularia

Length: 23–28 cm
Wingspan: 50–60 cm

Burrowing owls are loyal prairie inhabitants that nest underground in abandoned animal burrows. During the day, they may be seen atop fence posts or on the dirt mounds beside nest entrances. The extermination of tunnelling animals such as ground squirrels has greatly reduced burrowing owl nest sites. Other challenges include the loss of grassland habitat, poisoning of prey species and the effects of agricultural chemicals. • In Alberta, burrowing owls are mainly found east of Lethbridge, including the Suffield National Wildlife Area. **Where found:** open, short-grass haylands, pastures and prairies; occasionally on lawns and golf courses; endangered; uncommon and local in southeastern Alberta, Apr–Sept.

Great Gray Owl

Strix nebulosa

Length: 60–84 cm (female is slightly larger)
Wingspan: 1.37–1.52 m

This large, phantom-like owl glides down from a perch, hovers briefly, and then plunges headfirst into a snowbank to acquire a meal. With a face designed like a satellite dish, the great gray owl is able to detect and locate the faintest sound, even a tiny rodent covered by 60 cm of snow. This owl's facial discs funnel sound waves into its asymmetrically placed ears, enabling it, through triangulation, to pinpoint the precise location of its prey. • This magnificent bird is the largest North American owl. **Where found:** forest clearings, roadsides, bogs and open meadows; uncommon year-round throughout but absent from grasslands.

Short-eared Owl

Asio flammeus

Length: 33–43 cm (female is slightly larger)
Wingspan: 1.0–1.1 m

Short-eared owls fly low over wet meadows, often by day, beating their long wings with slow, butterfly-like wingbeats. • These owls perform spectacular aerial courtship "dances." Because they typically inhabit open country, visual courtship displays—called sky dances—are more effective than vocal ones for communicating. • This owl's life revolves around the population levels of voles, leading to nomadic movements in response to prey availability. **Where found:** open country including grasslands, wet meadows and cleared forests; highly erratic; uncommon to common east of the mountains, Mar–Nov; occasionally overwinters.

Northern Saw-whet Owl

Aegolius acadicus

Length: 18–23 cm
Wingspan: 43–55 cm

Although primarily a predator of forest mice, this owl is an opportunistic hunter that takes whatever it can, whenever it can, and may catch more than it can eat at a single sitting. In winter, extra food is usually stored in trees, where it quickly freezes. When hunting efforts fail, a hungry owl will thaw out its frozen cache by "incubating" it as it would a clutch of eggs. • By day, saw-whets roost quietly in the cover of dense lower tree branches and brush. **Where found:** coniferous and mixed forests; wooded city parks and ravines; uncommon to locally common year-round in central and northwestern Alberta.

Common Nighthawk

Chordeiles minor

Length: 22–25 cm
Wingspan: 61 cm

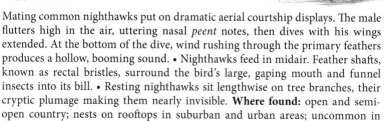

Mating common nighthawks put on dramatic aerial courtship displays. The male flutters high in the air, uttering nasal *peent* notes, then dives with his wings extended. At the bottom of the dive, wind rushing through the primary feathers produces a hollow, booming sound. • Nighthawks feed in midair. Feather shafts, known as rectal bristles, surround the bird's large, gaping mouth and funnel insects into its bill. • Resting nighthawks sit lengthwise on tree branches, their cryptic plumage making them nearly invisible. **Where found:** open and semi-open country; nests on rooftops in suburban and urban areas; uncommon in northern and central regions, common in the south, May–Sept.

Ruby-throated Hummingbird

Archilochus colubris

Length: 9.0–9.5 cm
Wingspan: 11.5 cm

Aerial extremists, hummingbirds beat their wings several dozen times per second and, like tiny helicopters, can fly in any direction. At full tilt, these nickel-weight speedsters have a heart rate of over 1000 beats per minute. Courting males fly in a pendulum-like arc, creating a loud hum with their wings. • Hummingbirds are attracted to feeders and flower gardens. Their tiny, lichen-shingled nests house 2 jellybean-sized eggs. • Ruby-throats winter in Central America, with many flying 800 nonstop kilometres over the Gulf of Mexico. **Where found:** open, mixed woodlands, wetlands, gardens and backyards; uncommon in central Alberta east of the mountains, May–Aug.

Rufous Hummingbird

Selasphorus rufus

Length: 8–9 cm
Wingspan: 11 cm

Rufous hummingbirds are tiny, delicate avian jewels, but their beauty hides a relentless mean streak—these birds buzz past one another at nectar sites, and males will chase rivals for some distance. • Rufous hummingbirds winter in tropical regions but migrate each summer as far north as southern Alaska. Their spring journey coincides with the flowering times of plants. **Where found:** nearly any habitat with abundant flowers including gardens, edges of coniferous and deciduous forests, burned sites, brushy slopes and alpine meadows; common in the mountains, May–Sept.

Belted Kingfisher

Megaceryle alcyon

Length: 28–36 cm
Wingspan: 51 cm

Chronically antisocial other than during the brief nesting period, belted kingfishers stake out productive fishing grounds and scold invaders with loud, rattling calls. They catch fish by plunging headfirst into water, diving to depths of up to 60 cm. • Mating pairs nest in a chamber at the end of a long tunnel dug into an earthen bank. • With an extra red band across her belly, the female kingfisher is more colourful than her mate. **Where found:** lakes, ponds and rivers; fairly common throughout except grasslands, Apr–Oct; a few may overwinter.

Yellow-bellied Sapsucker

Sphyrapicus varius

Length: 18–20 cm
Wingspan: 32 cm

Sapsuckers are known for the series of shallow parallel holes, or "sap wells," they drill into the bark of living trees and shrubs. Foraging sapsuckers fly from tree to tree, drinking the sap and eating the insects caught in the sticky juice. These wells also attract a variety of hummingbirds and songbirds and rarely harm the trees. • Sapsuckers don't actually suck sap. They lap it up with a fringed tongue that resembles a paintbrush. **Where found:** forests and wooded riparian areas; common throughout except grasslands, May–Sept.

Downy Woodpecker

Picoides pubescens

Length: 15–18 cm
Wingspan: 30 cm

Easily our most common woodpecker, downies are found everywhere from backyard feeders to dense forests. They closely resemble the less common hairy woodpecker (*P. villosus*) but are much smaller, with a proportionately tiny bill and black spots on the white outer tail feathers. • Downies and other woodpeckers have feathered nostrils that filter out the sawdust produced by their excavations. Their long tongues are designed to reach far into crevices to extract grubs and other morsels. The manoeuverable tip is sticky with saliva and finely barbed to help seize reluctant wood-boring insects. **Where found:** deciduous and mixed forests; common throughout year-round.

Northern Flicker

Colaptes auratus

Length: 32–33 cm
Wingspan: 51 cm

The northern flicker spends much of its time on the ground, feeding on ants. Flickers also clean themselves by squashing ants and preening themselves with the remains. Ants contain formic acid, which kills parasites on the birds' skin and feathers. • When these woodpeckers fly, they reveal a bold white rump and colourful underwings. The "yellow-shafted" race is a widespread breeder throughout most of Alberta and has yellow underwings. The "red-shafted" race nests throughout most of the Rockies and across southern Alberta, and has salmon-coloured underwings. **Where found:** open woodlands, forest edges, fields, wetlands and treed suburbia; common throughout, late Mar–Sept.

97

Pileated Woodpecker

Dryocopus pileatus

Length: 41–48 cm
Wingspan: 74 cm

This crow-sized bird, the sixth-largest woodpecker in the world, is an unforgettable sight. Its loud, maniacal, laughing calls give it away, but actually seeing one of these secretive woodpeckers is more difficult. • This woodpecker's large, distinctively oval-shaped nest holes also provide homes for wood ducks, American kestrels, owls and even flying squirrels. • Pileateds feed heavily on carpenter ants, and that's usually what they are digging for as they hammer into tree trunks. **Where found:** large, mature forests; uncommon to common year-round in the mountains, boreal forests and aspen parkland.

Least Flycatcher

Empidonax minimus

Length: 13–15 cm
Wingspan: 20 cm

Perfectly camouflaged least flycatches have olive-brown plumage, white eye rings and 2 white wing bars. In spring, courting males issue loud, two-part *che-bek* calls throughout much of the day. Vocalizations are key to identifying flycatcher species. • Flycatchers sally from exposed perches to snatch flying insects in midair, a foraging behaviour known as "flycatching" or "hawking." **Where found:** open deciduous or mixed woodlands, and forest openings and edges; common throughout, May–Sept.

Eastern Phoebe

Sayornis phoebe

Length: 15–18 cm
Wingspan: 27 cm

Eastern phoebes often build their mud nests on building ledges, the eaves of barns and sheds and under bridge trestles, and consequently are often found close to people. They utter loud, emphatic *fee-bee!* calls and are known for their tail-wagging behaviour. • Phoebes are among the earliest flycatchers to return in spring, and they immediately begin nest building. With such an early start, phoebe pairs regularly raise 2 broods during the nesting season, often reusing the same nest. **Where found:** open deciduous woodlands, forest edges and clearings, often near water; fairly common in foothills, aspen parkland and boreal forest, Apr–Aug.

Eastern Kingbird

Tyrannus tyrannus

Length: 22 cm
Wingspan: 38 cm

The eastern kingbird lives up to its scientific name, *Tyrannus tyrannus*. This avian tyrant will fearlessly attack crows, hawks and even humans that pass through its territory, pursuing and pecking at them until the threat has passed. • The kingbird prefers open landscapes and often perches prominently on roadside wires. • This bird is a gregarious fruit eater while wintering in South America and an antisocial, aggressive insect eater while nesting in North America. **Where found:** fields and agricultural landscapes with scattered trees; also shrubby roadsides, borders of marshes and treed suburbia; locally common throughout, May–Aug.

Northern Shrike

Lanius excubitor

Length: 25 cm
Wingspan: 37 cm

Shrikes are predatory songbirds that kill and eat smaller birds and rodents, swooping down on them from above. These birds lack powerful talons and rely on their sharp, hooked bills for catching prey. Males display their hunting competence to females by impaling their trophies on thorns or barbed wire. This may also be a means of storing excess food. • The similar-looking loggerhead shrike (*L. ludovicianus*) has white underparts and a black mask that extends above the bill. It is an uncommon summer resident in our southern grasslands. The 2 species have little seasonal overlap. **Where found:** open country including fields, forest clearings and shrubby riparian areas and roadsides; breeds in the extreme northeast; uncommon throughout, Oct–Mar.

Red-eyed Vireo

Vireo olivaceus

Length: 15 cm
Wingspan: 25 cm

Capable of delivering about 40 phrases per minute, male red-eyed vireos sing almost nonstop throughout the day. A patient researcher once tallied 21,000 individual songs delivered by one of these avian motormouths in a single day. Such incessant yammering has earned this vireo the nickname "preacher bird." • Red-eyed vireos are hard to spot because they forage sluggishly high in the canopy, hidden in dense, leafy cover. **Where found:** deciduous or mixed woodlands; common throughout, May–mid-Sept.

Gray Jay

Perisoreus canadensis

Length: 28–33 cm
Wingspan: 46 cm

Few birds can outdo the mischievous gray jay in curiosity and boldness. Attracted by any foreign sound or potential feeding opportunity, small family groups glide gently and unexpectedly out of spruce stands to introduce themselves to any passersby. These intelligent birds are known to hide bits of food under the bark of trees, to be retrieved in times of need. • The thicker-billed Clark's nutcracker (*Nucifraga columbiana*) has black and white tail and wing feathers and is found in mountain forests. **Where found:** coniferous and mixed forests; locally common year-round in the mountains, as well as central and northern areas. **Also known as:** Canada jay, whiskey jack, camp robber.

Blue Jay

Cyanocitta cristata

Length: 28–31 cm
Wingspan: 41 cm

This loud, striking and well-known bird can be quite aggressive when competing for sunflower seeds and peanuts at backyard feeders. It rarely hesitates to drive away smaller birds, squirrels or even cats. Even the great horned owl is not too formidable a predator for a group of these brave, boisterous mobsters to harass. **Where found:** habitat generalist; found everywhere from dense forests to suburbia; common in central Alberta year-round; rare and local in the south.

Black-billed Magpie

Pica hudsonia

Length: 46 cm
Wingspan: 64 cm

These exceptional architects construct large, domed stick nests that conceal and protect their eggs and young from harsh weather and predators. Abandoned nests remain in trees for years and are often reused by other birds. • It is hard to imagine Alberta without these beautiful, long-tailed chatterboxes, but magpies historically followed bison herds and disappeared from the province during the time of the great bison slaughters. They soon returned to the region, cleverly adapting to life in both rural and urban areas. **Where found:** farmyards, hedgerows, open groves and suburbia; common throughout year-round.

Common Raven

Corvus corax

Length: 61 cm
Wingspan: 1.3 m

Ravens are crafty, clever, adaptable birds that use their wits to survive in a wide variety of habitats. These birds produce complex vocalizations, form lifelong pair bonds and exhibit problem-solving skills. When working as a pair to confiscate a meal, one raven may act as the decoy while the other steals the food. • The smaller American crow (*C. brachyrhynchos*) issues a distinctive *caw-caw-caw* and inhabits urban areas, agricultural areas and shrublands from mid-March to October, when most migrate south for the winter. **Where found:** urban areas, forests and landfills; common throughout except prairies year-round.

Horned Lark

Eremophila alpestris

Length: 18 cm
Wingspan: 30 cm

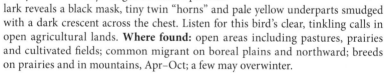

Rather nondescript, horned larks scurry like mice across open landscapes and often flush from rural roadsides as cars pass by. Watch for the blackish tail that contrasts with the sandy-coloured body. • A good look at a perched lark reveals a black mask, tiny twin "horns" and pale yellow underparts smudged with a dark crescent across the chest. Listen for this bird's clear, tinkling calls in open agricultural lands. **Where found:** open areas including pastures, prairies and cultivated fields; common migrant on boreal plains and northward; breeds on prairies and in mountains, Apr–Oct; a few may overwinter.

Tree Swallow

Tachycineta bicolor

Length: 14 cm
Wingspan: 37 cm

The first tree swallows return to our region in late April. Competition for nest sites is fierce, and the earliest swallows are the most likely to secure the best cavities in which to nest. Bluebird enthusiasts have greatly benefited this cavity-nesting species, as tree swallows readily adopt bluebird boxes. • When the hunting is good, these busy birds are known to return to their young 10 to 20 times per hour. **Where found:** wide range of open habitats, especially those near ponds, lakes and wetlands; often seen in areas with bluebird nest boxes; common throughout, May–Aug.

Barn Swallow

Hirundo rustica

Length: 18 cm
Wingspan: 38 cm

Barn swallows are a familiar sight under bridges, in picnic shelters and around farmsteads, where they nest in barns and other buildings. It is now almost unheard of for these birds to nest in natural sites such as cliffs. • Swallows construct their nests by rolling mud into small balls, one mouthful at a time. • Longer-tailed males tend to live longer and have greater reproductive success. **Where found:** open landscapes, especially in rural areas, often near water; common on the prairies, local elsewhere, May–Sept.

Black-capped Chickadee

Poecile atricapillus

Length: 13–15 cm
Wingspan: 20 cm

Curious and inquisitive, black-capped chickadees have even been known to land on people! They are very common and familiar visitors to backyard feeders. Chickadees cache seeds, and are able to relocate hidden food up to a month later. • These birds are omnivorous cavity nesters that usually lay 6 to 8 eggs in late winter or early spring. • The boreal chickadee (*P. hudsonicus*) has a grey-brown cap and flanks, a nasal call and inhabits mature coniferous forests. **Where found:** mixed and deciduous forests, parks and suburban backyards; common throughout year-round.

Red-breasted Nuthatch

Sitta canadensis

Length: 11 cm
Wingspan: 22 cm

The red-breasted nuthatch has a somewhat dizzying view of the world as it moves down tree trunks headfirst, searching for bark-dwelling insects. Food shortages periodically force these birds to stage southward invasions known as "irruptions" in some winters, so they may be absent at feeders some years and common in others. • The white-breasted nuthatch (*S. carolinensis*) has a white face and white underparts. It is a year-round inhabitant of central Alberta's forests and backyards. **Where found:** coniferous and mixed forests; common throughout except prairies year-round.

House Wren

Troglodytes aedon

Length: 12 cm
Wingspan: 15 cm

A familiar suburban sight and sound, house wrens have loud, bubbly warbles. They typically skulk in dense brush but won't hesitate to express their displeasure with intruders by delivering harsh, scolding notes. • These cavity nesters are easily lured to nest boxes. House wrens can be aggressive and highly territorial, and are known to puncture the eggs of other birds nesting nearby. • This wren ranges all the way from Canada to southern South America—the broadest longitudinal distribution of any wren. **Where found:** thickets, shrubby areas and woodland openings, often near buildings; uncommon to common in suburban central and southern Alberta, May–Sept.

Ruby-crowned Kinglet

Regulus calendula

Length: 10 cm
Wingspan: 18 cm

The ruby-crowned kinglet is impossibly tiny, barely larger than a ruby-throated hummingbird. Its loud, rolling, rising songs are one of the most frequently heard bird songs in Alberta's coniferous forests during May and June. • The male's small, ruby crown is held erect during courtship to impress prospective mates but remains hidden the rest of the year. • Like chickadees, kinglets can lower their body temperature at night to conserve energy. **Where found:** coniferous forests; common throughout except prairies, Apr–late Oct.

Mountain Bluebird

Sialia currucoides

Length: 18 cm
Wingspan: 36 cm

Bluebird enthusiasts have erected thousands of nest boxes throughout the range of this cavity-nesting thrush, greatly bolstering populations. Natural nest sites, such as woodpecker cavities or holes in sandstone cliffs, are in short supply because of habitat loss and increased competition from aggressive, introduced European starlings. • Male mountain bluebirds are a gorgeous, deep blue and issue short, pleasing warbles. Females are a duller blue-grey, and young birds have heavily spotted underparts, revealing their relationship to the thrushes. **Where found:** uncommon to common in the southern two-thirds of Alberta, mid-Mar–Sept.

103

American Robin

Turdus migratorius

Length: 25 cm
Wingspan: 43 cm

Among our most widely seen and familiar birds, American robins arrive in March to welcome spring with their cheery songs. The striking males have black heads, rich brick red underparts and streaked white throats. • Robins are master earthworm hunters, adeptly spotting worms and tugging them from the soil. In winter, these birds switch to a diet of berries. • The Swainson's thrush (*Catharus ustulatus*) and the hermit thrush (*C. guttatus*) are common throughout Alberta, except in southern grasslands, from May to October. Both species have brownish upperparts, spotted breasts and warbling songs with notes that spiral upward. **Where found:** habitat generalist; residential lawns, gardens, urban parks, forests and bogs; abundant throughout, Mar–Nov; a few may overwinter.

Varied Thrush

Ixoreus naevius

Length: 24 cm
Wingspan: 42 cm

Heard far more often than it is seen, the varied thrush remains hidden within the thick, moist spruce, fir and hemlock forests of the northern Rockies. The song of the male is designed to penetrate the dense foliage and consists of a number of long, whistled notes, always delivered at different pitches. • These colourful thrushes arrive early in spring and can be seen hopping under feeders and along shorelines in mountain townsites by the end of March. **Where found:** dense coniferous forests, especially with Engelmann spruce and lodgepole pine; foothills and mountains, Apr–Oct; a few may overwinter.

Gray Catbird

Dumetella carolinensis

Length: 22–23 cm
Wingspan: 28 cm

A catbird in full song issues a nonstop, squeaky barrage of warbling notes, interspersed with poor imitations of other birds. It will occasionally utter loud, cat-like meows that might even fool a feline. • Gray catbirds occupy habitats with thick brush and can be difficult to glimpse, but squeaking sounds may lure them into view. Perseverance pays off, as these handsome birds display tones of grey set off by a dark cap and striking cinnamon undertail coverts. **Where found:** dense thickets, brambles, shrubby areas and hedgerows, often near water; uncommon to common in central and southern Alberta, May–Sept.

Brown Thrasher

Toxostoma rufum

Length: 29 cm
Wingspan: 33 cm

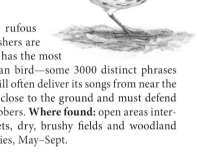

Looking somewhat thrush-like with their rufous
backs and spotted underparts, brown thrashers are
mimics, as is the gray catbird. This species has the most
extensive repertoire of any North American bird—some 3000 distinct phrases
have been catalogued. A singing thrasher will often deliver its songs from near the
tip of a small tree. • Brown thrashers nest close to the ground and must defend
their nests against snakes and other nest robbers. **Where found:** open areas interspersed with fencerows; also dense thickets, dry, brushy fields and woodland
edges; uncommon to common on the prairies, May–Sept.

European Starling

Sturnus vulgaris

Length: 22 cm
Wingspan: 41 cm

The European starling is perhaps the most
damaging nonnative bird ever introduced
into North America. About 60 of these birds
were released in New York City in 1890 and
1891 as part of an ill-fated effort to release into the U.S. all the
birds mentioned in Shakespeare's works. Now abundant throughout North
America, long-lived, aggressive starlings often drive native species such as bluebirds from nest cavities. **Where found:** cities, towns, farmyards, woodland
fringes and clearings; common throughout, Feb–Oct; a few may overwinter.

Bohemian Waxwing

Bombycilla garrulus

Length: 18 cm
Wingspan: 30 cm

With its black mask and slick hairdo, the Bohemian waxwing
has a suave look. These birds are most noticeable in winter,
when large, nomadic flocks plunder the fruit of mountain-ash
trees and various berry bushes, sometimes getting tipsy on
fermented fruit. Although largely frugivorous (fruit eating),
waxwings also take insects in summer, often near water.
• Cedar waxwings (*B. cedrorum*) visit the province from
May to October. They lack the Bohemian's reddish brown
undertail coverts and white wing markings and have yellowish underparts.
Where found: *Summer:* uncommon to common in open coniferous forests of
central and northern Alberta. *Winter:* common throughout in townsites.

Yellow Warbler

Dendroica petechia

Length: 13 cm
Wingspan: 20 cm

Warblers are among our most beautiful birds, and the yellow warbler is one of our showiest. It sings a loud, ringing *sweet-sweet-I'm-so-sweet* song. • This warbler is often parasitized by the brown-headed cowbird and has learned to recognize cowbird eggs. But instead of tossing the foreign eggs out, the yellow warbler will build another nest overtop the old eggs or abandon the nest completely. Occasionally, cowbirds strike repeatedly—a five-storey nest was once found! **Where found:** habitat generalist; moist, open woodlands, scrubby meadows, urban parks and gardens; common throughout, May–Sept.

Yellow-rumped Warbler

Dendroica coronata

Length: 13–15 cm
Wingspan: 23 cm

Yellow-rumped warblers are the most abundant and widespread wood-warblers in North America. There are 2 races of this species: the "myrtle warbler," which has a white throat, and the "Audubon's warbler," which has a yellow throat. Both occur in our region. Myrtles are more prevalent in the boreal forest, whereas Audubon's dominate in the Rockies, the foothills and the Cypress Hills. **Where found:** mature coniferous and mixed woodlands; common throughout, May–Sept, except on the prairies, where it is a migrant in May and late Aug–Sept.

American Redstart

Setophaga ruticilla

Length: 13 cm
Wingspan: 21 cm

Hyperactive American redstarts chronically flick their wings and fan their tails. It is thought that they flush insects from the foliage by flashing the bright orange or yellow spots in their plumage. A broad bill and rictal bristles help the redstart capture insects like a flycatcher. • Females and first-year males have yellow markings instead of orange ones. **Where found:** dense, shrubby understorey of deciduous woodlands, often near water; uncommon to common in central and northern regions, May–Aug; uncommon to common migrant on the prairies, May and mid-Aug–Sept.

Common Yellowthroat

Geothlypis trichas

Length: 11–14 cm
Wingspan: 18 cm

This little masked bandit's loud *witchity witchity witchity* song bursting from the cattails gives it away. Common yellowthroats are probably our most common breeding wood-warbler, reaching peak numbers in wetlands and damp, overgrown fields. They have wrenlike curiosity, and you can coax them into view by making squeaking or "pishing" sounds. Females can be difficult to identify but share the male's odd big-headed, slender-bodied, long-legged dimensions. **Where found:** wetlands, riparian areas and wet, overgrown meadows; common throughout, May–Sept.

Chipping Sparrow

Spizella passerina

Length: 13–15 cm
Wingspan: 22 cm

The chipping sparrow can be distinguished from other sparrows by its rufous crown and prominent, white eyebrow. Listen for this sparrow's rapid trill, which is slightly faster, drier and less musical than the similar trilling song of the dark-eyed junco. • Another common sparrow, the light-brown clay-colored sparrow (*S. pallida*), is found in forested and brushy sites throughout the province from May to September. Its song is a repeated, insect-like buzz. **Where found:** open conifer stands, mixed woodland edges and shrubby yards and gardens; common throughout, Apr–Sept.

Savannah Sparrow

Passerculus sandwichensis

Length: 13–17 cm
Wingspan: 22 cm

Like most sparrows, the savannah sparrow generally prefers to stay out of sight, though small flocks and individuals are sometimes seen darting across roads, fields or beaches. They are not apt to fly even if threatened, preferring to escape by running swiftly and inconspicuously through tall grasses. Listen for their clear, distinct *tea tea tea teeeea today!* song. **Where found:** moist meadows, marshy edges and weedy fields; very common throughout, late Apr–Oct.

Song Sparrow

Melospiza melodia

Length: 14–18 cm
Wingspan: 19 cm

You are likely to see the widespread, adaptable and ubiquitous song sparrow in your backyard. It has a bold, central breast spot and a long, rounded tail, which is conspicuous as the bird is flying away. • Song sparrows have one of the most beautiful songs of any bird—a bright, variable series of clear notes and trills. Young song sparrows (and many other birds) learn to sing by imitating their fathers or rival males. **Where found:** shrublands, riparian thickets, suburban gardens and fields; very common throughout, Apr–Oct.

White-throated Sparrow

Zonotrichia albicollis

Length: 17–18 cm
Wingspan: 23 cm

The white-throated sparrow sings in a distinctive, somewhat mournful minor key. Its clear, whistled *dear sweet Canada Canada Canada* is very characteristic of our boreal forests. • Unique among sparrows, there are 2 colour morphs—one has black and white stripes on the head, whereas the other has brown and tan stripes. So, a duller, tan-coloured bird is not necessarily a female, nor is a white-striped bird always a male. **Where found:** coniferous and mixed forests; common in central and northern areas, May–Oct; common migrant on the prairies, May and Sept–Oct.

Dark-eyed Junco

Junco hyemalis

Length: 14–17 cm
Wingspan: 23 cm

The dark-eyed junco is one of North America's most abundant songbirds, with a total population estimated at 630 million birds. • When flushed, juncos flash prominent white outer tail feathers, a strategy intended to distract a pursuing raptor and enable the bird to escape. • Four races of this species occur in Alberta, sharing similar habits but different colouration and ranges. The grey "slate-colored junco" nests in boreal forests; the rufous-sided "Oregon junco" nests in the southern Rockies; the "Northern Rockies junco" nests in Jasper National Park; and the "pink-sided junco" nests in the Cypress Hills. **Where found:** shrubby woodland borders and backyard feeders; common throughout, Mar–Nov.

Western Tanager

Piranga ludoviciana

Length: 18 cm
Wingspan: 29 cm

The western tanager brings the colours of a tropical visitor on a summer vacation to our area. Each summer, this bird raises a new generation of young and takes advantage of the seasonal explosion of food in our forests before heading back to its exotic wintering grounds in Mexico and Central America. • The male western tanager spends long periods of time singing from the same perch, sounding like a robin with a sore throat. **Where found:** mature coniferous and mixed forests; common throughout, May–Sept, except on the southern prairies, where it is a spring and fall migrant.

Rose-breasted Grosbeak

Pheucticus ludovicianus

Length: 18–21 cm
Wingspan: 32 cm

The rose-breasted grosbeak sounds like a robin that has taken singing lessons, though its call note is a squeaky sound reminiscent of a sneaker on a basketball court. Listening for grosbeaks is a good way to find them—they remain high in leafy canopies and are rather sluggish. Males have beautiful black-and-white plumage and a bold, inverted "V" of crimson pink on the breast. The plumage of females is muted, and they resemble big sparrows. Female grosbeaks are unusual for songbirds in that they also sing. **Where found:** deciduous and mixed forests; uncommon to common in central and northern Alberta, May–Aug; fairly common prairie migrant, May and Sept.

Red-winged Blackbird

Agelaius phoeniceus

Length: 18–24 cm
Wingspan: 33 cm

Red-winged blackbirds are one of North America's most abundant birds. The males are stunning, and when they court females by thrusting their wings forward to flare their brilliant scarlet orange epaulets, they appear as grand as any of our more colourful birds. • Male red-wings are avian polygamists, and one male may have as many as 15 females in his territory. • True harbingers of spring, male red-winged blackbirds utter loud, raspy *konk-a-ree* calls that can be heard in early April. **Where found:** cattail marshes, wet meadows, ditches, agricultural areas and overgrown fields; very common throughout, Apr–Oct.

Western Meadowlark

Sturnella neglecta

Length: 24 cm
Wingspan: 40 cm

The clear, ringing, whistled songs of the western meadowlark are characteristic sounds of grasslands and fields. From above, this bird's plumage is muted, with sombre hues of speckled brown, allowing it to blend in with the vegetation. Seen from below, however, its striking, lemon yellow breast is accented with a bold, black chevron. When flushed, meadowlarks reveal conspicuous, white outer tail feathers, and they fly with distinctive, stiff, shallow wingbeats. **Where found:** grassy meadows, roadsides, pastures, old fields and croplands; uncommon and local in central Alberta, common on the prairies, Mar–Oct.

Yellow-headed Blackbird

Xanthocephalus xanthocephalus

Length: 23–28 cm
Wingspan: 35–38 cm

You might be taken aback by the male yellow-headed blackbird's "song." When he perches on a cattail stalk and arches his dazzling golden head backward to sing, all he manages to produce is a pitiful, grinding sound. • In areas where yellow-headed blackbirds occur with red-winged blackbirds, the larger yellow-heads dominate, pushing their red-winged competitors to the periphery, where predation is highest. **Where found:** permanent marshes, sloughs, lakeshores and river impoundments with emergent vegetation; forages in fields; fairly common in central and southern Alberta, Apr–Sept.

Brown-headed Cowbird

Molothrus ater

Length: 15–20 cm
Wingspan: 30 cm

Cowbirds are reviled as nest parasites—they lay their eggs in other birds' nests and are known to parasitize more than 140 bird species. Upon hatching, baby cowbirds outcompete the host's young, leading to nest failure. This strange habit evolved with the cowbirds' association with nomadic bison herds. As the animals moved about, cowbirds couldn't stay in one place long enough to tend their own nests. Although bison no longer occur here in the wild, cowbirds still commonly forage around cattle. **Where found:** agricultural and residential areas and woodland edges; common throughout, Apr–Sept.

Baltimore Oriole

Icterus galbula

Length: 18–20 cm
Wingspan: 29 cm

The clear, flute-like whistles of this tropical black-bird are common sounds where large trees are found, including suburbia. Even a crudely whistled imitation of its song can bring the male oriole rocketing down to investigate.
• Baltimore orioles make hanging, pouch-like nests woven of plant fibres, which become conspicuous in autumn once the leaves have fallen. **Where found:** open deciduous and mixed forests, particularly riparian woodlands; common on the prairies, fairly common and local in central and southern Alberta, May–Aug.

Pine Grosbeak

Pinicola enucleator

Length: 20–25 cm
Wingspan: 35–38 cm

Pine grosbeaks do not regularly migrate from their northern nesting range and their winter visits are erratic, so it is a momentous occasion when these birds settle on your backyard feeder. The invasions are not com-pletely understood, but factors forcing these birds south in search of food may include widespread cone crop failures or changes to forest ecology. • During the nesting season, adult grosbeaks develop throat pouches for transporting seeds to their young. **Where found:** coniferous forests; townsites in winter; uncommon to common year-round in northern Alberta and the mountains; invades central areas in winter.

House Finch

Carpodacus mexicanus

Length: 12–15 cm
Wingspan: 22–25 cm

Formerly restricted to the arid American Southwest and Mexico, the aggressive house finch is now com-monly found throughout the continental U.S. and southern Canada. • The male house finch's plumage varies in colour from light yellow to bright red, but females will choose to breed with the reddest males. • The native purple finch (*C. purpureus*) nests in coniferous and mixed forests in central and northern Alberta. Males are more raspberry red than purple in colour, whereas females are dark brown with heavily streaked underparts. **Where found:** cities, towns and agricultural areas; common year-round and increasing in the southern half of Alberta.

111

Common Redpoll

Acanthis flammea

Length: 13 cm
Wingspan: 23 cm

Common redpolls are unpredictable winter visitors. Some winters, dozens of redpolls flock together, gleaning waste grain from bare fields or stocking up at feeders. In other years, they make only a modest appearance. • A large surface area relative to a small internal volume puts the common redpoll at risk of freezing in low temperatures. A high intake of food and the insulating layer of warm air trapped by its fluffed feathers keep this songbird from dying of hypothermia. **Where found:** irruptive; open fields, roadsides and backyard feeders; common throughout, Nov–May.

American Goldfinch

Spinus tristis

Length: 11–14 cm
Wingspan: 23 cm

Vibrant American goldfinches fill the air with their jubilant *po-ta-to-chip* calls and fly with a distinctive, undulating flight style. Commonly seen in weedy fields, gardens and along roadsides, these acrobatic birds regularly feed while hanging upside down. Finch feeders are designed with the seed openings below the perches to discourage the more aggressive, upright-feeding bird species. Use niger or black-oil sunflower seeds to attract American goldfinches to your feeder. **Where found:** weedy fields, riparian areas, parks and gardens; fairly common to common in central and southern regions, May–Sept; a few may overwinter.

House Sparrow

Passer domesticus

Length: 14–17 cm
Wingspan: 24 cm

A black mask and bib adorn the male of this adaptive, aggressive species. These well-known birds frequent fast-food restaurant parking lots, backyard feeders and farms. • This abundant and conspicuous bird was introduced to North America in the 1850s as part of a plan to control the insects that were damaging grain and cereal crops. As it turns out, these birds are largely vegetarian and usually feed on seeds and grain! **Where found:** any human environment; abundant throughout year-round.

AMPHIBIANS & REPTILES

Amphibians and reptiles are commonly referred to as cold blooded, but this term is misleading. Although these animals lack the ability to generate their own internal body heat, they are not necessarily cold blooded. Instead, the temperature of the surrounding environment governs their body temperature, and they obtain heat from sunlight or warm rocks and logs. Reptiles and amphibians hibernate in winter in cold regions, and some reptile species estivate (are dormant during hot or dry periods) in summer in hot regions. Both reptiles and amphibians moult (shed their skins) as they grow.

Amphibians are smooth skinned and most live in moist habitats. In Alberta, they are represented by the salamanders, frogs and toads. These species typically lay eggs without shells in jelly-like masses in water. The eggs hatch into gilled larvae, which later metamorphose into adults with lungs and legs. Amphibians can regenerate their skin and sometimes even entire limbs.

Reptiles are completely terrestrial vertebrates with scaly skin. In this guide, the representatives are turtles, lizards and snakes. Most reptiles bury their eggs in loose soil, but some snakes and lizards give birth to live young. Reptiles do not have a larval stage.

Salamanders
p. 114

Toads & Frogs
pp. 114–117

Turtles
p. 117

Lizards
p. 117

Snakes
pp. 118–119

113

Tiger Salamander

Ambystoma mavortium

Length: up to 40 cm

These whoppers can reach 40 cm in length and resemble mini Komodo dragons as they swagger along. Tiger salamanders are richly patterned, with dull yellow blotches that contrast with their greyish black body colour. They prefer more open landscapes than other mole salamanders and are often found far from woods or water during early spring migrations. • Tiger salamanders lay their eggs in shallow pools and even farm ponds but will vanish if fish are introduced. Most salamanders require fishless ponds—fish are voracious predators that quickly consume amphibian eggs and young. **Where found:** farms, prairies and wet woods near water; hibernates underground; central and southern Alberta.

Long-toed Salamander

Ambystoma macrodactylum

Length: 10–17 cm

These striking, secretive creatures often hide under rocks or decomposing logs, emerging at night to feed on invertebrates. They are more easily seen in the rainy months of April and May, when they migrate to breeding sites in silt-free ponds and lakes. Eggs are laid singly or in clumps on rocks or among vegetation and take about 3 weeks to hatch. • In Alberta, long-toed salamanders are active from spring to fall, but in warmer climates, they may remain active year-round. **Where found:** subalpine and alpine forests of foothills, mountains and forests; hibernates underground; western Alberta.

Plains Spadefoot Toad

Spea bombifrons

Length: 3.5–6 cm

Spadefoot toads are named for the pointed, dark-edged "spade" on each hind foot, which is used for digging. The toad tunnels backward into loose, sandy soil to make an underground burrow that allows it to take shelter and conserve moisture in dry habitats. Burrows going as deep as one metre underground have been found. • The call of the plains spadefoot toad is similar to the harsh bark of a wood frog. • This toad breeds in temporary ponds that form after spring rain showers. **Where found:** sandy or gravelly soils on short-grass prairie; hibernates underground; southeastern Alberta.

Western Toad

Bufo boreas

Length: 6–12 cm

Touching a toad will not give you warts, but the western toad does have a way of discouraging unwanted affection—when handled, it secretes a toxin from the large parotid glands behind its eyes that acts to irritate the mouth of a potential predator. • This large, grey, green or brown toad is a voracious predator of insects and other tasty invertebrates such as worms and slugs. **Where found:** near springs, streams, meadows and woodlands in foothills, mountains and adjacent forests; hibernates underground; central and western Alberta; special concern.

Canadian Toad

Bufo hemiophrys

Length: 4–7.5 cm

Listen for the Canadian toad's short, harsh trill in spring. This small, brown, grey or greenish toad is covered with warts and has a distinctive hump, called a "boss," between its protruding eyes. The Canadian toad is typically active during the day and retreats to a burrow at night, but may remain active on very warm nights. • This toad used to be common in boreal forests and aspen parkland but has recently suffered severe declines. **Where found:** open areas near wetlands; hibernates underground; south-central and eastern Alberta.

Great Plains Toad

Anaxyrus cognatus

Length: 4.5–11 cm

This relatively large toad has large, oval parotid glands and distinctive cranial crests that fuse to form an "M" around its eyes. It is mostly active at night and spends much of its time in an underground burrow. • When threatened, the Great Plains toad puffs itself up with air and stands on all 4 legs. **Where found:** ponds, dugouts, ditches, irrigation canals and river floodplains; hibernates underground; short-grass prairie of extreme southeastern Alberta; special concern.

Boreal Chorus Frog

Pseudacris maculata

Length: 2–4 cm

In early spring, you can hear chorus frogs calling from wetlands, often along with the *cluck cluck* of wood frogs. The chorus frog's commonly heard call resembles the sound made by running a finger down the teeth of a comb—but projected through a stack of Marshall amps. • This tiny frog has a grey-brown body, a dark eye stripe and 3 darker, sometimes broken, stripes running along its back. **Where found:** breeds in ponds, marshes and ephemeral water bodies; hibernates under leaf litter; throughout except alpine habitats.

Spotted Frog

Rana luteiventris

Length: 5–10 cm

The spotted frog forages throughout the day for insects and other invertebrates. It tends to be sluggish when approached but will jump for cover into water or aquatic vegetation when threatened. • This frog's back has ridges similar to those found on the northern leopard frog, and it may have a dark mask around the eyes. Variable in colour, the spotted frog has a brown to bronze-coloured back with irregular dark spots. In Alberta, this frog's undersides are salmon pink to red, especially on the inside of the hind legs. **Where found:** in or near subalpine and alpine lakes, ponds and streams with emergent vegetation; from Jasper National Park south; special concern.

Northern Leopard Frog

Rana pipiens

Length: 5–10 cm

Leopard frogs are seen only when flushed from grass in wet meadows or near wetlands, but you probably won't see more than a froggy blur shooting off in huge, zigzagging bounds. With a bit of patience, the leaper can usually be tracked down and admired. It's easy to see where the name comes from—these frogs are patterned with very distinctive, leopard-like spots. They emit a curious low, snoring sound, which is sometimes even delivered underwater. • Once widespread in Alberta, leopard frog populations have severely declined. **Where found:** meadows, fields and marshes; hibernates on lake bottoms; primarily southern areas but occurs locally as far north as Slave Lake; endangered.

Wood Frog

Rana sylvatica

Length: 3–6 cm

The wood frog is an amphibian with antifreeze. At below-zero temperatures, its heart rate, blood flow and breathing stop, turning it into a froggy ice cube. Special compounds, mainly glucose, allow it to survive the partial freezing and thawing of its tissues. Thus, the species is able to range above the Arctic Circle, farther north than any other amphibian. • In early spring, when ice still fringes woodland pools, vernal wetlands explode into life as wood frogs invade to mate and lay their eggs. Their collective calls sound like the quacking of distant ducks. **Where found:** moist woodlands, sometimes far from water; throughout except the extreme southeast.

Western Painted Turtle

Chrysemys picta belli

Length: 6–25 cm

Painted turtles can be seen basking in the sun on top of floating logs, mats of vegetation or exposed rocks. When alarmed, they slip into the water for a quick escape. • This turtle may live up to 40 years. There are four recognized subspecies, but only the largest, the western painted turtle, is found in Alberta. It has an olive green carapace with red or orange borders on the underside of its shell. **Where found:** marshes, ponds, lakes and slow-flowing streams; extreme southeastern Alberta.

Short-horned Lizard

Phrynosoma hernandesi

Length: 4–7 cm

Short, flat and horned, this small lizard typically basks on warm, south-facing slopes and waits for a meal to pass by. Beetles, ants and grasshoppers are its preferred prey. • These well-camouflaged creatures emerge from their shallow winter burrows and mate in mid-May. Females give birth to live young, unlike most lizards, which lay eggs. • This lizard reaches the northern limit of its range in Alberta, making it one of the only lizards in the world that can survive cold climates and high latitudes. **Where found:** coulees and short-grass prairie with vegetative cover such as sagebrush; patchy distribution south of the South Saskatchewan River valley; endangered.

Western Hog-nosed Snake

Heterodon nasicus

Length: 40–90 cm

An extraordinary actor, the western hognose snake is a master of the bluff. If threatened, it will hiss and expand its neck, giving it the look of a cobra. If this response fails to frighten, the snake will flip over and play dead, even lolling its tongue out the side of its mouth for effect. • This snake favours sandy or gravelly soil and uses its snout to dig for toads, frogs or salamanders to prey upon. • The western hognose snake has large, dark blotches on a lighter background and a distinctly upturned snout. **Where found:** sandy soil or gravelly areas adjacent to prairies, scrublands or floodplains; extreme southeastern Alberta.

Bullsnake

Pituophis catenifer sayi

Length: 90–200 cm

This large, beautiful constrictor is often mistaken for a rattlesnake because of its similar colouration, patterning and aggressive defensive strategy. When threatened, it produces a convincing rattling sound by hissing and exhaling forcefully through its vocal cords or by vibrating its tail against vegetation. • The bullsnake frequently over-winters in communal dens with other snakes, including rattlesnakes and gartersnakes. **Where found:** open, dry grasslands or sagebrush; also agricultural areas and fields, often near rock piles or boulders; southern one-third of Alberta.

Wandering Gartersnake

Thamnophis elegans vagrans

Length: 45–100 cm

Wandering gartersnakes are often, but not always, found near water, and they may slip into the water or under vegetation when threatened. They have a mildly venomous bite, which is used to immobilize prey such as fish, amphibians, molluscs, small mammals or birds. These snakes also feed on carrion. • Wandering gartersnakes are typically brown, grey or green with darker spots, yellowish brown dorsal and side stripes and greyish undersides. **Where found:** all habitat types, often near water; primarily south and west of the Red Deer River but occurs locally farther north.

Plains Gartersnake

Thamnophis radix

Length: 50–100 cm

Two rows of dark spots form a checker-
board pattern along the sides of the plains
gartersnake, distinguishing it from the similar-looking red-sided gartersnake.
From above, this snake appears dark and has an orange or red stripe running
down its back. • Plains gartersnakes are active from spring to autumn and feed
primarily on earthworms. In fall, they gather in underground hibernacula to
mate and spend the winter. In July, females give birth to 5 to 40 live young. **Where
found:** open, moist, grassy or brushy areas, often near water; eastern Alberta.

Red-sided Gartersnake

Thamnophis sirtalis

Length: 40–100 cm

Probably our most commonly encountered
snakes, gartersnakes can vary in colour but are
normally prominently striped with alternating
bands of yellow and dark. The red-sided subspecies (*T. s. parietalis*) has red markings along its
sides. • Gartersnakes spend the winter in hibernacula,
located in animal burrows, rock piles or sink holes. • The name "gartersnake" comes
from the pattern of longitudinal stripes on the bodies of these reptiles, suggestive of
the colourful garters that men once used to support their socks. • Gartersnakes are
efficient hunters of amphibians, fish, small mammals, slugs and leeches. **Where
found:** meadows, marshes, gardens and suburban and urban areas; throughout.

Prairie Rattlesnake

Crotalus viridis

Length: up to 1.5 m

Our only venomous snake, the prairie
rattlesnake warns away intruders by
shaking the rattle at the tip of its tail.
Those that ignore the warning risk a poisonous bite. A rattlesnake's deadly fangs are
hinged and can be folded back into its mouth. • Prairie rattlesnakes are light
brown with dark blotches overall, with a triangular head, vertical pupils and
special heat-sensing facial pits for locating warm-blooded prey. • During winter,
rattlesnakes den communally in protected hibernacula such as abandoned animal
burrows or rock crevices. **Where found:** mixed or short-grass prairie, badlands
and sage flats, often near coulee or river bottoms; southwestern Alberta.

FISH

Fish are ectothermic vertebrates that live in the water, have streamlined bodies covered in scales and possess fins and gills. A fundamental feature of fish is the serially repeated set of vertebrae and segmented muscles that allow the animal to move from side to side, propelling it through the water. A varying number of fins, depending on the species, further aid fish to swim and navigate. Most fish are oviparous and lay eggs that are fertilized externally. Spawning is an intense time for fish, often involving extraordinary risks. Eggs are either produced in vast quantities and scattered, or they are laid in a spawning nest (called a "redd") under rocks or logs. All these methods are designed to keep the eggs healthy and surrounded by clean, oxygen-rich water. Parental care may be present in the defence of such a nest or territory.

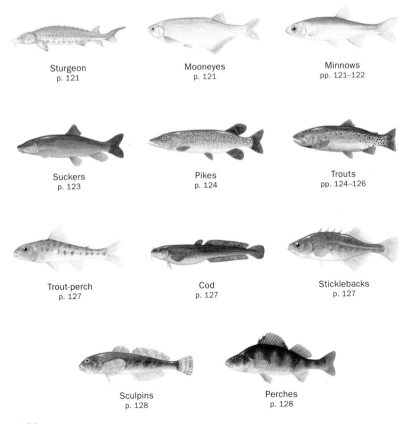

Sturgeon
p. 121

Mooneyes
p. 121

Minnows
pp. 121–122

Suckers
p. 123

Pikes
p. 124

Trouts
pp. 124–126

Trout-perch
p. 127

Cod
p. 127

Sticklebacks
p. 127

Sculpins
p. 128

Perches
p. 128

Lake Sturgeon

Acipenser fulvescens

Length: 75–100 cm (maximum 1.7 m)

For 100 million years, the lake
sturgeon has nosed along river bottoms,
using the 4 barbels that surround its mouth to detect prey. This scaleless relic has
5 rows of hard plates called "scutes" running down the sides of its body. Unfortu-
nately, this formerly abundant species is now threatened because of overharvesting
of eggs for caviar, overfishing and habitat degradation. • Lake sturgeon can live
up to 80 years, and individuals once grew to over 2 m in length, making it our
largest freshwater fish. **Where found:** large lakes and rivers; North and South
Saskatchewan river basins. **Also known as:** black sturgeon, bony sturgeon, rock fish.

Goldeye

Hiodon alosoides

Length: 35 cm (maximum 50 cm)

Goldeyes are found in large
river systems but prefer the muddy back-
waters of rivermouths. Large, yellow eyes allow this fish to see in silty waters.
• Goldeye eggs are semi-buoyant and transparent, and they float safely down the
river, hidden by the turbid water, until they hatch 2 weeks after spawning. Eggs
released in Alberta most likely hatch in Saskatchewan. When an individual
matures, it travels upstream, retracing the path that its egg followed. • The
closely related mooneye (*H. tergisus*) occurs in the North and South Saskatchewan
river basins. **Where found:** large, turbid waterways; primarily in central and
southern drainages.

Lake Chub

Couesius plumbeus

Length: 5–9 cm (maximum 17 cm)

This widespread, abundant minnow
can survive in almost any pool or stream, but
prefers water bodies with gravelly bottoms and rocky shores. It can even thrive in
pulp-water effluent! A pulp mill near Boyle has a great display of lake chub in the
main lobby's aquarium. • Sheer numbers make this fish an important link in
the food chain. Lake chub can be so abundant that they are sometimes eaten by
animals that do not normally eat fish. **Where found:** prefers areas with hiding
places such as large rocks; throughout.

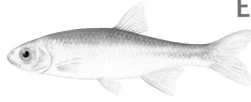

Emerald Shiner

Notropis atherinoides

Length: 5–7.5 cm (maximum 12 cm)

This minnow is common in larger rivers and lakes and is important to many predators, both aquatic and avian. Its populations fluctuate greatly, thus influencing the populations of many other fish species. • Emerald shiners spend much of their time in open water feeding on plankton, which they follow up to the surface at dusk. In fall, large schools of these little jewels gather near shorelines and docks. **Where found:** lakes, large rivers and along shallow lakeshores in spring and autumn; eastern Alberta.

Fathead Minnow

Pimephales promelas

Length: 4–8 cm

This minnow is considered a "plastic" species because it can tolerate low oxygen levels, high levels of acidity or alkalinity and silty conditions. Native to the interior United States and Canada, the fathead minnow is now found throughout the continent because of range expansion and bait-bucket releases. • A spawning male develops a fleshy forehead pad with bumpy nuptial tubercles, which he uses to scrub his well-guarded nest site when he is preparing it for a visit from a spawning female. **Where found:** muddy pools, ditches and lakes; eastern Alberta.

Longnose Dace

Rhinichthys cataractae

Length: 9–17 cm

Adapted for living along the rocky bottoms of fast-flowing mountain streams, the longnose dace is a benthic (bottom-living) species. This minnow thrives on the aquatic larvae of mosquitoes, midges and other insects. • A dark lateral band is often present in young dace, and a breeding male displays a reddish orange tinge on its head, body and fins. **Where found:** various aquatic habitats including fast-flowing streams, cold- and warm-water springs and lakes; throughout.

Longnose Sucker

Catostomus catostomus

Length: 30–50 cm (maximum 64 cm)

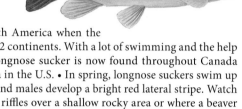

Scientists believe that suckers originated in Asia and then expanded their range to North America when the Bering land bridge linked the 2 continents. With a lot of swimming and the help of bait-bucket releases, the longnose sucker is now found throughout Canada and southeast to Pennsylvania in the U.S. • In spring, longnose suckers swim up smaller tributaries to spawn, and males develop a bright red lateral stripe. Watch for suckers wherever a stream riffles over a shallow rocky area or where a beaver dam creates a brushy waterfall. **Where found:** prefers cold lakes and rivers; occasionally found in warmer waters; throughout.

White Sucker

Catostomus commersoni

Length: 25–41 cm (maximum 61 cm)

This abundant generalist species lives in habitats ranging from cold streams to warm, even polluted, waters. It avoids rapid currents and uses shallow areas to feed. • In early spring, hundreds of spawning white suckers noisily splash and jostle in shallow streams or along lakeshores, providing food for other animals such as eagles and bears. Once hatched, the fry are a critical food source for other young fish. In the past, streams were so thick with spawning white suckers that Canadian pig farmers could pitchfork loads of them out of the water to feed livestock. **Where found:** variable habitats; prefers cool, clean waters with sandy or gravel substrate, throughout.

Shorthead Redhorse

Moxostoma macrolepidotum

Length: 30 cm (maximum 45 cm)

This distinctive, short-headed fish has reddish fins. The caudal (tail) fin turns bright red during spawning. • The genus name *Moxostoma* is Greek for "sucker mouth," and *macrolepidotum* describes this species' very large scales. • The shorthead redhorse is very sensitive to silty waters and moves to less muddy tributaries during spring breakup. It can endure warmer waters than many fish. **Where found:** clear waters of larger rivers and tributaries from the North Saskatchewan to the South Saskatchewan.

Northern Pike

Esox lucius

Length: 40–50 cm (maximum 1.2 m)

If you canoe, watch for adult northern pike hanging motionless among reeds or along the edges of dense aquatic plant beds. This carnivorous fish lies in wait for prey—other fish, ducklings or shorebirds—then attacks with a quick stab of its long snout, clamping down on its victim with heavily toothed jaws. **Where found:** vegetated edges of warmer lakes and rivers; throughout except mountain habitats. **Also known as:** jackfish, pickerel, water wolf.

Lake Whitefish

Coregonus clupeaformis

Length: 40 cm (maximum 63 cm)

Biologists call the lake whitefish a "plastic" species because it changes behaviour, food habits and appearance in different habitats. Different forms of this species may be identified by the number of gillrakers. Fish that live in open water develop extended gillrakers that are better for filtering plankton. Lake whitefish caught closer to the surface tend to have higher gillraker counts than those that live near lake bottoms. • The cisco (*C. artedii*), found in northeastern Alberta, has a small head and jaws, small scales and a terminal mouth. **Where found:** cool, deep water at the bottom of larger lakes; occasionally in rivers; throughout.

Mountain Whitefish

Prosopium williamsoni

Length: 25–45 cm (maximum 63 cm)

Mountain whitefish of Alberta's Eastern Slopes have endured habitat change and increased fishing pressures remarkably well. These fish can be sedentary, but many populations are known for their migratory behaviour—one tagged fish swam 500 kilometres from the mouth of the La Biche River all the way up the Athabasca River into Jasper National Park. Some seem to be in perpetual migration between seasonal feeding habitats and spawning grounds, and they move in large groups from pool to pool. **Where found:** fast, clear or silty streams and rivers; also cold, deep lakes; throughout the foothills and the Athabasca and Peace river drainage basins to northeastern Alberta.

Arctic Grayling

Thymallus arcticus

Length: 30–40 cm (maximum 55 cm)

The Arctic grayling's large dorsal fin, the aquatic equivalent of deer or moose antlers, and its vivid colouration identify this species immediately. • During spawning, this fish ventures from lakes and large rivers to smaller tributaries, where each male aggressively defends its selected spawning ground. • A fish of cold, clear streams, the Arctic grayling is vulnerable to changes in the environment. This fish needs to see its food to catch it, so clean, clear water is important. **Where found:** clear, cold waters of large rivers, rocky creeks and lakes; northern half of Alberta.

Cutthroat Trout

Oncorhynchus clarki

Length: 20–40 cm (maximum 74 cm)

Named for the red streaking in the skin under its lower jaw, cutthroat trout seen in the water can be mistakenly identified as the similar-looking rainbow trout. The cutthroat's reddish belly and throat become brighter during spawning. • Fourteen species of cutthroats have been described so far. Despite its name, the "westslope cutthroat" (*lewisii* ssp.) is native to Alberta's East Slopes. • Our native cutthroat trout populations declined in the early 1900s and were restocked with an introduced Yellowstone subspecies, as well as rainbow trout and hybrids of the two. **Where found:** clean, clear, well-oxygenated alpine lakes, mountain streams and tributaries.

Rainbow Trout

Oncorhynchus mykiss

Length: 30–45 cm (maximum 81 cm)

Because of its popularity among anglers, this species has spread from western North America to 6 continents, becoming the most widely introduced species in the world. Its trademark colourful appearance and heavily spotted back and sides vary in hue with the fish's lifestyle and habitat. • Rainbow trout in streams are bottom feeders but will often rise to the surface to leap for a struggling insect. They are highly respected by fly fishers because of their spectacular jumps and fighting strength. **Where found:** cool, well-oxygenated waters; streams with swift currents; southern two-thirds of Alberta.

Brown Trout

Salmo trutta

Length: 25–40 cm (maximum 87 cm)

Early European settlers introduced the "brownie" to North America and many other regions of the world. Today, some of the largest brown trout populations in western Canada are found in the rivers of central Alberta. • Brownies are drift feeders, preferring streams with cover and an intermediate water flow. They can handle warmer water temperatures and higher turbidity than other members of the trout family, so this species can be introduced into streams disturbed by logging or industrial activity. **Where found:** streams, larger rivers, beaver ponds and lakes; central Alberta and the foothills. **Also known as:** brownie, English brown trout, German brown trout.

Brook Trout

Salvelinus fontinalis

Length: 15–25 cm (maximum 86 cm)

The unique vermiculations, or "worm tracks," on the top part of the brook trout's body distinguish it from other Alberta trout species. This trout is the only char in the province with blue halos surrounding the red or yellow dots on its sides. • Introduced brook trout are very effective breeders, and many populations overcrowd their habitat, outcompeting or hybridizing with native bull trout (*S. confluentus*). **Where found:** cold, clear, slow-moving waters and clear, shallow areas of lakes; mountains and foothills.

Lake Trout

Salvelinus namaycush

Length: 45–65 cm (maximum 1 m)

Large, solitary lake trout prefer ice-cold water. In summer, they follow the retreat of colder water to the bottom of a lake, rarely making excursions into the warm surface layer. • Despite their slow growth, lake trout can reach old ages and large sizes. Large trout are often over 20 years old, with one granddaddy of a specimen reaching a phenomenal 62 years of age! • Lake trout can take 6 years or more to reach maturity and may spawn only once every 2 to 3 years, which makes recovery from overfishing difficult. **Where found:** deep, cool lakes; northeastern Alberta and the foothills.

Trout-perch

Percopsis omiscomaycus

Length: 7–10 cm (maximum 13 cm)

Transparent skin makes the trout-
perch fascinating—you can peer
straight through to the body cavity if you look carefully, and you can actually see
the 2 huge otoliths (ear bones) lying alongside the brain. • An important prey
species for larger fish such as lake trout and burbot, trout-perch hide under rocks
and usually feed at night. • Shine a flashlight into the shallows on a dark June
night, and you may see the big eyes and chunky pale bodies of spawning trout-
perch. • This species is one of the few non-salmonids with an adipose fin. **Where
found:** usually deeper water, but spawns and feeds in shallows; throughout except
mountain habitats.

Burbot

Lota lota

Length: 40–60 cm (maximum 1 m)

The burbot is the only member of the cod family confined to fresh water. • Both the
single chin barbel and the pectoral fins contain taste buds. As these fish grow,
they satisfy their ravenous appetite for whitefish and suckers by eating larger fish
instead of increasing numbers of smaller ones, sometimes swallowing fish almost
as big as themselves. A 30-centimetre-long walleye was once found in the stomach of
a large burbot. **Where found:** bottom of cold lakes and rivers; hides near boulders;
throughout except mountain habitats.

Brook Stickleback

Culaea inconstans

Length: 5 cm (maximum 9 cm)

This plentiful little fish is distinguished by the 4 to 6 spines along
its back. It is one of the easiest fish to see and
can be found along the vegetated edges of water bodies. • Brook sticklebacks tolerate
low oxygen levels and can live in waters where other fish cannot, spreading into
flooded fields that may eventually leave them high and dry. These little fish have
even been found in artesian wells, indicating that they are present in underground streams! **Where found:** various habitats including ponds, saline sloughs,
rivers, creeks and lake edges; throughout except a small area west of Jasper and
Grande Cache.

Slimy Sculpin

Cottus cognatus

Length: 6 cm (maximum 9 cm)

Female mottled sculpins literally fall "head over tails" in love.
After entering the nesting burrow, the female turns upside down to
deposit her sticky eggs on the underside of the rock or ledge that covers the den.
More than one topsy-turvy female may visit the nest, and the male will guard
his territory for up to 5 weeks. • Slimy sculpins are particularly fond of living
under bridges, always a promising place to look for local fish species. **Where
found:** bottom dweller; cool, clean boreal rivers and large lakes with gravelly or
rocky substrates; northern Alberta.

Yellow Perch

Perca flavescens

Length: 20–25 cm (maximum 39 cm)

The yellow perch, with its
recognizable black "saddles,"
is often pictured in biology
textbooks and dissected in science labs.
It also falls prey to almost every piscivorous predator around, including other fish
and birds. • Yellow perch lay eggs in gelatinous, accordion-folded ribbons that can
be as long as a human is tall! These zigzag streamers are draped over aquatic
vegetation, an excellent strategy that keeps them away from suffocating bottom silt.
Occasionally, wind or waves cast segments onto shore, a unique find for lucky
beachcombers. **Where found:** common in lakes, less common in rivers; from the
Peace River south except mountains and foothills.

Walleye

Stizostedion vitreum

Length: 30–40 cm (maximum 66 cm)

The walleye, prized for its tasty
flesh and sporting qualities, has black and
gold flecks all over its body and 2 dorsal fins. The first dorsal fin is spiny, whereas
the second is fleshy. • In "two-storey" lakes, brown trout inhabit the cool bottom
"storey," whereas walleye stick to the warmer surface waters and shallows. **Where
found:** large rivers and relatively deep lakes; prefers low light levels; throughout
except mountains and foothills. **Also known as:** pickerel.

INVERTEBRATES

More than 95 percent of all animal species are inverte-brates, and there are thousands of invertebrate species in our region. The few mentioned in this guide are fre-quently encountered and easily recognizable. Invertebrates can be found in a variety of habitats and are an important part of most ecosystems. They provide food for birds, amphibians, shrews, bats and other insects, and they also play an important role in the pol-lination of plants, as well as aiding in the decay process.

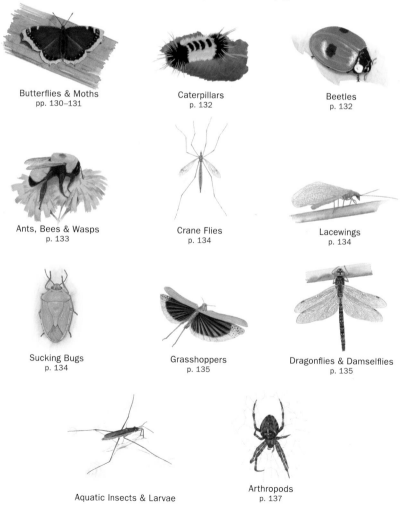

Butterflies & Moths
pp. 130–131

Caterpillars
p. 132

Beetles
p. 132

Ants, Bees & Wasps
p. 133

Crane Flies
p. 134

Lacewings
p. 134

Sucking Bugs
p. 134

Grasshoppers
p. 135

Dragonflies & Damselflies
p. 135

Aquatic Insects & Larvae

Arthropods
p. 137

Cabbage White

Pieris rapae

Wingspan: 50 mm

Although it is a European introduction, this species is probably our most widely seen butterfly. Cabbage whites were accidentally introduced near Montréal, Québec, in the 1860s; since then, they have spread continent-wide. • The larvae feed on many types of mustards and can become localized pests. The green caterpillars are nearly 3 cm long and are marked with 5 yellowish stripes—you probably encounter them on your cabbage plants. • This adaptable butterfly is easily the most urban of our species and can appear anywhere, even in large cities. **Where found:** any open habitat; shuns large, dense forests; throughout.

Canadian Tiger Swallowtail

Papilio canadensis

Wingspan: 100 mm

Few butterflies are more striking than this jumbo swallowtail. Tigers are fast, powerful fliers and often course high in the treetops. Fortunately, they often come down to our level for flower nectar. They turn up in gardens and are especially fond of dandelions. • The green caterpillars feed on various trees including aspens, willows and crabapples. They produce sticky silk and roll leaves to form tent-like shelters during the day—a good bird-avoidance strategy. **Where found:** mature forests with appropriate host plants; adults range widely; throughout.

Spring Azure

Celastrina ladon

Wingspan: 25 mm

As spring arrives in our region, the tiny spring azure can be seen fluttering along the forest floor before the last snows have melted. With its brilliant blue upperwings, the male appears like a tiny flower come to life. Males patrol sheltered areas in search of their dull brown mates, and they can often be found near red-osier dogwood or buffalo-berry bushes. • Spring azures belong to a subfamily of butterflies commonly known as "blues." **Where found:** common in forest clearings; throughout.

Mourning Cloak

Nymphalis antiopa

Wingspan: 70 mm

These long-lived butterflies may survive for up to 10 months. Adults typically emerge in May or June to feed for a short time before taking shelter until autumn, when they become active again. As winter approaches, mourning cloaks shelter under a piece of bark or within a woodpile and hibernate until spring mating season. You may be surprised to see a mourning cloak fluttering over the snow, but they will come out of hiding in temperatures above 10°C, even in the middle of winter! **Where found:** widespread in forested areas; throughout.

Monarch

Danaus plexippus

Wingspan: 95 mm

This familiar butterfly stages the most conspicuous and spectacular migration of any North American insect. In late summer and fall, millions of monarchs begin moving southward to Mexico, where they over-winter in masses in high-elevation fir forests. • Monarchs lay their eggs on milkweeds (*Asclepias* spp.), and their large, yellow-, white- and black-banded caterpillars are often easily found if you search milkweed plants. When the caterpillars feed on these plants, they absorb a toxic chemical into their bodies that makes both the caterpillars and the adults poisonous to birds. **Where found:** any open area that supports milkweeds; southern two-thirds of Alberta.

Polyphemus Moth

Antherea polyphemus

Wingspan: 110 mm

This large moth's spectacular colours and design make it highly noticeable. Many people assume it's a butterfly, but moths have fuzzy or thin and pointy antennae, whereas butterflies have slender antennae with thick tips. • The large eyespots exist for defensive purposes; if the wings are closed and a predator such as a bird approaches, the Polyphemus moth will flash its wings like eyelids, creating the illusion of a much larger creature to startle the predator. • Polyphemus was a one-eyed giant in Greek mythology—too bad that this moth has 4 fake eyes and 2 real ones, for a total of 6! **Where found:** deciduous forests; throughout.

Woolly Bear Caterpillar

Lophocampa maculata (larva)

These fuzzy, black-and-yellow beasts are the offspring of the spotted tussock moth and a common sight in late summer. They are often seen crawling through yards, gardens or along trails, when they climb down from their host plants and wander along the ground in search of a pupation site. They often spin their cocoons under railway ties, rain barrels or logs. Larvae host plants include Manitoba maple, alder, willow, cherry and linden. **Where found:** throughout.

Two-spot Ladybug

Adalia bipunctata

Length: 6 mm

The two-spot ladybug often spends cold Alberta winters hibernating in buildings and appears on our windowpanes in January or February. They may be coaxed back to sleep if they are placed in a cooler place in the house. These native ladybugs typically have 2 dark spots on a red background, but variations include 4 spots or red patches on a black background. • There are 35 ladybug species in Alberta that may be identified by features such as body shape, colour and arrangement and number of spots. **Where found:** variety of habitats; throughout.

Spruce Sawyer

Monochamus scutellatus

Length: 20 mm, plus long antennae

Finding this miniature replica of the Asian longhorn beetle in your backyard is a thrill. The exotic-looking spruce sawyer has a white-flecked, ebony body and long, curved antennae. These marvellous beasts pupate inside dead spruce trees, and the larvae hollow out winding galleries through the wood. When the awkward, noisy adults emerge to mate, they fly with their bodies held vertically and their legs sticking out in all directions. **Where found:** forested areas with spruce trees; throughout.

Carpenter Ant

Camponotus pennsylvanicus

Length: 10–15 mm

Woe to homeowners who have a colony of these wood-borers in their house. Carpenter ants damage the wooden infrastructure of a home. Their presence is characterized by small tunnels, or "galleries," with occasional slit-like openings where they expel sawdust. The ants don't actually eat the wood, as do termites; they are making nests. • In the wild, these ants excavate trees and form extensive galleries. Pileated woodpeckers readily tune into these colonies and often rip apart large sections of bark to get at the ants. **Where found:** trees and logs in forested areas; sometimes enters homes; throughout.

Bumblebee

Bombus spp.

Length: 14–20 mm

Intimidating but not aggressive, these large, fuzzy bees can be closely approached. Their dense, hairy coats help keep them warm, and "bumbles" can often fly in cooler weather than many other insects. Their hairy coats also make them extremely effective pollinators; as they visit flowers, the pollen adheres readily to their "fur" and is transferred to other plants. • Bumblebees usually build nests in underground burrows, and only young queens survive the winter to start new colonies the following spring. **Where found:** open habitats; frequent visitor to flowers and gardens; throughout.

Yellow Jacket

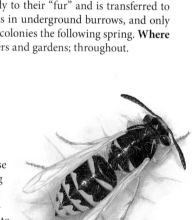

Vespula spp.

Length: 10–15 mm

Big and boldly striped in black and yellow, these ill-tempered hornets are attracted to anything sweet, including soda pop. • Yellow jackets nest in trees or in old rodent ground burrows, building papery nests made of wood fibre chewed into a pulp. People mowing lawns or walking through the woods sometimes agitate a colony and are attacked. A yellow jacket can inflict multiple painful stings, unlike a honeybee. • These predators kill a variety of other insects and sometimes eat nectar at flowers such as goldenrod. **Where found:** open areas; throughout.

Giant Crane Fly

Tipula spp.

Length: up to 25 cm

These innocent insects are not giant mosquitoes or harvestmen ("daddy longlegs") but very benign and harmless crane flies. Giant crane flies do not bite—the adults do not eat and live just long enough to mate and lay eggs. The larvae scavenge in soil and rotting logs, then burrow down into the soil to overwinter. • These long-legged creatures are more comfortable in the forest than when they accidentally find themselves inside your house. • There are 30 species of giant crane flies in Alberta. **Where found:** throughout.

Green Lacewing

Chrysopa spp.

Length: about 10 mm

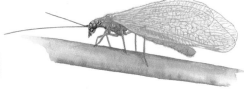

Lacewings are frequent visitors to your garden, where their lime green bodies are camouflaged against the pale foliage of young plants. They have elegant, filigreed wings (hence the name "lacewing"), large, golden eyes and, if you pick one up, you will notice that they produce an odd scent. • Both the adults and the larvae of these beneficial insects feed on aphids. **Where found:** shrubby or forested areas and gardens; widespread throughout.

Stinkbug

Chlorochroa sayi

Length: 14–19 mm

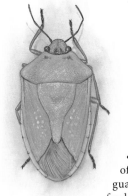

There is no question about it—stinkbugs really do stink. This insect is easily recognized by its unique odour, which is produced by its scent glands, its shield-shaped body and the triangular plate (scutellum) in the centre of its back. There are many species of stinkbugs in our region, both green and yellowish brown in colour. • Stinkbugs are devoted mothers. The female lays clusters of intricately shaped eggs on the surfaces of leaves and guards the eggs until they hatch, then she leaves the brood to fend for themselves. **Where found:** southern half of Alberta.

Road Duster Grasshopper

Dissosteira carolina

Length: 30–40 mm

One of North America's largest and most conspicuous grasshoppers, this big bug is easy to miss when motionless, but wait until it flushes. In flight, the road duster flashes large, black wings rimmed with pale gold, suggesting a mourning cloak butterfly. In flight, its wings make loud, crackling sounds called "crepitations."

• The male grasshopper engages in a courtship display in which it hovers like a tiny helicopter low over the ground. • Road dusters sometimes become so abundant locally that they damage plants. **Where found:** nearly any open ground, often along weedy roadsides and in lots; southern two-thirds of Alberta.

Variable Darner

Aeshna interrupta

Length: 70 mm

Variable darners, like all dragonflies, are voracious hunters. Each time they zig and zag in the air, they seize small insect prey. In turn, darners are an important prey item for falcons, and young merlins learn to hunt by chasing these dragonflies as they dart through the air. • Darners have incredible vision—each compound eye is composed of thousands of tiny facets, each of which is, in effect, a tiny eyelet. **Where found:** near ponds and lakes; throughout.

Cherry-faced Meadowhawk

Sympetrum internum

Length: 35 mm

The little red or yellow dragonflies that can be so common in parks and gardens are meadowhawks, and the cherry-faced meadowhawk is one of the most common species. Males have a cherry red face and a deep red body; the females and young males are yellowish. • Meadowhawks breed in ponds because their larvae are aquatic, but they will wander far from water to feed and may show up in gardens or parks. You can tiptoe up and watch them, because they often perch on or close to the ground. **Where found:** wetlands, parks, lawns and gardens; throughout.

Water Strider

Limnoporus dissortis

Length: about 13 mm

This unique bug lives on the surface of the water, relying on surface tension and its 4 long, water-repellent legs to keep it afloat. The water strider's legs distribute its body weight over the water's surface and allow it to zing about at speeds up to 1.5 metres per second, leaving rings of water in its wake. • This sucking bug uses its 2 short, front legs to catch larvae or other insects that fall into the water. In turn, water striders are eaten by fish or birds. **Where found:** ponds, lakes and slow-moving streams; throughout. **Also known as:** pond skater.

Giant Diving Beetle

Dytiscus spp.

Length: 27 mm

Equipped with a hard exoskeleton, large, efficient swimming limbs and sharp, chewing mouthparts, diving beetle are ferocious and impressive aquatic hunters. To breathe underwater, they dive with a bubble of air taken from the surface. • These beetles breed and lay their eggs on land, where the young pupate in damp forest soils before flying to water as adults. There are many species of diving beetles in our region. **Where found:** marshes, ponds and slow-moving streams; throughout.

Caddisfly Larvae

Order Trichoptera

Length: up to 60 mm (with case)

Caddisfly larvae are tiny architects that build a protective casing or shell around their soft bodies by gluing together sand, twigs or leaves using saliva and silk. The tube-shaped or coiled casings act as camouflage. • Search for caddisfly larvae on the bottom of shallow ponds or small creeks. Watch for pieces of moving debris with eyes and wiggly legs at one end. The larvae emerge as mothlike adults with long, wispy antennae and are an important food source for fish. **Where found:** ponds, lakes, rivers and streams; throughout.

Orbweaver

Araneus spp.

Length: to 15 mm

Spiders that make the classic "orb" webs belong to the orbweaver group, like the famous spider in *Charlotte's Web*. Their familiar, flat webs have radiating spokes connected by spiral silk strands. When prey hits the web, the spider rushes forth and quickly enwraps its prey in silk from its spinnerets. After completely immobilizing the victim, the spider administers the *coup de grâce*—several venom-filled bites from its sharp fangs. There are about 2 dozen orbweaver species in our region. **Where found:** various habitats; throughout.

Harvestman

Order Opiliones

Length: about 5 mm (body only)

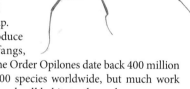

Although this poorly studied group of spider relatives called "daddy longlegs" includes numerous species, most are readily recognizable as harvestmen. They climb about in shrubs or on the forest floor, hunting small insects and occasionally feeding on plant sap. Unlike true spiders, harvestmen cannot produce silk and do not have venom glands or fangs, so they are utterly harmless. • Fossils from the Order Opilones date back 400 million years. Today, the order includes over 10,000 species worldwide, but much work remains to sort them out. **Where found:** nearly all habitats; throughout.

Garden Centipede

Lithobius spp.

Length: up to 30 mm

A centipede moves its many legs very quickly, but if you manage to see one sitting still, you can count one pair of legs per body segment—significantly fewer than 100 feet, as the name suggests. • This predator has venomous fangs with which it subdues its prey. It is not dangerous to people but should nevertheless be avoided, especially by small children. • Centipedes require a moist environment to survive and will quickly desiccate if they find their way into a house. **Where found:** under moist debris or other cover in gardens and forests; throughout.

137

PLANTS

Plants belong to the Kingdom Plantae. They are autotrophic, which means they produce their own food from inorganic materials through a process called photosynthesis. Plants are the basis of all food webs. They supply oxygen to the atmosphere, modify climate, and create and hold soil in place. Plants disperse their seeds and pollen through carriers such as wind, water and animals. Fossil fuels come from ancient deposits of organic matter—largely that of plants. In this book, plants are separated into 3 categories: trees; shrubs and vines; and forbs, ferns and graminoids.

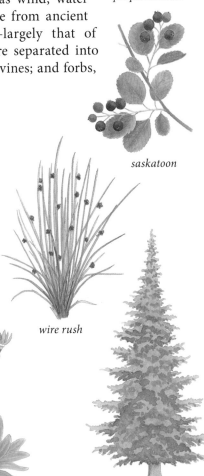

purple clematis

saskatoon

ostrich fern

wire rush

water birch

saline shootingstar

balsam fir

TREES

Trees are long-lived, woody plants that are normally taller than 5 metres. There are 2 types of trees: coniferous and broadleaf. Conifers, or cone-bearers, have needles or small, scale-like leaves. Most conifers are evergreens, but some, such as larches, shed their leaves in winter. Most broadleaf trees lose their leaves in autumn and are often called deciduous trees (meaning "falling off" in Latin). This book gives measurements for average tree heights in Alberta.

A single tree can provide a home or a food source for many different animals. Roots bind soil and play host to a multitude of beneficial fungi, and even support certain semi-parasitic plants such as common red paintbrush. Trunks provide a substrate for numerous species of mosses and lichens, which in turn are used by many animals for shelter and nesting material. Tree cavities are used by everything from owls to squirrels to snakes. Leafy canopies support an amazing diversity of life. Myriad birds depend on mature trees, as do scores of insects. Both the seed cones of coniferous trees and the fruits of deciduous trees are consumed by all manner of wildlife.

A group of trees can provide a windbreak, camouflage or shelter, and can hold down soil, thus preventing erosion. Streamside (riparian) woodlands are vital to protecting water quality. Their dense root layers filter out sediments and other contaminants that would otherwise enter watercourses. It is no mystery why Canada's healthiest rivers are also those that have abundant, undisturbed woodlands buffering them. There are many types of forest communities, and their species composition is largely dictated by the types of soils on which they occur. To some extent, the types of trees within a forest determine what other species of plants and animals are present. Old-growth forest is critical habitat for many species that use the fallen or hollowed-out trees as nesting or denning sites. Many species of invertebrates live within or under the bark, providing food for birds. Fallen, decomposing logs provide habitat for snakes, salamanders, mosses, fungi and invertebrates. The logs eventually completely degrade into nutrient-rich soil to perpetuate the continued growth of plant life and retain organic matter in the ecosystem. Large forests retain carbon dioxide, an important preventive factor of global warming. One giant old-growth tree can extract 7 kg of airborne pollutants annually and put back 14 kg of oxygen. Responsibly managed forests can also sustain an industry that provides wood products and jobs.

Firs
p. 141

Spruces
pp. 142–143

Tamarack
p. 143

Pines
pp. 144–145

Birches
p. 146

Alders & Poplars
pp. 147–148

Maples
p. 149

Subalpine Fir

Abies lasiocarpa

Height: 20–30 m
Needles: 2–4 cm long, bluish green, flattened, usually blunt
Seed cones: 5–10 cm long, erect, barrel-shaped

The fragrance of these resinous evergreens often permeates the air near treeline. In sheltered valleys, the spire-like crowns can reach their maximum height, but on high, exposed slopes, these trees grow stunted and twisted like bonsai. • Small subalpine fir needles have lines of white dots on the lower surface. The erect, deep purple, barrel-shaped cones usually grow on upper branches. • The oil-rich seeds are eaten by many species of birds, porcupines and squirrels. **Where found:** montane to subalpine zones of western Alberta.

Balsam Fir

Abies balsamea

Height: up to 25 m
Needles: 1.5–2.5 cm long, flat, flexible
Seed cones: 4–10 cm long, erect, greyish brown

The balsam fir is found in northern Alberta and is recognizable by the erect, barrel-shaped cones that grow near the top of the tree's spire-like crown. The needles have white lines on the lower surface. • Cut trees have a wonderful fragrance and do not immediately shed their needles, making the balsam fir a popular Christmas tree. The resin was traditionally used as a glue to waterproof canoe seams. Today, this tree is used in the manufacturing of glues, as a cement for mounting microscope slides, and in candle and soap making. **Where found:** low, swampy ground to well-drained hillsides; requires moist soil; central and northern Alberta. **Also known as:** Canada balsam.

White Spruce

Picea glauca

Height: 25–40 m
Needles: 1.5–2 cm long, stiff, 4-sided
Seed cones: 2.5–3.5 cm long, cylindrical, pale brown

Small white spruce trees often grow beneath old lodgepole pines. This species can live for 200 years and eventually replaces pines in mature forests. • Spruce needles roll between your fingers, unlike the flat, 2-sided needles of most other conifers. The needles are an exceptional source of vitamin C in winter and also have antioxidant properties, but they should be used in moderation. • This tree is an important source of food and shelter for many forest animals, including grouse and other seed-eating birds, porcupines and red squirrels. **Where found:** various soils and climates, but prefers moist, rich soil; throughout except southern grasslands.

Black Spruce

Picea mariana

Height: up to 15 m (rarely up to 30 m)
Needles: 0.5–1.0 cm long, stiff, 4-sided
Seed cones: 2–3 cm long, dull greyish brown to purplish brown

This slow-growing wetland tree, which may live for 200 years, is an important source of lumber and pulp. • Northern explorers used black spruce to make spruce beer, a popular drink that prevented scurvy. Spruce gum was also chewed or boiled into cough syrup to relieve sore throats, though spruce should be used in moderation. • Snowshoe hares love to eat young spruce seedlings and red squirrels harvest the cones, but in general, black spruce is not favoured as a wildlife food source. • Many black spruces have a club-shaped crown. **Where found:** cool, damp, boggy sites; central and northern Alberta. **Also known as:** bog spruce, swamp spruce.

Engelmann Spruce

Picea engelmannii

Height: up to 35 m
Needles: 1.5–2.5 cm long, flexible, slightly curved
Seed cones: 3–7 cm long, yellowish brown, cylindrical, shiny

A narrow, spire-like crown, whorls of drooping lower branches and sharp, 4-sided needles help to identify this aromatic evergreen. • This western spruce is an important forestry species and is used for lumber and especially for pulp because of the wood's long, light-coloured, resin-free fibres. The lumber often contains small knots, but it is still used for home construction, prefabricated products and also high-end, specialty items such as violins, pianos and aircraft parts. **Where found:** low to upper subalpine slopes of the Rockies.

Tamarack

Larix laricina

Height: up to 20 m (rarely to 25 m)
Needles: 2–5 cm long, soft, deciduous, in tufts of 15–60
Seed cones: 1–2 cm long, 20 or fewer scales, pale brown

The needles of this slender, exotic-looking tree are unusual among conifers because they turn golden yellow and drop in autumn. They grow on stubby twigs in tightly spiralled tufts. • Straight tamarack trunks are used as poles, piers and railway ties. The tannin-rich bark was once used for tanning leather. • In the mountains of southern Alberta, tamarack is replaced by subalpine larch (*L. lyallii*), which has bluish green leaves in tufts of 30 to 40 and occurs from 1500 m to treeline, higher than any other tree. **Where found:** moist, well-drained soils, bogs and muskeg; central and northern Alberta. **Also known as:** American larch, hackmatack.

143

Jack Pine

Pinus banksiana

Height: up to 20 m (maximum 27 m)
Needles: 2–4 cm long, in pairs, slightly twisted
Seed cones: 25–75 mm long, closed, point toward the branch tip

Jack pines are the first conifers to colonize areas burned by fire. The cones are held shut with a tight resin that melts when heated, allowing the seeds to disperse. • The cones of jack pine usually occur in groups of 2 to 3 and point toward the tip of the branch. Jack pine is found in central and eastern Canada, and lodgepole pine is found in western regions. In Alberta, the ranges of these 2 closely related species overlap, and hybrids with intermediate features occur. **Where found:** dry, infertile, acidic, often sandy or rocky soils; central and northeastern Alberta.

Lodgepole Pine

Pinus contorta var. *latifolia*

Height: up to 30 m
Needles: 3–7 cm long, in pairs, strongly twisted
Seed cones: 3–6 cm long, closed, at right angles to branch or pointing back

Lodgepole pines regularly colonize burned areas because fire melts the resin that holds the cones closed and releases the seeds. • The tall, straight trunks were traditionally used to support tipis or to build lodges and are an important source of timber today. Mountain pine beetle outbreaks are a serious problem, killing large stands. • A closely related variety of this pine found in western Canada is the short, scrubby shore pine (*P. c.* var. *contorta*), which thrives along the Pacific Coast. **Where found:** variety of habitats from dry sites to bogs; western Alberta.

Limber Pine

Pinus flexilis

Height: up to 12 m
Needles: 4–7 cm long, in bundles of 5
Seed cones: 8–12 cm long, narrowly cylindrical, short stalked

Limber pines are unique to western North America and are ecologically important. These gnarled, twisted trees can cling tenaciously to exposed bluffs and cliffs for over 1000 years. The name *flexilis* refers to the flexible branches, a necessary adaptation for survival under such windy conditions. These slow-growing trees providing valuable cover for wildlife on exposed, high-elevation slopes. Birds, small mammals and grizzly bears collect the nutritious, oil-rich seeds for food. **Where found:** warm ridges and rocky slopes; montane and subalpine zones of southern Alberta.

Whitebark Pine

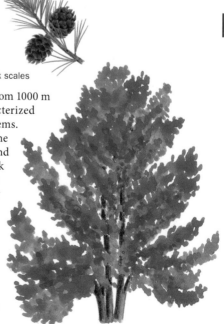

Pinus albicaulis

Height: up to 20 m
Needles: 4–7 cm long, soft, finely toothed, in bundles of 5
Seed cones: 5–8 cm long, oval, stalkless, thick scales

Whitebark pine, found at elevations from 1000 m to treeline in the mountains, is characterized by whitish bark and often multiple stems. Its size and appearance varies with the growing conditions. • Various birds and small mammals feed on whitebark pines, but the Clark's nutcracker is a major seed disperser. One bird may transport up to 90 seeds at a time, holding them in a pouch under its tongue. Each year, a single nutcracker may cache over 30,000 seeds for winter use or for feeding young. Seeds that are not retrieved contribute to new growth. **Where found:** montane and subalpine zones of western Alberta. **Also known as:** scrub pine.

Paper Birch

Betula papyrifera

Height: up to 25 m
Leaves: 5–10 cm long, coarsely toothed, 5–9 straight veins per side
Flowers: tiny, male and female flowers in separate catkins, 2–4 cm long
Fruit: tiny, flat, 2-winged nutlets

This small, showy tree, with its peeling, papery, white bark, occurs across North America. First Nations peoples used the waterproof bark as the outer skin of canoes, for roofing material and to make baskets and storage containers. Never cut bark from living trees because bark removal may weaken or kill the tree. • Recent studies have shown that the betulinic acid in birch bark may be useful in treating skin cancer and exhibits anti-HIV, anti-malarial and anti-inflammatory properties. **Where found:** open, often disturbed sites; also forest edges on a variety of substrates; throughout except the extreme south. **Also known as:** white birch.

Water Birch

Betula occidentalis

Height: up to 12 m
Leaves: 2–5 cm long, broadly oval, sharply toothed, 4–5 veins per side
Flowers: catkins, 2–6 cm long
Fruit: hairy, winged nutlets in slender catkins, 2.5–4 cm long

This tall shrub grows in moist, riparian areas and is often found in pure, dense stands or mixed with streamside shrubs such as willows or alders. When mature, water birch has dark purplish brown bark that does not peel off like that of paper birch. • Liquid, slightly sweet birch sap can be collected in spring and used as a beverage or boiled into syrup. **Where found:** moist areas and streamsides; throughout.

Speckled Alder

Alnus incana ssp. *tenuifolia*

Height: up to 8 m
Leaves: 5–10 cm long, deeply veined, double-toothed
Flowers: tiny, in catkins, 5–8 cm long
Fruit: narrow-winged nutlets, in ovoid catkins, 1.0–1.5 cm long

These tall, clumped, deciduous shrubs often grow near lakes and rivers but do not tolerate shade. The woody, cone-like fruits are made of tiny, winged nutlets. The leaves are shiny and finely toothed. • In the past, alder wood was an important fuel for smoking fish, meat and hides. The twigs and inner bark produce a red-brown dye that was used to colour hides and birchbark baskets. • Green alder (*A. viridis* ssp. *crispa*) is shade tolerant and grows as an understorey plant on both wet sites and dry, upland areas. **Where found:** streamsides and moist sites; throughout except grasslands.

Trembling Aspen

Populus tremuloides

Height: 10–20 m
Leaves: 2–8 cm long, finely toothed
Flowers: tiny, in slender, hanging catkins, 2–10 cm long
Fruit: hairless capsules, in hanging catkins, 10 cm long

Suckers from the shallow, spreading roots of this deciduous tree can colonize many hectares of land. Single trees are short lived, but a colony of clones can survive for thousands of years. • The greenish, photosynthetic bark produces a white powder that protects the trees from ultraviolet radiation in open areas. This powder can be used as sunscreen. • These trees are sometimes called "asbestos trees" because the trunks will not burn easily when a fast-moving fire passes through the forest. **Where found:** dry to moist sites; throughout except southern grasslands. **Also known as:** quaking aspen, aspen poplar.

Western Cottonwood

Populus deltoides

Height: up to 25 m
Leaves: 5–10 cm long, triangular, tapered at tip
Flowers: tiny, in catkins, 5–7 cm long
Fruit: small capsules, in hanging catkins 1.5–2.5 cm long

Cottonwoods grow on floodplains or shorelines because the seeds require wet mud to germinate. The trees begin to "snow" in late May or early June, as rivers swollen from spring runoff begin to recede. • These fast-growing trees can reach massive proportions—old cottonwoods are among the largest trees in many areas. Young trees can grow more than 3.5 m per year, and even big ones can add 1.5 m annually. • Ungulates browse on the young trees, and bees collect the sticky, aromatic resin from the buds to cement and waterproof their hives. Baltimore orioles frequent cottonwoods and often build their nests in these trees. **Where found:** moist, warm, low-lying sites including floodplains and sand dunes near lakes; southern Alberta.

Balsam Poplar

Populus balsamifera

Height: up to 25 m
Leaves: 5–12 cm long, broadly ovate, long stalked
Flowers: tiny, in catkins, 7–10 cm long
Fruit: small, oval capsules, in catkins, 10–13 cm long

The trunks of these trees can reach girths of up to 1 m, with the bark becoming deeply furrowed and dark grey when old. • This tree had several traditional uses in Native medicines, as well as being a source of sugar, fragrance, ink and firewood. • The male and female flowers are in catkins on separate trees. The seeds are in capsules attached to parachutes of cottony down. Young seedlings have extremely large leaves to ensure maximum energy absorption. **Where found:** moist, low-lying areas, often in river valleys; mountains, central and northeastern Alberta, and Cypress Hills.

Manitoba Maple

Acer negundo

Height: up to 20 m
Leaves: 5–12 cm long, opposite,
compound, divided into 3–5 irregularly coarsely toothed leaflets
Flowers: tiny, pale yellowish green, male flowers on slender
stalks in bundles, female flowers in clusters
Fruit: pairs of winged samaras, 3–5 cm long,
hanging in clusters

This species might not be recognized as a maple at first glance because of its trifoliate leaves. Manitoba maple is our only maple with compound leaves. • This widely planted, fast-growing shade or shelterbelt tree can withstand drought and freezing temperatures, but snow, ice and wind can cause its brittle branches to break. • The samaras usually spread at less than a 45° angle, and the hanging clusters of fruit persist through winter. **Where found:** low, moist sites and disturbed ground, especially along streams; central and southern Alberta. **Also known as:** box-elder, ashleaf maple.

SHRUBS & VINES

The difference between a tree and a shrub is sometimes rather sketchy, but in general, shrubs are small, woody plants less than 6 metres tall. They are typically bushy, having multiple small trunks and branches that emerge from near the ground, and many species produce soft berries. Some shrubs occur in open, sunny areas, whereas others are important dominant components of the understorey in forests. Shrubs provide habitat and shelter for a variety of animals, and their berries, leaves and often bark are crucial sources of food. The tasty berries of some shrubs have been long been a staple of Native and traditional foods, and they are still enjoyed by people throughout our region.

Evergreens
p. 151

Birches
p. 152

Bayberries
p. 152

Willows
p. 153

Dogwoods
p. 153

Roses & Currants
pp. 153–158

Oleasters
p. 158

Asters
p. 159

Goosefoots
p. 159

Heaths
pp. 160–162

Honeysuckles
pp. 162–164

Buttercups
p. 164

Legumes
p. 164

Common Juniper

Juniperus communis

Height: evergreen, up to 1 m
Needles: 5–12 mm long, narrow, lance-shaped, in whorls of 3
Cones: female cones 6–10 mm across, bluish, berry-like; male cones catkin-like

Common juniper grows over much of the world and is most famous as the flavouring for gin. The blue-grey "berries" of this shrub are, in fact, tiny cones with 3 to 8 fleshy scales. These strongly flavoured fruits are occasionally added to wild game dishes but are generally considered distasteful. Pregnant women or people with kidney problems should not eat juniper. **Where found:** dry, open sites; throughout.

Creeping Juniper

Juniperus horizontalis

Height: creeping evergreen, up to 25 cm
Needles: about 1.5 mm long, overlapping, scale-like
Cones: male cones small, catkin-like; female cones 5–7 mm across, bluish, berry-like

Creeping juniper is a low shrub with trailing branches and scalelike leaves in 4 vertical rows.
• The branches of this aromatic evergreen were traditionally burned in smudges or to repel insects, and the bluish berries (actually fleshy cones) make a pleasant addition to potpourris. The berries also have antiseptic properties, and strong juniper tea was once used to sterilize bandages and needles. Oil-of-juniper is used today in aromatherapy applications. **Where found:** dry, rocky soils and sterile fields; throughout.

Crowberry

Empetrum nigrum

Height: creeping evergreen, to 15 cm
Leaves: 3–8 mm long, needle-like
Flowers: tiny, purplish crimson
Fruit: black, berry-like drupes, 4–8 mm across

This creeping, evergreen shrub forms dense mats on the forest floor. Next to cranberries and blueberries, crowberries are one of the most abundant edible wild fruits found in northern Canada and were a popular food among Arctic aboriginal groups. The berries are high in vitamin C and antioxidant anthocyanins (the black pigment that gives them colour) and have a high water content, making them a valuable snack in waterless high-country areas. Freezing or cooking improves the bland taste of these fruits. **Where found:** coniferous forests, acidic peatlands and alpine heaths; low elevations to alpine; throughout.

Dwarf Birch

Betula pumila

Height: up to 2 m
Leaves: 1–4 cm long, round, coarsely toothed, leathery, shiny
Flowers: male catkins 1–2 cm long, hanging; female catkins 1 cm long, erect
Fruit: round, winged nutlets, 2 mm across

Dwarf birch is a common shrub of the northern boreal forest and is typically found in wet environments such as bogs or swamps. • The smooth, dark grey or reddish brown bark of older shrubs has raised pores called "lenticels." The leaves turn a deep orange to russet in fall. The branches, with their small, attractive leaves, make a unique addition to flower arrangements. **Where found:** marshes, sloughs and bogs; throughout, except southern grasslands. **Also known as:** bog birch, swamp birch.

Beaked Hazelnut

Corylus cornuta

Height: up to 3 m
Leaves: 5–10 cm long, elliptical, heart-shaped or round base, irregularly double-toothed
Flowers: male in hanging catkins, 4–7 cm long; female tiny, crimson, thread-like, emerging from a scaly bud
Fruit: spherical nuts, 1–1.5 cm long

Plentiful, edible wild hazelnuts are rich in protein, but sometimes become infested with grubs just when they are ready to harvest. A bristly, greenish, beaked husk surrounds each round nut. Nuts may be single or in groups of 2 or 3. They can be roasted and eaten whole or ground into flour. • If you have sharp eyes, you may spot the hazelnut's thread-like, red female flowers in spring emerging from buds at the ends of leafy shoots. **Where found:** moist, well-drained woodlands; central Alberta.

Sweet Gale

Myrica gale

Height: to 2 m
Leaves: 3.5–6 cm long, lance-shaped, toothed on upper one-third
Flowers: waxy, yellowish green catkins, to 1.5 cm long
Fruit: oval nutlets, 3 mm long, in conelike catkins, 8 mm long

This unusual member of the bayberry family bears flowers of only one sex each year, alternating between female flowers one year, then male flowers the next. • Nitrogen-fixing sweet gale can pull nitrogen out of the air and make it available to the plant, which allows it to survive where other plants cannot. • The nutlets have spongy, wing-like scales that work like tiny life preservers to keep the fruits afloat in water and aid in dispersal. • Before hops became widely available, sweet gale was used to flavour English ale. **Where found:** wet, low-elevation areas such as bogs and streamsides; northeastern Alberta.

Bebb's Willow

Salix bebbiana

Height: up to 6 m
Leaves: 3–7 cm long, narrow to elliptical, dull green above, whitish hairs beneath
Flowers: catkins, 1–4 cm long, on leafy shoots
Fruit: sparsely hairy, long-beaked capsules, 6–8 mm long

There are more than 40 willow species in Alberta, and many are tough to differentiate. Bebb's willow has reddish brown stems and is one of the most common lowland willows in Alberta. Some stems are marked by diamond-shaped patches caused by fungal infections that produce orange to brown patterns in the pale wood. When peeled and sanded, these "diamond willow" branches are used to make walking sticks, furniture and plaques. • Grayleaf willow (*S. glauca*) has grey stems and is a common mountain species. **Where found:** moist sites; throughout. **Also known as:** diamond willow, beaked willow.

Red-osier Dogwood

Cornus sericea

Height: to 3 m
Leaves: 2–10 cm long, oval or lance-shaped, smooth edges
Flowers: 3–6 mm across, white, 4 petals, in dense, flat-topped clusters
Fruit: white, berry-like drupes, 7–9 mm across

This attractive, hardy, deciduous shrub has distinctive purple to red branches with white flowers in spring, red leaves in autumn and white, berry-like fruits in winter. The opposite leaves have 5 to 7 prominent veins. Dogwood is easily grown from cuttings and makes an interesting addition to a native plant garden. • Native peoples smoked the dried inner bark alone or mixed it with tobacco or bearberry leaves. The flexible branches can be woven into baskets. **Where found:** moist sites; throughout except the extreme southeast. **Also known as:** *C. stolonifera.*

Pin Cherry

Prunus pensylvanica

Height: up to 12 m
Leaves: 3–10 cm long, oval to lance-shaped, sharp-pointed, finely toothed
Flowers: 1 cm across, white, 5 petals, in clusters
Fruit: red, berry-like drupes, 6–8 mm across

Pin cherries have a lifespan of about 40 years, and mature trees produce edible but sour fruit. These tart wild cherries can be cooked, strained and sweetened for use in jellies, jams or syrup. The stones, bark, wood and leaves of cherry trees contain hydrocyanic acid and are toxic, so only the cherry flesh can be used. • Pin cherries can also be planted as ornamentals, and the flowering plants attract an audible number of bees in spring. Songbirds feast on the berries and disperse the seeds. **Where found:** open woodlands or recently burned sites; southwestern, central and northeastern Alberta. **Also known as:** bird cherry.

Chokecherry

Prunus virginiana

Height: up to 6 m
Leaves: 3–10 cm long, broadly oval with sharp tip, finely toothed
Flowers: 1–1.5 cm across, white, 5 petals, cup-shaped, in hanging, cylindrical clusters
Fruit: reddish to blackish, berry-like drupes, 8–12 mm across

Chokecherry has long, bottlebrush-like clusters of flowers and hanging clusters of shiny, crimson fruit that turns black with age. The sour fruit of mature trees can be eaten raw or or preserved, but the stones, bark, wood and leaves contain toxic hydrocyanic acid. • Many species of moths and butterflies, including swallowtails, use chokecherry as a host plant. **Where found:** open sites, fencerows, streams and forest edges; southern two-thirds of Alberta.

Western Mountain-ash

Sorbus scopulina

Height: 1–4 m
Leaves: compound, divided into 9–13 opposite, elliptical leaflets, each 3–6 cm long
Flowers: 8–15 m across, white, 5 petals, in dense, flat-topped clusters, 9–15 cm wide
Fruit: shiny, red-orange, berry-like pomes, 7–8 mm across

This extremely showy shrub has sharp-tipped leaves and bright clusters of white flowers or glossy clusters of reddish berries. The juicy berries attract many birds such as cedar waxwings, and the more northerly Bohemian waxwing's range seems largely tied to the western mountain-ash. The decorative berries are edible, but only when fully ripe. • European mountain-ash (*S. aucuparia*) is a commonly planted, escaped species with white-hairy buds, 13 or more leaflets and bright red fruit. **Where found:** moist, open or shaded sites; west-central Alberta.

Round-leaved Hawthorn

Crataegus rotundifolia

Height: up to 5 m
Leaves: 2–7 cm long, round to oval, toothed
Flowers: 1–1.5 cm across, white, 5 petals, in clusters
Fruit: deep red haws (pomes), 1 cm across

This easily recognized, widespread species has numerous black thorns, 2 to 6 cm long, and clusters of white, unpleasant-smelling flowers. The red haws resemble tiny apples and remain on the plant throughout winter. The haws of all hawthorn species are edible but are usually seedy or mealy. • Hawthorn thickets provide shelter and food for many small animals that, in turn, help distribute the fruit. **Where found:** open, gravelly, riparian areas; southern Alberta. **Also known as:** *C. chrysocarpa* var. *rotundifolia*.

Saskatoon

Amelanchier alnifolia

Height: up to 4 m
Leaves: 2–5 cm long, oval to round, toothed near tip
Flowers: about 1 cm across, white, showy, 5 petals, in clusters
Fruit: dark purple, berrylike pomes, 5–10 mm across

Saskatoons make excellent ornamental shrubs. They
are hardy, easily propagated, with beautiful white blossoms in spring,
delicious, edible fruit in summer and scarlet leaves in autumn. Several
native butterflies use saskatoon as a host plant, including the coral hairstreak
(*Harkenclenus titus*). • Saskatoon berries were an important food source for many
Native peoples and are still popular today. Many animals also feast on the berries,
including black bears, snowshoe hares, flying squirrels and birds. **Where found:**
dry, often sandy woods, rocky sites and forest edges; throughout.

Wild Red Raspberry

Rubus idaeus

Height: 1–2 m
Leaves: 4–8 cm long, compound with 3–5 oval, toothed leaflets
Flowers: 8–12 mm wide, white, 5 petals, solitary
Fruit: red raspberries (drupelets), 1 cm across

Delicious, plump raspberries can be eaten straight off the bush
or made into jams, jellies or pies. Fresh or completely dried
leaves make excellent tea, but wilted leaves can be toxic. • Dwarf
raspberry or dewberry (*R. pubescens*) hugs the ground, has
pinkish flowers and bears a single red raspberry. It is found in wet
forests across central and northern Alberta. **Where found:** thickets,
clearings and open aspen forests; southern two-thirds of Alberta.

Prickly Wild Rose

Rosa acicularis

Height: 20–120 cm
Leaves: compound with 3–9 oval, coarsely toothed leaflets,
each 2–5 cm long
Flowers: 5–7 cm across, showy, pink, 5 petals, solitary
Fruit: red hips, about 15 mm long

The sweet-smelling, widespread wild rose is Alberta's provincial flower.
This shrub's stems are covered with many small, prickly bristles. • Rose
hips are high in vitamins A, B, E, K and especially vitamin C—3 hips
contain as much vitamin C as an orange. Only the fleshy outer layer should be eaten;
the sliver-like hairs on the seeds can irritate the digestive tract. • The common wild
rose or wood rose (*R. woodsii*) has fewer, scattered thorns, usually at stem nodes.
Where found: dry to moist sites; southwestern, central and northeastern Alberta.

Prairie Rose

Rosa arkansana

Height: 20–50 cm
Leaves: compound with 7–11 oval, sharply toothed leaflets, each 1–5 cm long
Flowers: 3–7 cm across, showy, pink to white, 5 petals, in clusters of 2–5
Fruit: red hips, 1–2 cm across

The prairie rose has reddish brown, prickly stems that die back to ground level each autumn. • Rose petals may be eaten fresh or preserved. Early Ukrainian pioneers gathered the ever-abundant prairie rose petals for fragrant preserves that were used as a filling for dainty pastries. Petal preserves were made by removing the bitter yellow crowns, and then boiling the rose petals with sugar, water and lemon. **Where found:** grasslands and prairie roadsides; southern Alberta.

White Mountain-avens

Dryas octopetala

Height: trailing shrub, hairy flowering stems 5–20 cm tall
Leaves: 1.0–1.5 cm long, lance-shaped, toothed margins, woolly below
Flowers: 2–3 cm wide, white, 8 petals, solitary
Fruit: achenes, <3 mm across, with a feathery plume at the tip

This alpine wildflower stays low, avoiding cold, drying winds in summer and blanketed by snow in winter. Its thick, evergreen leaves are wrinkled above and densely white-hairy beneath to help conserve water and produce food when temperatures rise above freezing. The parabolic flowers follow the sun, warming the stigmas and developing seeds. • Entire-leaved mountain-avens (*D. integrifolia*) has white flowers and smaller leaves with smooth margins and undersides. • Yellow mountain-avens (*D. drummondii*) has nodding, yellow flowers and tapered leaves. **Where found:** gravelly slopes and riparian areas; mountains of western Alberta.

Shrubby Cinquefoil

Dasiphora floribunda

Height: up to 1–1.5 m
Leaves: 2 cm long, pinnately compound with 3–7 (usually 5) linear to oblong, leathery leaflets
Flowers: 2–3 cm wide, yellow, saucer-shaped, 5 petals, solitary or in small clusters at branch tips
Fruit: tiny, egg-shaped, hairy achenes in compact clusters

Commonly planted in parking-lot islands, shrubby cinquefoil is a common garden ornamental with many cultivars. In the wild, it is often an indicator of high-quality habitats. • Traditionally, the leaves were used to flavour meat and were boiled into a tea that was in high calcium. A medicinal tea made of the leaves, stems and roots has mild astringent properties and was used to treat congestion, tuberculosis and fevers. **Where found:** wet prairies, fens and rocky shores; in suitable habitat throughout. **Also known as:** *Dasiphora fruticosa, Pentaphylloides floribunda, Potentilla fruticosa.*

Narrow-leaved Meadowsweet

Spiraea alba

Height: up to 1.5 m
Leaves: 3–6 cm long, narrow, elliptical, finely toothed
Flowers: 5–8 mm across, white, 5 petals, in tall, pyramidal clusters
Fruit: clusters of small pods

Narrow-leaved meadowsweet's pyramid-shaped flower clusters appear throughout the summer. The flowers look slightly fuzzy because they are covered in fine hairs. Mature branches have peeling, purplish grey bark. • The leaves of this plant were traditionally steeped into a flavourful tea. **Where found:** moist, sandy or rocky sites, riparian areas, lakeshores and ditches; east-central Alberta. **Also known as:** white meadowsweet.

Wild Black Currant

Ribes americanum

Height: up to 1 m
Leaves: 2–8 cm wide, maple-like with 3–5 pointed, double-toothed lobes
Flowers: 2–5 mm across, creamy white to yellowish, bell-shaped, 5 petals, in drooping clusters
Fruit: black berries, up to 1 cm wide

Wild black currant is a small shrub with smooth, black berries. The fruit may be eaten raw, cooked or dried. Currants are high in pectin and make excellent jams and jellies. Mixed with other berries, they are used to flavour liqueurs or make wines. Raw currants tend to be very tart, but these common shrubs provide a safe emergency food source. **Where found:** open, wooded areas, riparian areas and swamps; central and southern Alberta.

Skunk Currant

Ribes glandulosum

Height: up to 1 m
Leaves: 2–7 cm across; maple-like with 5–7 rounded, coarsely toothed lobes
Flowers: 6 mm wide, yellowish green, 5 petals, in erect clusters of 6–15
Fruit: bristly red berries, 6 mm across

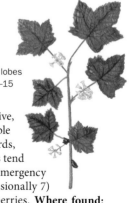

The crushed leaves and stems of this plant emit a distinctive, skunky odour. • The bristly red berries are not very palatable but are eaten by moose, chipmunks, martens and birds, including thrushes, thrashers and waxwings. Raw currants tend to be very tart, but these common shrubs provide a safe emergency food source. • Currants have leaves with 3 to 5 lobes (occasionally 7) that resemble those of maples and red, yellow or black berries. **Where found:** damp forests, swampy areas and clearings; central and northeastern Alberta.

Wild Gooseberry

Ribes oxyacanthoides

Height: up to 1.5 m
Leaves: 2–5 cm wide, 3–5 pointed, double-toothed lobes
Flowers: 4–9 mm across, greenish white, bell-shaped, 5 petals,
in short, hanging clusters
Fruit: purple-black berries, 1–1.5 cm across

Gooseberries are often eaten fresh, and they are delicious alone or mixed with other fruit in pies. Their high pectin and citric acid content makes them a good choice for jellies. Timing is important when picking the fruit because green berries are very sour and ripe fruit quickly drops to the ground. • Wild gooseberry is a sprawling shrub with prickly branches, often with 1 to 3 spines up to 1 cm long at the base of each leaf. **Where found:** wet forests, thickets, clearings, open woods and rocky sites; throughout.

Wild Red Currant

Ribes triste

Height: to 1 m
Leaves: 5–8 cm wide, maple-like with 3–5 pointed,
coarsely toothed lobes
Flowers: 4–6 mm wide, greenish pink to purple-red, 5 petals,
in drooping clusters of 6–20
Fruit: bright red berries, 4 mm across

Almost 30 native species of currants and gooseberries (*Ribes* spp.) are found across Canada. All currants and gooseberries are edible, but flavour varies greatly with species, habitat and season. Gooseberry stems have prickles and currants stems do not, but currant stems are sometimes dotted with yellow, crystalline resin glands that have a sweet, "tomcat" odour. **Where found:** moist, coniferous forests; also swamps, streambanks and rocky montane slopes; central and northern Alberta and Cypress Hills.

Canada Buffaloberry

Shepherdia canadensis

Height: 1–3 m
Leaves: 2–6 cm long, elliptical, greenish above, silvery below, smooth edges
Flowers: 4 mm wide, greenish yellow, in leaf axils
Fruit: bright red, oval berries, 4–6 mm across

This deciduous shrub has dark green leaves that are silvery below, with star-shaped hairs and rust-coloured scales. The tempting, juicy, translucent red berries are quite sour, but many Native peoples enjoyed them. • Buffaloberries contain a bitter, soapy substance called saponin that foams when beaten. The berries were whipped like egg whites to make a foamy "ice cream" dessert, which was sweetened with other berries and, later, with sugar. **Where found:** open woods and streambanks; throughout except southern grasslands. **Also known as:** soapberry.

Wolf Willow, Silverberry

Elaeagnus commutata

Height: 1–3 m
Leaves: 3–8 cm long, silvery grey, oblong to lance-shaped,
wavy edges
Flowers: 3 mm across, yellowish green, funnel-shaped,
in groups of 2–5 in leaf axils
Fruit: silvery, dry, mealy berries, 6 mm across

This beautiful silvery shrub flowers in June, giving
off a sweet, musky scent. The flowering dates of wolf willow can be reported to
PlantWatch, a nationwide volunteer program that helps scientists track changes
in the environment. • Traditionally, the beautifully striped, stony seeds inside the
berries were cleaned, oiled and polished, then used as decorative beads. **Where
found:** edge habitats, dry hillsides and open areas; in suitable habitat throughout.

Silver Sagebrush

Artemisia cana

Height: 40–125 cm
Leaves: 1–4 cm long, elliptical, silvery, hairy, aromatic when crushed
Flowers: minute, yellowish green
Fruit: small achenes

This common shrub is a true prairie plant, with a sage-like aroma
and greyish, shredding bark. The green, leafy branches were traditionally burned as ceremonial smudges to cleanse participants of impuri-
ties and evil spirits, and they are still used in this way today. Sagebrush
has been used in a wide variety of medicines, and its extracts are
reputed to kill many types of bacteria, but some classify this plant as toxic. The
aromatic, volatile oils have been used in shampoos and as insect repellents.
Where found: uplands and overgrazed areas; southern Alberta.

Greasewood

Sarcobatus vermiculatus

Height: to 3 m
Leaves: 1–4 cm, linear, fleshy
Flowers: 2 mm long, green, in catkin-like clusters
Fruit: winged achenes, about 6 mm long

Greasewood is a halophyte, one of only a few plants in Alberta
that is able to grow in saline habitats. Only about 2 percent of all
plants worldwide are able to tolerate salt. • Greasewood is named for
its fleshy leaves and spiny branches—in Greek, *sarco* means "thorn"
and *batus* means "flesh." • This plant is poisonous to livestock. **Where found:**
sunny, saline flats or alkaline soils; also roadside ditches; southeastern Alberta.

Pink Mountain-heather

Phyllodoce empetriformis

Height: up to 40 cm
Leaves: 5–12 mm long, needle-like, grooved
Flowers: 5–8 mm long, purplish pink, bell-shaped, 5 petals, nodding
Fruit: round, dry capsules, 3–4 mm across,

These bright, rose pink clusters of tiny bells on deep green mats delight hikers on alpine slopes. Needle-like leaves help these ground-hugging plants to survive in areas where frozen soil and cold, dry winds limit water. • Yellow heather (*P. glandulifera*) has pale yellow, bell-shaped flowers, needle-like leaves and grows in similar habitats. **Where found:** dry to moist slopes in subalpine and alpine zones of the western mountains. **Also known as:** pink heather, purple heather.

White Mountain-heather

Cassiope tetragona

Height: up to 30 cm
Leaves: 2–4 mm long, evergreen, oval, grooved, overlapping
Flowers: 5–6 mm long, white, bell-shaped, 4–5 petals, nodding, solitary
Fruit: reddish brown capsules, 3–4 mm long

White mountain-heather is a circumpolar plant that hugs the ground on Arctic tundra and high alpine slopes. The thick, evergreen leaves surround the branches on all sides, giving them the appearance of a braided rope. • The genus name *Cassiope* comes from Greek mythology; Cassiopeia was a beautiful, vain queen and the mother of Andromeda. **Where found:** moist slopes in subalpine and alpine zones of the western mountains.

Labrador Tea

Rhododendron groenlandicum

Height: up to 1.5 m
Leaves: 1–5 cm long, oblong, leathery, rusty below, rolled edges
Flowers: 8–10 mm across, white, 5 petals, in umbrella-shaped clusters
Fruit: dry, drooping capsules, 5–7 mm long

This evergreen shrub saves energy by keeping its leaves year-round. The leaves have a thick, leathery texture, rolled edges and distinctive rusty-coloured, woolly hairs on their undersides, all adaptations that help the plant conserve moisture. Labrador tea may also produce chemicals that discourage other plants from growing nearby. • First Nations peoples and early settlers made the leaves and flowers into a tea that was rich in vitamin C. However, consuming large amounts can be toxic. • Do not confuse this plant with poisonous heaths such as bog rosemary. **Where found:** moist, acidic, nutrient-poor soils; often associated with black spruce; central and northern Alberta. **Also known as:** *Ledum groenlandicum.*

Bearberry, Kinnikinnick

Arctostaphylos uva-ursi

Height: to 10 cm
Leaves: 1–3 cm long, dark green, oval, leathery, smooth edges
Flowers: 4–6 mm wide, pinkish, urn-shaped, 4–5 petals, in nodding clusters
Fruit: dull red, berry-like drupes, 6–10 mm across

Thick, leathery, evergreen leaves conserve moisture and help this common, mat-forming shrub survive on dry, sunny slopes where others would perish. The flowers nod in small clusters, and trailing branches, which may be up to 1 metre long, send down roots. • The red "berries" are edible but are rather mealy and tasteless. They were traditionally mixed with grease and cooked to reduce their dryness. **Where found:** sandy, well-drained, open or wooded sites; throughout except southern grasslands.

Velvetleaf Blueberry

Vaccinium myrtilloides

Height: 10–50 cm
Leaves: 1–4 cm long, oblong to elliptical, covered with short, soft hairs
Flowers: 3–5 mm wide, greenish to pinkish white, bell-shaped, 5 petals, in clusters
Fruit: blue berries, 4–8 mm across

Plentiful blueberries were the most important fruits for northern First Nations peoples, and blueberry picking remains a favourite family tradition today. Traditionally, the berries were eaten fresh, dried or preserved in grease. The roots and stems were boiled into various medicinal teas. Today, young and old alike enjoy blueberry pie, jam, pancakes and even blueberry wine. **Where found:** sandy soils in forests and clearings; central and northern Alberta.

Bog Cranberry

Vaccinium vitis-idaea

Height: creeping, 10–20 cm
Leaves: 6–15 mm long, leathery, elliptical to oval, dotted below
Flowers: 5 mm long, pinkish, bell-shaped, 4 petals, in 1-sided clusters
Fruit: red berries, 5–10 mm across

In northern regions, mixed patches of bog cranberry, lichen and Labrador tea carpet the ground in a mosaic of reddish brown. The smooth, dark green leaves of bog cranberry have dark spots on their undersides. • The acidic, edible berries are best collected after the first frost. They were traditionally used in pemmican or cooked with grease, fish or meat. The berries were also boiled into a dye for porcupine quills or dried as beads for necklaces. **Where found:** various habitats including bogs, moist areas and dry woods; central and northern Alberta. **Also known as:** lingonberry.

Leatherleaf

Chamaedaphne calyculata

Height: up to 1 m
Leaves: 1–4 cm long, lance-shaped or elliptical, leathery
Flowers: 5–6 mm across, white, urn-shaped, in clusters
Fruit: round, brownish capsules, 3–5 mm across

Leatherleaf is a genuine wetland species that can be found in almost every boreal bog. This low, evergreen shrub forms patches of dense thickets or floating mats at the edges of lakes or swamps. Its delicate, urn-shaped flowers grow in long clusters, which then give way to fruit capsules that contain abundant tiny seeds. • The genus name *Chamaedaphne* stems from the Greek words *chamai*, "on the ground," and *daphne*, "laurel." **Where found:** wet, coniferous bogs, swamps and lakeshores; northern Alberta.

Bog Rosemary

Andromeda polifolia

Height: 10–40 cm
Leaves: 1–5 cm long, dull green, linear to elliptical, leathery, rolled edges
Flowers: 6 mm across, pinkish white, urn-shaped, 5 petals, in clusters
Fruit: round, pinkish capsules, 6 mm across

Despite resembling and sharing the name of a common kitchen herb, bog rosemary contains poisonous andromedotoxin compounds that can cause breathing problems, vomiting and even death if ingested. • The leathery leaves of this plant curl under, and the undersides are covered with fine hairs to help prevent moisture loss. • Bog rosemary has rounded stems and bluish green, alternate leaves, unlike bog laurel (*Kalmia polifolia*), which has flattened stems and shiny, green, opposite leaves. **Where found:** wet areas, coniferous swamps, sphagnum bogs and lakeshores; central and northeastern Alberta.

Common Snowberry

Symphoricarpos albus

Height: 50–75 cm
Leaves: 2–4 cm long, oval, hairy below, smooth edges
Flowers: 4–7 mm long, pink to white, bell-shaped, 4–5 petals, hairy centres, in 2s or 3s
Fruit: white, waxy, berry-like drupes, 6–10 mm across

The name "snowberry" refers to the white fruits that remain in small clusters near branch tips through winter. Some Native groups called the fruits "corpse berries," because they were believed to be the ghosts of saskatoons and therefore part of the spirit world, not to be eaten by the living. • All parts of this deciduous shrub are toxic and will cause vomiting and diarrhea. **Where found:** moist, wooded sites; throughout except southern grasslands.

Buckbrush

Symphoricarpos occidentalis

Height: to 1 m
Leaves: 2–6 cm long, thick, oval to oblong
Flowers: 5–9 mm long, pink to white, funnel-shaped, 4–5 petals, in clusters
Fruit: greenish white to purple, berry-like drupes, 6–10 mm across, in dense clusters

This common, widespread shrub is easily recognized by its compact clusters of greenish white fruits that turn purple in autumn and often persist throughout the winter. The inedible berries are mildly poisonous and can cause an upset stomach and vomiting. • Traditionally, the thicker branches were used to make pipe stems or arrow shafts. **Where found:** dry slopes and open forests; throughout.

Highbush Cranberry

Viburnum opulus ssp. *trilobum*

Height: up to 4 m
Leaves: 5–11 cm long, 3 pointed, spreading, coarsely toothed lobes
Flowers: 1–2 cm wide, white, 5 petals, in flat-topped clusters
Fruit: orange to red, berry-like drupes, 1 cm across

Shiny, red to orange highbush cranberry fruit makes a tart, tasty trailside snack and is easy to pick for use in jams and jellies. The fruits remain above the snow in winter. Raw fruits should not be eaten in large quantities because they can cause vomiting and severe cramps. • Several *Viburnum* species grow in Alberta, including lowbush cranberry or mooseberry (*V. edule*), which is found in moist habitats and along wetland margins and steamsides throughout Alberta, except grasslands. **Where found:** moist, rich sites near water in cool woodlands; central and northern Alberta. **Also known as:** *V. trilobum*.

Twining Honeysuckle

Lonicera dioica

Height: climbing vine, to 5 m
Leaves: 5–8 cm long, opposite, oval, hairy below, smooth edges
Flowers: 2–2.5 cm long, yellow to orange, funnel-shaped, 5 petals, in clusters of 3–9
Fruit: red berries, 8–12 mm across, in clusters surrounded by leafy cups

This vine twines itself around deciduous tree trunks and may reach heights of 5 metres or more. The flowers produce sweet nectar and attract ruby-throated hummingbirds and butterflies. The hollow stems have light-coloured, shredding bark and were traditionally used for children's drinking straws. The berries are extremely bitter and inedible. **Where found:** dry woods, thickets and rocky slopes; throughout.

Bracted Honeysuckle

Lonicera involucrata

Height: climbing vine, 1–3 m
Leaves: 5–10 cm long, oval to oblong, prominently veined, smooth edges
Flowers: 1–2 cm long, yellow, tubular, in pairs, cupped by purplish bracts, 1–2 cm long
Fruit: purplish black berries, 8 mm across, in pairs

The unusual, shiny berries of this deciduous shrub, with their broad, spreading, backward-bending, shiny red to purplish bracts, catch the eyes of passersby and also of hungry bears and birds. Despite their tempting appearance, these berries are unpalatable, and they can be toxic. • There are 11 honeysuckle species in our region. **Where found:** moist to wet, usually shaded sites; central Alberta and the mountains.

Purple Clematis

Clematis occidentalis

Height: climbing vine, up to 2 m
Leaves: opposite, divided into 3 oval, smooth-edged leaflets, each 2–6 cm long
Flowers: 1–6 cm across, purple, 4 petals, star-like, solitary
Fruit: small achenes with long, feathery bristles

With its eye-catching, purple flowers and large, fluffy seedheads, this woody-stemmed vine makes an excellent ornamental. Flowers appear from May to July. Propagated from seed or by layering sections of vine, purple clematis grows best in sunny spots where the plant's base is shaded. • Western clematis (*C. ligusticifolia*) occurs in coulees and badlands of southern Alberta and bears white, 4-petalled, star-like flowers in July. **Where found:** moist to dry, open sites; central and southwestern Alberta and Cypress Hills.

Caragana

Caragana arborescens

Height: 3–4 m
Leaves: compound with 8–12 oval, smooth-edged leaflets, each 10–25 mm long
Flowers: 15–25 mm long, bright yellow, pea-like, in clusters
Fruit: narrow legumes, 4–5 cm long

This member of the legume family was introduced from Siberia and China and has been widely planted as a hedge, ornamental or windbreak. This weedy, invasive species should not be encouraged, because it spreads quickly, choking out native vegetation and reducing biodiversity. The pea-like pods drop off and rapidly grow into new plants. • The young pods and seeds are edible and were used by early North American settlers as a food source. **Where found:** well-drained soils, roadsides and forest edges; escaped. **Also known as:** Siberian pea tree.

FORBS, FERNS & GRASSES

Forbs include all non-woody, flowering plants that are not grass-like (grasses, sedges and rushes are all graminoids). Forbs are often perennials that grow from a persistent rootstock, but many are short-lived annuals. A great variety of plants are forbs, including all our spring wildflowers, several flowering wetland plants, herbs grown for food or medicine and numerous weeds. Many herbs are used for adding flavour to foods and in herbal remedies, aromatherapy and dyes. Various forbs also flower into unique, delicate and beautiful colours and forms. They are the inspiration of artists and poets and are often symbols of romance or have meanings attached to them through folklore, legend or superstition. Forbs are also vital to the ecology of the plant communities in which they occur as food sources for pollinating insects and other animals, host plants for moths and butterflies, nest material for birds and cover for many animal species.

The forbs illustrated here are only the most frequent and likely to be seen examples. Alberta hosts hundreds of species of native forbs, far more than we could hope to include, and many similar species. For example, there are 11 different violet (*Viola*) species found in Alberta, but only 2 are included here.

At the end of the wildflower section, a fern, horsetail and several graminoids are described—only a few representatives of much larger groups. We have included common, widespread, ecologically important species, as well as representatives found in each region: mountains, boreal, aspen parkland and grasslands. These species should provide a good starting point for those wishing to delve further into the spectacular and diverse flora of our region.

Arums
p. 168

Lilies
pp. 168–169

Irises
p. 170

Orchids
pp. 170–171

Nettles
p. 171

Sandalwoods
p. 171

Buckwheats
p. 172

Goosefoots
p. 173

Pinks
p. 173

Pond-lilies
p. 174

Buttercups
pp. 174–177

Mustards
p. 177

Sundews
p. 178

Pitcher-plants
p. 178

Stonecrops
p. 178

Saxifrages
pp. 179–180

Roses
pp. 180–181

Legumes
pp. 181–184

Geraniums
pp. 184–185

Flaxes
p. 185

Touch-me-nots
p. 185

Mallows
p. 186

Violets
p. 186

Cacti
p. 187

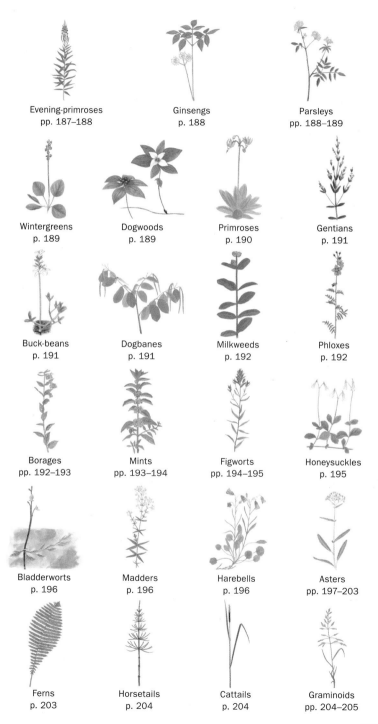

Evening-primroses
pp. 187–188

Ginsengs
p. 188

Parsleys
pp. 188–189

Wintergreens
p. 189

Dogwoods
p. 189

Primroses
p. 190

Gentians
p. 191

Buck-beans
p. 191

Dogbanes
p. 191

Milkweeds
p. 192

Phloxes
p. 192

Borages
pp. 192–193

Mints
pp. 193–194

Figworts
pp. 194–195

Honeysuckles
p. 195

Bladderworts
p. 196

Madders
p. 196

Harebells
p. 196

Asters
pp. 197–203

Ferns
p. 203

Horsetails
p. 204

Cattails
p. 204

Graminoids
pp. 204–205

Water Arum

Calla palustris

Height: 10–20 cm tall, aquatic perennial from rootstock
Leaves: 5–10 cm long, oval to heart-shaped, on long stalks
Flowers: showy, white bract (spathe), 2.5–7 cm long, surrounds
a cluster of tiny, pale yellow flowers (spadix), 2 cm long
Fruit: red, berry-like, in clusters, 1.5–5 cm long

These beautiful plants have a fiery side—all parts contain calcium oxalate crystals that inflame soft tissues and cause a strong burning sensation in the mouth and digestive tract if ingested. Animals tend to leave this plant alone. • The genus name *Calla* comes from *kallos*, the Greek word for "beautiful." **Where found:** still, shallow, boggy water; from the North Saskatchewan River northward through the boreal forest. **Also known as:** water-dragon.

Western Wood Lily

Lilium philadelphicum

Height: 30–60 cm
Leaves: 3–10 cm long, lance-shaped, in whorls of 4–8
Flowers: 5–6 cm wide, showy, goblet-shaped, 6 orange tepals
with purplish dotted throat, solitary or in clusters of 2–5
Fruit: erect, cylindrical capsules, 2–4 cm long

Almost shocking in their beauty, the brilliant orange flowers of the western wood lily spring up along roadsides and in woodlands across much of Canada. But please don't pick or dig these plants out of the ground! Picking the flowers can kill the entire plant, and overzealous collectors have caused these lilies to disappear in some locales. • Native peoples ate the peppery bulbs, tiny tubers and flowers raw or cooked. **Where found:** dry woods and meadows; southern two-thirds of Alberta.

Wild Lily-of-the-Valley

Maianthemum canadense

Height: 15 cm
Leaves: 2–8 cm long, oval to oblong, 2 per plant
Flowers: 4–6 mm wide, white, star-shaped, in erect clusters
Fruit: red berries, 4–6 mm wide

This small understorey herb has 2 (occasionally 3) leaves with parallel veins and heart-shaped bases. The berries are brownish green and turn red when ripe. The red or green berries are edible, but their taste is unremarkable, and they should not be eaten in large amounts. • The leaves of wild lily-of-the-valley resemble those of European lily-of-the-valley (*Convallaria majalis*), for which it is named. **Where found:** moist woodlands; throughout except southern prairies.

Star-flowered Solomon's-seal

Maianthemum stellatum

Height: 15–60 cm
Leaves: 3–12 cm long, elliptical, smooth edges, prominent veins
Flowers: 6 mm wide, white, star-shaped, in spike-like clusters
Fruit: brown-striped, greenish berries, <1 cm across, becoming dark blue to black when mature

The species name *stellatum*, from the Latin *stella*, "star," aptly describes the radiant, white blossoms of this woodland wildflower. • This unbranched, slightly arching plant produces clusters of dark blue or reddish black berries that are greenish yellow with purplish brown stripes when young. • A larger relative, false Solomon's-seal (*M. racemosum*) has wavy (rather than straight-edged) leaves and puffy, pyramidal flower clusters, 5 to 15 cm tall, that produce showy, red berries. **Where found:** moist to dry sites; throughout. **Also known as:** *Smilacina stellata*.

Prairie Onion

Allium textile

Height: to 50 cm
Leaves: 10–15 cm long, thin, basal
Flowers: 5–7 mm long, white, 3 petals, 3 sepals, in clusters of 8–20
Fruit: oblong capsules, 4 mm across

When they are not in flower, wild onions are distinguished from their poisonous relative, meadow death-camas (*Zigadenus venenosus*), by their strong onion smell. Do not try the taste test. • Wild onions were traditionally used as a vegetable and as flavouring for other foods. Bears, ground squirrels and marmots also enjoy wild onions. • Nodding onion (*A. cernuum*) has nodding, pink or white flowers and grows on open slopes, meadows and rock slides in the mountains and parkland. **Where found:** dry to mesic, open areas such as bluffs, open forests and meadows; prairies and parkland in the southern half of Alberta.

White Death-camas

Zigadenus elegans

Height: 20–60 cm
Leaves: up to 25 cm long, linear, basal
Flowers: 7–12 mm long, greenish white, 3 petals, 3 sepals, foul smelling, in tall spikes
Fruit: egg-shaped capsules, 1.5 cm long

Deadly poisonous, the bulbs of this plant are very similar in appearance to those of the prairie onion and the common camas (*Camassia quamash*), which grows alongside death-camas in southwestern Alberta. The edible variety is easily identifiable by its colourful, purple-blue flowers. • This plant is notorious for poisoning sheep and occasionally other livestock. The plant's toxic alkaloids cause tingling in the mouth upon contact, but ingestion results in convulsions, coma and death. **Where found:** mesic to moist meadows in lowland to montane areas; southern half of Alberta.

Common Blue-eyed Grass

Sisyrinchium montanum

Height: 10–50 cm
Leaves: 1–3.5 mm wide, grass-like, basal
Flowers: 8–10 mm across, blue to violet, 6 pointed tepals, yellow eye, solitary or in a small cluster
Fruit: black capsules, 3–6 mm wide

Common blue-eyed grass is not a true grass but a member of the iris family. The stems of this plant are flat or 2-sided, not round like those of grasses. • Dozens of blue-eyed grass species are found around the world, but some can have white, yellow or purple blossoms. These beautiful flowers have been much reduced by people picking them or transplanting them as garden plants. They're best enjoyed by leaving them where they grow. **Where found:** moist meadows and streambanks in prairie to montane areas; throughout.

Yellow Lady's-slipper

Cypripedium parviflorum var. pubescens

Height: 10–70 cm
Leaves: to 20 cm long, lance-shaped, prominent veins
Flowers: 4 twisted petals, 3–6 cm long, around a yellow, sac-like pouch, 2–4 cm long
Fruit: erect, oblong capsules, 2–3 cm long

Finding any one of Alberta's 26 native orchid species is always a treat, but none top this stunner. The large, sac-like flowers are adapted for pollination by bumblebees. • This plant depends on special mycorrhizal fungi in the soil for nutrient intake. Do not transplant this unusual orchid—it will likely not survive without the fungi. • Yellow lady's-slipper and 16 other orchid species are found at Wagner Natural Area, just west of Edmonton. **Where found:** moist to dry forests in lowland to subalpine areas; central Alberta.

Rattlesnake-plantain

Goodyera repens

Height: 20–40 cm
Leaves: 1–3 cm long, basal, oblong, often mottled or striped with white, in a rosette
Flowers: 8–10 mm, dull white to green, pouch-like lip, in a tall spike
Fruit: erect capsules, 1 cm long

Rattlesnake-plantain and various bog orchids (*Platanthera* or *Habenaria* spp.) are some of Alberta's most common orchids. • This plant's mottled leaves resemble snakeskin (hence the name), and early settlers believed the leaves could be used to treat rattlesnake bites. The basal leaves resemble those of common plantain (*Plantago major*), thus the second half of the name. • Children used to play with the leaves, rubbing them to separate the layers, and then inflating the leaves like balloons! **Where found:** moist forests; northern two-thirds of Alberta.

Northern Green Orchid

Platanthera aquilonis

Height: 10–60 cm
Leaves: 2–10 cm long, lance-shaped
Flowers: 4–7 mm long, yellowish green, in a tall, many-flowered spike, 2–10 cm long
Fruit: erect capsules, 1 cm long

The northern green orchid is relatively unknown because of its subtle colours and tendency to grow in boggy habitats, but this orchid is quite common and widespread across Canada. The plant's 20 to 45 flowers are arranged in a loose to dense spike.
• The scientific name *Platanthera*, Greek for "wide anthers," refers to the flowers, and *aquilonis*, "of the north," refers to the plant's range. **Where found:** wet mea dows, bogs, moist woods and riparian areas; throughout. **Also known as:** *Platanthera hyperborea*.

Stinging Nettle

Urtica dioica

Height: 0.5–2 m
Leaves: 4–15 cm long, oval to lance-shaped, coarsely toothed, covered with stinging hairs
Flowers: 1–2 mm long, green to purplish, in drooping clusters
Fruit: achenes, 1–2 mm long

The stinging hairs on the stems and undersides of this plant's leaves contain formic acid, which causes itching and burning. The sting can last from 10 minutes to several days, depending on how sensitive you are. • Young, tender nettle leaves are delicious and can be steamed or cooked in soup. Just remember to wear gloves when picking nettles to avoid a rash. Cooking destroys the formic acid, but eating large amounts may irritate the digestive system. **Where found:** shady woodlands and disturbed sites; throughout.

Bastard Toadflax

Comandra umbellata

Height: 10–30 cm
Leaves: 1–3 cm long, slender
Flowers: 3–5 mm across, white to pinkish, in oval clusters
Fruit: brownish, berry-like drupes, 4–8 mm long

Pretty white flowers disguise this plant's sinister side. Bastard toadflax is a semi-parasitic plant that steals water and nutrients from neighbouring plants by extending underground stems and attaching sucker-like organs to nearby roots. • This plant reproduces both vegetatively and, less commonly, sexually. A single plant sends out numerous shoots and can cover a huge area. **Where found:** moist woodlands and open areas with gravel; throughout. **Also known as:** pale comandra.

171

Yellow Umbrellaplant

Eriogonum flavum

Height: 10–20 cm, occasionally to 40 cm
Leaves: 3–5 cm long, basal, paddle-shaped, felted
Flowers: 12 mm wide, pale yellow, 6 petal-like sepals, in flat-topped clusters
Fruit: tiny, hairy, seed-like achenes

Yellow umbellaplant's delicate, modest flowers have a strong scent that may be unpleasant to humans but is irresistible to bees and other insects. Several flat-topped flower clusters appear at once, creating a showy display that attracts pollinators. The thick, felted leaves help the plant retain moisture. **Where found:** dry, eroded areas, hillsides and badlands; southern one-third of Alberta. **Also known as:** golden wild buckwheat, sulphur plant.

Western Dock

Rumex occidentalis

Height: 0.5–1.5 m
Leaves: 5–20 cm long, lance-shaped, heart-shaped base
Flowers: tiny, greenish to reddish, in dense clusters, 10–40 cm long
Fruit: papery achenes, 2–4 mm long

Edible dock leaves are a good source of protein, calcium, iron, potassium and vitamins A and C. Raw leaves may be bitter, but cooked leaves add a lemony zing to soups or stews. • Dock leaves, like those of the closely related beet (*Beta vulgaris*), contain oxalic acid, which is safe in moderation but toxic if consumed in large quantities. • Fifteen *Rumex* species are found in Alberta, including curled dock (*R. crispus*), an introduced, weedy species that grows in prairies and parkland. **Where found:** moist, often disturbed ground; throughout.

Water Smartweed

Polygonum amphibium

Height: terrestrial form up to 90 cm tall
Leaves: 2–15 cm long, lance-shaped, pointed, often reddish
Flowers: 4–5 mm long, pink, in dense, spike-like clusters
Fruit: brownish black achenes, 3 mm long

This species is easily the showiest of our many native smartweeds, sending forth large, flaming pink spikes of flowers. There are 2 forms: *P. a.* var. *stipulaceum* grows in deep water and has floating leaves, whereas *P. a.* var. *emersum* is found in moist soil and is stiffer and more upright. • Smartweed achenes are a winter staple for birds, and chipmunks, squirrels, other small rodents and deer eat the plants and fruit. The edible leaves have a hot, peppery taste and are very high in vitamins C and K. • The achenes can remain dormant in soil for decades, germinating when conditions become suitable. **Where found:** shallow ponds, lakes, streams, wetlands; throughout. **Also known as:** *Persicaria amphibia*.

Strawberry-blite

Chenopodium capitatum

Height: to 50 cm
Leaves: 3–7 cm long, triangular, coarsely toothed
Flowers: minute, green, sepals become fleshy and bright red at maturity,
in strawberry-shaped clusters
Fruit: tiny, black achenes

The genus *Chenopodium* includes several plants of minor to moderate
importance as food crops, including quinoa (*C. quinoa*), canihua
(*C. pallidicaule*) and lamb's-quarters (*C. album*). • This plant's nutritious leaves contain significant amounts of protein, fibre, calcium,
phosphorus, iron and vitamins A and C. They may be eaten raw in small amounts
but are best cooked or steamed and served like spinach. • Saponins in the seeds
are potentially toxic. The leaves contain toxic oxalic acid, but this is mainly
removed by cooking. **Where found:** roadsides and cultivated fields; throughout
except southern grasslands.

Sea-blite

Suaeda calceoliformis

Height: to 70 cm, stems prostrate to erect
Leaves: 1–4 cm long, fleshy, widest at base
Flowers: 1–4 mm wide, rounded, in small clusters
Fruit: black nutlets, 1.5 mm across

Sodium chloride, common table salt, is poisonous to most plants, but
sea-blite has adapted to saline conditions. Salt-tolerant plants, known
as halophytes, make up only about 2 percent of all plant species.
Several sea-blite species grow across North America in salt marshes or
along seashores. • These unusual plants have a salty taste. In some areas,
they were eaten as vegetables or the seeds were ground to make a salt substitute.
• Sea-blite is rare in Alberta and should not be picked. **Where found:** saline
sloughs and salted roadsides; southwestern Alberta.

Field Chickweed

Cerastium arvense

Height: 5–50 cm long, stems trailing or erect
Leaves: 1–3 cm long, narrow, lance-shaped
Flowers: 8–12 mm wide, white, 5 deeply notched petals, in open, flat-topped clusters
Fruit: capsules, 6–10 mm long

The cheerful flowers of field chickweed brighten rocky mountain slopes.
• The genus name *Cerastium* comes from the Greek *kerastes*, "horned,"
in reference to the curved, cylindrical capsules, which open by 10 small
teeth at the tip. The leaves of this loosely clumped perennial often
have secondary, leafy tufts in their axils. **Where found:** open, moist
to dry slopes and open forests; all elevations; throughout.

Yellow Pond-lily

Nuphar lutea

Height: floating aquatic perennial
Leaves: 7–35 cm wide, heart-shaped, smooth edges, floating
Flowers: 3.5–6 cm across, yellow, 6 petal-like sepals, solitary
Fruit: spongy, purplish brown berries, 20–45 mm across

This pond-lily forms floating carpets in shallow water, growing from massive, buried rootstocks. Some Native groups sliced the rootstocks and roasted or boiled them in soups or stews, but other groups considered them inedible. The roots are poisonous in large amounts. The seeds were an important food for some tribes. The dried capsules were broken open to release the seeds, which were dried, fried or popped like popcorn kernels. **Where found:** still water; boreal forest and parkland. **Also known as:** *Nuphar variegatum.*

Prairie Crocus

Pulsatilla patens

Height: to 10 cm high (stems)
Leaves: 4–10 cm wide, basal, grey-green, much divided
Flowers: 4 cm wide, pale blue to mauve, 5–7 petal-like sepals covered in woolly hairs
Fruit: feathery achenes, 3–4 mm long, on long stalks

This low, furry plant appears in early spring and blooms right after the snow melts. The leaves appear as the flowers fade. • True crocuses are part of the lily family, but prairie crocuses are related to anemones and are part of the buttercup family. **Where found:** dry, open woods, sandy soils and prairies; throughout. **Also known as:** *Anemone patens*; pasqueflower.

Canada Anemone

Anemone canadensis

Height: 20–70 cm
Leaves: 5–15 cm long, 3–5 deep lobes, prominent veins
Flowers: 2–4 cm across, white, 5 petal-like sepals, solitary
Fruit: green, seed-like achenes, 3–5 mm across, clustered in round heads

Beautiful, delicate Canada anemone flowers unfold above unique, deeply lobed leaves. The flowers have 5 showy, petal-like sepals rather than true petals. • The name "anemone" comes from the Greek word for "wind." These plants, also called windflowers, were once thought to bloom only on windy spring days. • The leaves of cut-leaved anemone (*A. multifida*) are divided into 3 leaflets, each divided again 2 to 3 times. Found throughout Alberta in open woods and grassland, it has white, yellowish or pinkish flowers tinged with purple and woolly, spherical fruits. **Where found:** moist, open sites, roadsides and gravelly shores; central and northern Alberta; absent from mountains.

Marsh-marigold

Caltha palustris

Height: 20–60 cm
Leaves: 5–17 cm wide, basal, toothed edges, heart- or kidney-shaped
Flowers: 1.5–4 cm across, yellow, 5–9 petal-like sepals surround numerous stamens
Fruit: follicles, 1–1.5 cm long, in clusters

One of spring's great botanical spectacles is a mass blooming of these gorgeous buttercups in swampy woods. Early wildflowers, marsh-marigolds have come and gone by the time spring's procession of wildflowers reaches peak abundance. • The raw leaves contain a toxin that can irritate skin and are poisonous if eaten. **Where found:** swampy woods and sometimes wet meadows, bogs and fens; central and northern Alberta.

Red and White Baneberry

Actaea rubra

Height: 30–100 cm
Leaves: 2–10 cm long, divided 2–3 times into groups of 3 toothed leaflets, about 6 cm long
Flowers: 4 mm wide, white, 5–10 petals, in rounded clusters
Fruit: glossy, red or white berries, 6–8 mm across

Although birds and small mammals eat the tempting, shiny berries of this perennial, baneberry is very poisonous to humans. As few as 2 berries can cause cramps, headaches, vomiting, bloody diarrhea and dizziness. • Some Native peoples considered baneberry to be sacred and used it in religious ceremonies, but this plant was always treated with respect because it could kill the user. **Where found:** moist, often shady sites; throughout.

Blue Columbine

Aquilegia brevistyla

Height: up to 80 cm
Leaves: to 5 cm long, mostly basal, compound, divided into 3 leaflets, each with 3 lobed, rounded tips
Flowers: 3 cm long, tubular, blue, 5 petals, 4 spurs, nodding, solitary
Fruit: 5-parted, slightly spreading pods (follicles)

A striking member of the buttercup family, the native blue columbine grows best in open meadows and forests. The colourful flowers entice hummingbirds and long-tongued butterflies, which pollinate the plants. • Yellow columbine (*A. flavescens*) has nodding, yellow flowers and grows in the mountains. • The introduced European columbine (*A. vulgaris*) occasionally escapes from gardens to grow in the wild. **Where found:** moist, rocky meadows, forest openings and clearings; throughout except southern grasslands.

Veiny Meadowrue

Thalictrum venulosum

Height: 20–70 cm
Leaves: 1–2 cm long, rounded, compound, twice divided into 3s
Flowers: 2–4 mm across, green to pinkish, in pyramidal clusters
Fruit: seed-like achenes, 3–5 mm across

Tiny meadowrue flowers appear in showy, many-flowered clusters. The plants are usually either male or female. The male flowers have dangling stamens, and the less-showy female flowers give way to small fruits. • The dried seeds and leaves may be used as a fragrant potpourri. Some Native peoples used these plants in love potions. **Where found:** moist prairie, thickets and open woods; throughout.

Meadow Buttercup

Ranunculus acris

Height: 60–100 cm
Leaves: 5 cm wide, basal, deeply divided into 3–5 lobes
Flowers: 2.5 cm across, bright yellow, 5 petals, solitary
Fruit: smooth, round achenes, 5–7 mm across

Pretty yellow meadow buttercups flower over deeply parted, palmate leaves. This plant was introduced from Europe and often grows in pastures or open woods. • Eschscholtz's buttercup (*R. eschscholtzii*) is a very common mountain species native to western North America. It has yellow flowers and grows to 15 cm tall. • Buttercups contain toxic ranunculin in their sap, which may cause dermatitis, mouth blisters and intense burning pain of the digestive tract when ingested. **Where found:** disturbed ground and fields; common throughout.

White Water Crowfoot

Ranunculus aquatilis

Height: mat-forming, floating perennial
Leaves: 4–10 mm long, submersed, repeatedly divided into numerous hair-like segments
Flowers: 10–15 mm across, white, 5 petals, solitary
Fruit: oval, seed-like achenes, 2 mm long

White water crowfoot belongs to the buttercup family and can only survive in water. Clumps or floating mats of this thread-leaved plant provide hiding places for water bugs, shrimp and tadpoles. A variety of different water crowfoot species are found across our region and have either white or yellow flowers. • The name "crowfoot" comes from the resemblance of the leaves to a crow's foot. **Where found:** still, shallow water; common in the mountains; also in suitable habitat in central Alberta.

White Globeflower

Trollius laxus ssp. *albiflorus*

Height: 10–40 cm
Leaves: 4–8 cm long, 5–7 parted, lobed or toothed at the tip, prominently veined
Flowers: 4 cm wide, white, 5–8 petal-like sepals, yellow centre
Fruit: greenish to purple follicles, 1 cm long

White globeflower is a prominent mountain species with large, white flowers that have bright yellow centres. During severe weather, the petal-like sepals curve protectively inward, so that the flowers appear round. • This is the only *Trollius* species that occurs in Alberta. **Where found:** moist riparian areas, coniferous woods and meadows; subalpine to alpine zones of the mountains. **Also known as:** *Trollius albiflorus.*

Wormseed Mustard

Erysimum cheiranthoides

Height: 20–60 cm
Leaves: 2–10 cm long, lance-shaped, hairy
Flowers: 6 mm wide, yellow, 4 petals, in dense clusters, 2–3 cm wide
Fruit: erect, linear pods, 1–3 cm long

This widespread weed is sparsely covered with rough hairs and grows on cultivated sites and wastelands across Canada. • The genus name comes from the Greek *erysio,* meaning "to draw out pain," because poultices were often made from *Erysimum* species. • The seeds contain mustard oil (allyl isothiocynate), which can be dangerous to livestock in large quantities. **Where found:** disturbed sites, lakeshores and streambanks; throughout.

Marsh Yellow Cress

Rorippa palustris

Height: 20–60 cm
Leaves: 6–15 cm long, oblong, deeply lobed
Flowers: 2 mm long, yellow, 4 petals, in clusters
Fruit: sausage-shaped pods, 3–7 mm long

Marsh yellow cress is edible and has a peppery flavour similar to that of radishes. Leaves may be eaten raw in salads, steamed or added to soups, stews or sauces. Sprigs of flowers can make a pretty, peppery addition to salads. Traditionally, the seeds of *Rorippa* species have been dried, ground and mixed with salt and vinegar to make water mustard. Cress is rich in vitamins A, B2, C, D and E and iodine, and was used to prevent and cure scurvy. **Where found:** marshy ground; prairies to subalpine; throughout.

Round-leaved Sundew

Drosera rotundifolia

Height: 5–10 cm (occasionally taller)
Leaves: up to 4 cm across, round, basal, covered with sticky, red hairs, in a rosette
Flowers: 3–5 mm across, pink or white, 5 petals
Fruit: black capsules, 1–3 mm long

Like something from a horror movie, this insect-eating plant has sticky, round leaves covered in gooey, reddish hairs that attract, trap and digest prey. The hairs are tipped with the botanical equivalent of glue, and investigating insects are caught and held fast. The hairs then slowly curl around the victim in a death-grip. Next, the sundew secretes an enzyme that dissolves the prey within 48 hours, leaving only the exoskeleton. **Where found:** peaty wetlands, primarily bogs and fens; boreal forest.

Pitcher-plant

Sarracenia purpurea

Height: up to 40 cm (flower stalks)
Leaves: to 30 cm long, basal, green with reddish veins, often water-filled
Flowers: 5–7 cm wide, purplish red, 5 petals, nodding, solitary
Fruit: many-seeded capsules

This carnivorous plant's purple-streaked, hollow leaves (pitchers) secrete a chemical that attracts insects. An insect that enters the tubular leaf is prevented from escaping by stiff, downward-pointing hairs. The smooth, glassy inner leaf sends the insect plunging into the juice below, which is made up of rainwater enriched with enzymes that reduce buoyancy and speed decomposition. The plant then absorbs the insect's proteins and nitrogen, which is how it gets sustenance in nutrient-poor bog soils. **Where found:** peaty bogs and fens; a rare plant of northeastern Alberta; also occurs at Clyde Fen, 100 km north of Edmonton.

Lance-leaved Stonecrop

Sedum lanceolatum

Height: 5–20 cm
Leaves: 1–1.5 cm long, lance-shaped, fleshy
Flowers: 1 cm long, bright yellow, 5 petals, in flat-topped clusters
Fruit: erect follicles, in clusters

This small, hardy perennial graces rugged slopes with flashes of bright yellow. Its succulent, green or reddish leaves (sometimes coated with a whitish, waxy powder) and low growth form help it to survive in dry, rocky sites. • Many stonecrops are cultivated in rock gardens or as house plants. **Where found:** dry, stony, open sites from plains to alpine zones; mountains of western Alberta.

Marsh Grass-of-Parnassus

Parnassia palustris

Height: up to 40 cm
Leaves: to 6 cm long, roundish, mostly basal, typically 1 smaller stem leaf
Flowers: about 1 cm wide, white with green veins, 5 petals, solitary
Fruit: 4-valved capsules, 8–12 mm long

Grass-of-Parnassus does not look like a grass at all and is not even closely related. Dioscorides, a Greek botanist, apparently named this plant after a grass that grew on Mount Parnassus in Greece. Although the foliage is glossy and attractive, the flowers are the most striking aspect of this plant. The white petals are boldly striped with green, and they almost glow. • Grass-of-Parnassus requires the specialized, wet, alkaline soils of fens, a habitat that has largely been destroyed in many areas. Consequently, this beautiful plant is rare in some parts of our region. **Where found:** wet, calcareous, seep-fed meadows and fens; also along roadsides and railways; throughout.

Bishop's-cap

Mitella nuda

Height: 3–20 cm
Leaves: 2–5 cm wide, mostly basal, heart-shaped, round-toothed, hairy
Flowers: 5–6 mm wide, greenish yellow, star-shaped, 5 petals, in few-flowered clusters
Fruit: capsules, 2–3 mm wide

Bishop's-cap grows close to the forest floor and is easily overlooked. The unusual, star-shaped flowers have delicate, thread-like petals that resemble a television antenna. The leaves have scattered, stiff hairs on the upper surface. • This plant's seeds are dispersed by a "splash cup" mechanism. The seed capsules catch drops of water and eject the seeds out with a splash. **Where found:** throughout except southern grasslands; also Cypress Hills. **Also known as:** mitrewort.

Purple Saxifrage

Saxifraga oppositifolia

Height: to 10 cm
Leaves: 2–5 mm long, wedge-shaped, fleshy, hairy edges, in 4s, appearing whorled
Flowers: 5–8 mm long, purple, 5 petals, solitary
Fruit: brown capsules, 7 mm long

Dense cushions of scale-like, overlapping leaves dotted with purple flowers characterize this tiny alpine wildflower. The stiff leaves come off the stem in 4s and often persist for many years, hugging the ground to conserve energy in harsh, high-elevation environments. • Lyall's saxifrage (*S. lyallii*), also found in the Rockies, often has tiny, white flowers on erect, dark red or purplish stems and fan-shaped, basal leaves. **Where found:** moist to well-drained, rocky slopes in subalpine and alpine zones; throughout the Rockies.

Spotted Saxifrage

Saxifraga bronchialis

Height: up to 15 cm (flower stalks)
Leaves: up to 1.5 cm long, basal, lance-shaped, leathery, sharply pointed
Flowers: 5 mm across, white with red or yellow spots near the tip, 5 petals, in flat-topped clusters
Fruit: 2-beaked capsules, 5 mm long

Saxifrage means "stone breaker," referring to the preference of some species for rocky habitats such as mountain ridges or even stone walls. • This species displays all the characteristics of a typical saxifrage: a leafless stem rising above large, round, crowded, basal leaves, and many gracefully hanging flowers with tapered white petals and contrasting yellow or red dots. **Where found:** rocky crevices, rock faces and open slopes; foothills to alpine; throughout the mountains.

Common Wild Strawberry

Fragaria virginiana

Height: 5–15 cm
Leaves: 5–10 cm long, compound, divided into 3 oblong, coarsely toothed leaflets, 1–3 mm long
Flowers: 1.5–2 cm wide, white, 5 petals, in open clusters
Fruit: small, red strawberries dotted with tiny achenes

Few things beat finding a patch of fresh, wild strawberries. They are delicious, but many other animals know that, and good luck beating them to the crop. This plant is the ancestor of 90 percent of our cultivated strawberries, and each tiny, red berry contains all the flavour of a large domestic strawberry. • Wood strawberry (*F. vesca*) has yellow-green leaflets with the end tooth projecting beyond adjacent teeth; common wild strawberry has a shorter end tooth. **Where found:** dry fields and open woods; throughout.

Three-flowered Avens

Geum triflorum

Height: 10–30 cm
Leaves: 5–20 cm long, mostly basal, pinnately compound, divided into 9–19 oval, finely toothed leaflets, 1–5 cm long
Flowers: 1–2 cm wide, reddish purple, 5 petals, nodding, at the end of a long stem, in small clusters
Fruit: dense heads of feathery achenes on a style, 3 cm long

At first glance, a field of these plants in seed appears to be covered with low-lying haze—hence the alternate names "prairie smoke" and "old man's whisker's." This soft-hairy perennial has 3-flowered clusters of purplish to dusty pink flowers. Each seed-like fruit has a long, feathery style that acts like a parachute, carrying the fruit on the wind. **Where found:** dry to moist, open sites; throughout but less common northward. **Also known as:** prairie smoke, old man's whiskers.

Common Silverweed

Argentina anserina

Height: low, creeping
Leaves: to 30 cm long, basal, hairy, compound, divided into numerous, sharply toothed leaflets
Flowers: 15–25 mm across, bright yellow, 5 petals, solitary
Fruit: achenes, 2 mm across

This circumpolar plant carpets the ground with its sharply toothed leaflets and bright yellow flowers. The leaves, especially the undersides, are covered in silky, silver hairs, from which the plant gets its name. • Silverweed roots may be eaten raw or cooked and are said to taste like parsnips or sweet potatoes. Traditionally, the roots were ground and steeped into a medicinal tea, which was used to aid in childbirth or treat diarrhea. **Where found:** well-drained to wet, open sites including meadows, ditches and riversides; throughout. **Also known as:** *Potentilla anserina*.

Ground-plum

Astragalus crassicarpus

Height: trailing, prostrate stems up to 70 cm long
Leaves: compound, divided into 17–25 oblong leaflets, 2 cm long
Flowers: 4–5 cm long, yellowish white tinged with purple, 5 petals, in open clusters
Fruit: fleshy, red, spherical pods, 2 cm wide, becoming brown and hard at maturity

Edible ground-plum is named for its sweet, watery, edible, plum-like fruit. The young, thick-walled fruits are fleshy and reddish, becoming brown and hard when mature. • The genus *Astragalus* is a large, complex group of plants, including both harmless and extremely poisonous species. These nitrogen-fixing plants are valued as forage and soil-building crops. **Where found:** grasslands; southern Alberta. **Also known as:** buffalo bean.

Purple Prairie-clover

Dalea purpurea

Height: 30–80 cm
Leaves: compound, divided into 3–7 narrow leaflets, 5–20 cm long
Flowers: 1–5 cm long, rose pink to purple, 5 petals, in dense spikes
Fruit: small pods

Hardy purple prairie-clover is well adapted to prairie life and is able to withstand temperature extremes and drought. With a long, clumped, woody root system, this plant can reach for water. Its small, rolled leaves also help reduce sun exposure and conserve moisture. • This attractive perennial is a popular choice for habitat restoration and prairie gardens and is easy to grow from commercially available seed. **Where found:** dry, open sites; parkland and prairie; southern half of Alberta.

Alfalfa

Medicago sativa

Height: up to 1 m
Leaves: compound, divided into 3 oval, slightly hairy leaflets, toothed at the tip
Flowers: 6–12 mm long, purple-blue, pea-like, in rounded clusters
Fruit: small, curved or coiled pods

Alfalfa is an important forage crop that is adaptable to a wide range of agricultural regions. Native to Iran, alfalfa was cultivated as horse feed in Greece as early as 490 BC, then imported to South America by the Spaniards. Today, this legume is harvested as hay and is often used to feed cattle. Tasty, young alfalfa sprouts are also sold as salad and as a sandwich garnish. • The name "alfalfa" is derived from the Arabic *al-fasfasah,* meaning "best fodder." **Where found:** disturbed sites; southern boreal forest, parkland and grasslands.

Yellow Sweet-clover

Melilotus officinalis

Height: 0.5–2 m
Leaves: compound, divided into 3 lance-shaped, toothed leaflets, 1–2.5 cm long
Flowers: 4.5–7 mm long, yellow, pea-like, fragrant, in long, narrow clusters
Fruit: wrinkled pods, 3 mm long

This hardy forage crop blankets roadsides and abandoned fields in yellow, invading native grasslands and reducing plant diversity. Each pollinated plant can release as many as 350,000 seeds that remain viable for decades. • Yellow sweet-clover is valued as a forage crop, soil enhancer and honey plant. The genus name comes from *meli,* Greek for "honey," and refers to this plant's abundant, nectar-producing flowers. • White-flowered sweet-clover is known as *M. alba.* **Where found:** open, disturbed sites; southern boreal forest, parkland and grasslands.

Showy Locoweed

Oxytropis splendens

Height: 10–30 cm
Leaves: 5–25 cm long, basal, compound, divided into 7–15 lance-shaped, hairy leaflets
Flowers: 1–1.5 cm long, purple-blue, pea-like, in dense spikes, 3–10 cm long
Fruit: woolly, oval pods, 8–15 mm long

Showy locoweed is easily identified by its silky-hairy, greyish green leaves, whorled (rather than paired) leaflets and showy clusters of purplish flowers. • Many locoweeds can be dangerous because they contain locoine, a poisonous alkaloid that causes horses, sheep and cattle to go crazy, or "loco." • Inflated oxytrope (*O. podocarpa*) grows on exposed, rocky ridges in mountains and has purple or blue flowers. **Where found:** well-drained, usually open sites; common in the mountains and foothills; less common in boreal forest and parkland.

Early Yellow Locoweed

Oxytropis sericea

Height: to 50 cm (flower stalks)
Leaves: 5–30 cm long, basal, compound, divided into 7–17 opposite, oblong, sharply pointed leaflets
Flowers: 20 mm long, pale yellow, pea-like, in dense clusters
Fruit: leathery, beaked pods, up to 2.5 cm long

Like many locoweeds, this plant is poisonous to horses, sheep and cattle. Locoweeds contain toxic alkaloids, and some ostensibly edible species also take selenium from the soil, which can render them toxic to some animals. After eating large quantities of locoweed for several weeks, cattle, horses and sheep develop locoism, a disease that mainly affects the nervous system. **Where found:** prairies and dry hillsides; southern half of Alberta.

Wild Licorice

Glycyrrhiza lepidota

Height: 30–100 cm
Leaves: compound, divided into 11–19 lance-shaped leaflets, each 2–4 cm long
Flowers: yellowish white, pea-like, in erect, 2–6 cm long clusters
Fruit: reddish brown burs, 1–2 cm long

Wild licorice has been used to flavour candy, root beer and chewing tobacco. It contains glycyrrhizin, a substance that is about 50 times sweeter than sugar and quenches (rather than increases) thirst. Wild licorice has a milder flavour but is very similar to its close relative, European licorice (*G. glabra*), from which commercial licorice is obtained. • European and Chinese licorice (*G. uralensis*) are among the most widely used medicinal plants in the world. **Where found:** disturbed sites, roadside ditches and edges of wet fields; southern one-third of Alberta.

Golden-bean

Thermopsis rhombifolia

Height: 10–50 cm
Leaves: compound, divided into 3 oval leaflets, each 2–3 cm long, plus 2 lobes (stipules)
Flowers: 1–2 cm long, bright yellow, pea-like, in clusters
Fruit: flattened, curved pods, 3–7 cm long

Yellow golden-bean blossoms signal the arrival of spring on the prairies. The Blackfoot called this plant "buffalo-bean" because its flowering time coincided with the spring buffalo hunt. • Golden-bean provides bees with pollen and nectar and also attracts native butterflies. Small, brown duskywing butterflies (*Erynnis* spp.) and their caterpillars use golden-bean as both a nectar and food source, and yellow sulphur butterflies (*Colias* spp.) lay eggs on the plants. • Golden-bean is poisonous and should never be eaten. **Where found:** open, well-drained sites; prairies and grasslands; southern half of Alberta.

American Vetch

Vicia americana

Height: 20–120 cm
Leaves: compound, divided into 8–14 oblong, prominently veined leaflets, 1.5–3.5 cm long
Flowers: 1.5–2 cm long, bluish purple, pea-like, in clusters
Fruit: pods, 2–3 cm long

Twining tendrils wrap around nearby stems and leaves as this slender vine climbs upward over its neighbours. Its flat, hairless "pea pods" are attractive to young children, but they are not edible. • When an insect lands on a vetch flower, anthers spring out to dust the insect's belly with pollen. The next blossom collects the pollen on its stigma and applies another load of pollen to the insect. **Where found:** moist, fairly open sites; throughout.

Alsike Clover

Trifolium hybridum

Height: to 80 cm
Leaves: compound, divided into 3 oval leaflets, 2–4 cm long
Flowers: 8–9 mm long, pinkish, in dense heads, 2–8 cm long
Fruit: 2–4-seeded pods

Clovers are one of the most familiar flowering plants, beloved for their promise of luck to those who find a "leaf of four." Although clovers are quickly identifiable, they can be quite diverse in colour, ranging from white to bright fuchsia, and in size, varying from tiny species that hide in the grass to tall, proud species with lofty leaves. • The flowerheads of clovers are a tight cluster of tiny flowers that are identifiable as members of the pea family (Fabaceae) for their banner, wings and hidden keel formations. **Where found:** various grassy habitats; low to subalpine elevations; often invasive; throughout.

Northern Crane's-bill

Geranium bicknellii

Height: up to 60 cm
Leaves: 2–7 cm wide, opposite, deeply cut into 5 toothed, wedge-shaped segments
Flowers: 1 cm wide, showy, pink-purple, 5 petals, solitary or in pairs
Fruit: long-beaked capsules, up to 2 cm long

Northern crane's-bill is a characteristic spring bloomer found in rich woodlands, often growing in profusion with other wildflowers. This native is an excellent landscaping plant in central and southern areas of the province. • Rubbing a fresh geranium plant, which has a strong smell, on exposed skin and clothes is said to repel mosquitoes. You can try it, but don't discard the bug spray. **Where found:** rich woods; mountains, boreal forest, parkland and Cypress Hills.

Sticky Purple Geranium

Geranium viscosissimum

Height: 40–90 cm
Leaves: 5–11 cm wide, opposite, compound, divided into 5–7 sharply toothed lobes with sticky hairs
Flowers: 2 cm wide, rose-purple or (rarely) white with dark veins, 5 petals, in clusters
Fruit: capsules, 3 cm long

The purple veins on this plant's showy pink to magenta petals reflect ultraviolet light. Many insects, such as bees, can see these wavelengths and follow the lines to the nectar at the base of the petals. • The name "geranium" comes from the Greek *geranos*, "a crane," because the long, slender seed capsules resemble crane's bills. Many geraniums are called "crane's-bills" or "stork's-bills." **Where found:** dry to moist, fairly open sites in foothills and montane zones; southwestern Alberta and Cypress Hills.

Wild Blue Flax

Linum lewisii

Height: 30–90 cm
Leaves: 1.5–3.5 cm long, lance-shaped, numerous
Flowers: 2–3 cm wide, blue, 5 fragile petals, in few-flowered clusters
Fruit: round capsules, 6 mm long

The beautiful, delicate, pale to sky blue blossoms of wild blue flax usually open in the morning and fade in the hot sun later the same day. Most plants produce only one flower at a time, with the next bud opening the following morning. • The stems contain long, tough fibres, similar to those of cultivated or common flax (*L. usitatissimum*), which have traditionally been used to make ropes, cords, fishing lines and nets. The ground seeds are high in fibre and make a tasty addition to breads and other baked goods. **Where found:** dry, open sites; southern boreal forest, parkland and grasslands.

Spotted Touch-me-not

Impatiens noli-tangere

Height: 20–80 cm
Leaves: 3–12 cm long, oval, coarsely toothed
Flowers: 2.5 cm long, orange-yellow spotted with purple, sac-like sepals
Fruit: green capsules, 2.5 cm long

This exceptionally succulent plant seems to be made from water and practically wilts before your eyes if picked. The seeds are enclosed in fleshy capsules and held by tightly coiled elastic attachments. Press a ripe pod and the seeds shoot forth explosively, hence the name "touch-me-not." The seeds taste like walnuts, and the flowers are irresistible to hummingbirds. • The crushed leaves can be used to treat rashes caused by poison ivy and stinging nettle. **Where found:** moist forests and wetlands; central and northern Alberta. **Also known as:** jewelweed.

Scarlet Globemallow

Sphaeralcea coccinea

Height: 10–20 cm
Leaves: 2–5 cm long, grey-green, deeply cut into 3–5 narrow, hairy lobes
Flowers: 1–2 cm wide, orange to brick red, 5 petals, in clusters
Fruit: many-segmented, cheese-wheel-shaped capsules containing several hairy carpels, 3 mm long

Drought-tolerant scarlet globemallow is a good choice for native wildflower gardens. • The segmented fruits look like miniature cheese rounds, so children sometimes call globemallow fruits "fairy cheeses." • These mucilaginous plants are slimy when crushed. Traditionally, globemallow plants were crushed into poultices and used to soothe irritated tissues. **Where found:** dry, open sites; prairie and grasslands.

Early Blue Violet

Viola adunca

Height: up to 10 cm
Leaves: 1–3 cm long, broadly heart-shaped, toothed
Flowers: 1–1.5 cm wide, blue to violet, 5 petals, solitary
Fruit: capsules, 4–6 mm long

Few of these dainty flowers are fertilized each spring. When no seed is produced, small, inconspicuous blooms appear in autumn, hidden away among debris near ground level. These never open. Instead, they fertilize themselves, producing abundant, fast-growing seeds. • There are 13 violet species in Alberta. **Where found:** dry to moist sites; low to subalpine elevations; throughout.

Canada Violet

Viola canadensis

Height: up to 40 cm
Leaves: 5–10 cm long, broadly heart-shaped, toothed
Flowers: 2 cm wide, white with purple veins and yellow centre, 5 petals, solitary
Fruit: capsules, 8–10 mm long

Of all our native violets, Canada violet is perhaps the most stately and handsome. You can easily recognize this species by its tall, upright stems and bright white flowers with lemon yellow centres. • The seeds are often dispersed by ants, which carry them to their nests, then bite off the elaiosome bodies—oily, tasty "ant snacks." • Violet flowers make a pretty garnish for salads, and the cooked or raw leaves are high in vitamins A and C. The seeds and rhizomes are poisonous. **Where found:** damp woods; low to subalpine elevations; throughout.

186

Prickly-pear Cactus

Opuntia spp.

Height: prostrate, 5–40 cm tall
Leaves: absent; spreading stems segmented into oval pads,
5–7 cm wide, with spines to 5 cm long
Flowers: 4–8 cm wide, brilliant yellow, bell-shaped, solitary
Fruit: red-purple, fleshy, spiny berries, 15–25 mm long

The prickly-pear cactus, though native here, is scattered and local, inhabiting dry, sandy areas—relict habitats of a long-ago, hotter, drier time. But watch your step! These fleshy cacti are copiously beset with spines. • Prickly-pears were widely used for food by Native peoples. The raw fruits are said to taste like cucumber, and once the spines and seeds were removed, the fleshy pads were eaten raw, used to thicken stews and soups or dried for later use. The berries can also be boiled whole and then strained to make jellies or syrups. **Where found:** rocky outcrops, gravelly soils and sand dunes; grasslands of southern Alberta.

Common Fireweed

Chamerion angustifolium

Height: 3 m (occasionally taller)
Leaves: 2–20 cm long, lance-shaped, prominently veined
Flowers: 2 cm wide, pink to purple, 4 petals, in long, erect clusters
Fruit: narrow, pod-like capsules, 4–8 cm long

Aptly named, common fireweed reaches peak abundance immediately after a fire and can turn freshly scarred landscapes pink with its blossoms. Fireweed serves an important ecological role by stabilizing barren ground, which eventually allows other species of plants to recolonize burned-over areas. The erect, linear pods split lengthwise to release hundreds of tiny seeds tipped with fluffy, white hairs (comas). • Young shoots can be eaten like asparagus, and the flowers can be added to salads. **Where found:** open, often disturbed sites and burned areas; throughout. **Also known as:** *Epilobium angustifolium*.

Scarlet Butterfly-weed

Gaura coccinea

Height: 10–40 cm
Leaves: 1–3 cm long, narrow to oblong
Flowers: 1 cm wide, white becoming scarlet red, 4 petals, cross-shaped, in clusters
Fruit: nut-like capsules, 6 mm long

Once open, scarlet butterfly-weed flowers begin to change colour. At first, the 4 spoon-shaped petals are white, but they soon take on a pinkish hue. Within a few hours of opening, the whole flower has turned scarlet. • The paired petals of this plant's flowers resemble spreading butterfly wings. **Where found:** dry, open sites; parkland and prairies. **Also known as:** scarlet beeblossom.

Common Evening-primrose

Oenothera biennis

Height: 0.5–1.5 m
Leaves: 10–20 cm long, lance-shaped, slightly toothed
Flowers: 2.5–5 cm across, yellow, 4 petals, in leafy spikes
Fruit: cylindrical capsules, 2–3 cm long

The flowers of this well-named species open near dusk, bloom through-out the night and generally close by mid-morning. Moths are the prime pollinators, so this strategy best accommodates them. The flowers open amazingly quickly, blossoming in just 15 to 20 minutes. • Common evening-primrose is best known for its abundant, oil-rich seeds. They are processed into evening-primrose oil, which is used to treat a variety of ailments. **Where found:** dry, open sites; scattered in southern boreal forest and parkland, more common in southern prairies. **Also known as:** yellow evening-primrose.

Wild Sarsaparilla

Aralia nudicaulis

Height: to 60 cm
Leaves: 3–15 cm long, basal, compound, in 3 divisions of 3–5 oval, toothed leaflets, 3–6 cm long
Flowers: 2–5 mm wide, greenish white, 5 petals, in ball-shaped clusters
Fruit: greenish, berry-like drupes, 6 mm long, turning purple with age

The roots of this fragrant plant were once widely used to flavour root beer and to make medicinal teas. The root tea was valued as a blood purifier, tonic and stimulant and was used for treating lethargy, general weakness, stomach aches, fevers and coughs. • Wild sarsaparilla, a member of the ginseng family, is sometimes substituted for true sarsaparilla (*Smilax* spp.), a member of the lily family. **Where found:** rich, moist woods; parkland, boreal forest and Cypress Hills.

Spotted Water-hemlock

Cicuta maculata

Height: 0.6–2 m
Leaves: compound, divided into several lance-shaped, sharply toothed leaflets, 3–10 cm long
Flowers: 2 mm wide, greenish white, 5 petals, in flat-topped clusters
Fruit: seed-like schizocarps, 2–4 mm wide

Spotted water-hemlock is one of the most poisonous plants in North America. All parts of the plant are poisonous, but most of the toxin is contained in the roots. A single bite can be fatal to humans, and this plant is easily confused with common water-parsnip (*Sium suave*). Children have been poisoned from using the hollow stems as peashooters. Cattle are particularly at risk in early spring, when the plants are smaller, more palatable and easily uprooted. **Where found:** wet areas; throughout.

Common Cow-parsnip

Heracleum maximum

Height: 1–2.5 m
Leaves: 10–30 cm long, compound, divided into 3 large, coarsely toothed leaflets
Flowers: 2–6 mm across, white, 5 petals, in flat-topped clusters
Fruit: seed-like schizocarps, 7–12 mm across

The young, fleshy stems of common cow-parsnip can be peeled and eaten raw or cooked. They are said to taste like celery. Care must be taken not to confuse cow-parsnip with the deadly poisonous water-hemlocks (*Cicuta* spp.). Cow-parsnip is an important food source for many animals, including bears. • Although toy flutes or whistles can be made from the dry, hollow stems, they may irritate the lips and cause painful blisters. **Where found:** moist sites; throughout.

Common Pink Wintergreen

Pyrola asarifolia

Height: 10–30 cm
Leaves: 2–6 cm long, basal, evergreen, rounded, leathery, in a rosette
Flowers: 8–12 mm across, pink, bell-shaped, 5 petals, nodding, in spikes
Fruit: rounded capsules, 5–10 mm across

Wintergreens grow in intimate association with soil fungi (mycorrhizae). Some species produce all their food by photosynthesis, but others take their food almost entirely from dead organic matter via the mycorrhizae. These fungi are unlikely to be found in a garden environment, so wintergreen plants should not be transplanted. **Where found:** moist, often shady sites; throughout including Cypress Hills, but absent from southern grasslands.

Bunchberry

Cornus canadensis

Height: 5–20 cm
Leaves: 2–8 cm long, elliptical to diamond-shaped, deeply veined, smooth edges, in whorls of 4–6
Flowers: tiny, white, in clusters of 5–15, surrounded by 4 white, petal-like bracts
Fruit: round, red, berry-like drupes, 6–8 mm across

These small flowers are really miniature bouquets of tiny blooms surrounded by showy, white, petal-like bracts. The true flowers, at the centre, are easily overlooked. The large, white bracts attract insects and provide good landing platforms. • The fruits are edible, raw or cooked. They are not very flavourful, but the crunchy, poppy-like seeds are enjoyable. **Where found:** dry to moist sites; throughout including Cypress Hills, but absent from southern grasslands.

Saline Shootingstar

Dodecatheon pulchellum

Height: 5–30 cm
Leaves: 3–20 cm long, basal, oval, smooth edges
Flowers: 15–25 cm across, pinkish purple with yellow "collar,"
5 upswept petals, in clusters of 3–20
Fruit: capsules, 5–15 mm long

The upswept petals of this flower resemble a shooting star. The band in the centre of the flower can be yellow, orange or reddish purple, and this highly variable species can have either hairy or hairless leaves. • The rapid vibrations of a bee's wings release the fine, powdery pollen from the downward-facing anthers of this flower. **Where found:** salt flats and moist, open areas; common in foothills and mountains; southern half of Alberta.

Fringed Loosestrife

Lysimachia ciliata

Height: up to 1.2 m
Leaves: 5–12 cm long, opposite, oval to lance-shaped, on hairy stalks
Flowers: 1.3–2.5 cm wide, yellow, 5–6 fringed petals, in 2s or 3s
Fruit: rounded capsules, 4–6 mm across

An often-abundant native summer wildflower of rich woods, fringed loosestrife is named for the prominent fringes of hairs along the leaf stalks. • The common name "loosestrife" is applied to a number of plants, including the invasive, non-native purple loosestrife (*Lythrum salicaria*). According to legend, the name arose when King Lysimachus stopped a charging bull by waving a loosestrife stem, and the enraged animal was "loosened from strife." **Where found:** moist or wet sites, especially wooded floodplains; southern boreal forest and parkland.

Sweet-flowered Androsace

Androsace chamaejasme

Height: 2–10 cm (flower stems)
Leaves: 1 cm long, basal, lance-shaped, hairy
Flowers: 1 cm wide, white with yellow centre, 5 petals, fragrant, in clusters of 4–5
Fruit: capsules, 2–3 mm long

Fragrant sweet-flowered androsace forms loose mats or cushions on high mountain slopes. Hugging the ground helps this plant avoid the wind in its harsh, high-altitude environment, and short, silky hairs cover the leaves to aid in water and nutrient absorption. • The species name *chamaejasme*, "dwarf jasmine," refers to both the plant's scent and its preferred habitat. **Where found:** rocky slopes; montane to alpine zones; mountains of western Alberta.

Felwort

Gentianella amarella

Height: 10–40 cm
Leaves: 5 cm long, opposite, elliptical
Flowers: 2 cm long, violet to pinkish, tubular, 4–5 fringed petals, usually solitary
Fruit: capsules, 1–2 cm long

The flowers of this late bloomer stand up to the first frosts. Before the widespread introduction of hops, gentians were used in Europe for brewing beer. • Gentian roots have been used in many forms to treat various ailments and in bitter tonics to aid digestion. Present-day herbalists recommend gentian-root tea as one of the best vegetable bitters for stimulating appetite, aiding digestion, relieving bloating and preventing heartburn. **Where found:** moist meadows, open forests and other open areas; lowland to montane zones; throughout. **Also known as:** northern gentian.

Buck-bean

Menyanthes trifoliata

Height: 10–30 cm
Leaves: 3–8 cm long, compound, divided into 3 oval to elliptical leaflets
Flowers: 2 cm across, white, funnel-shaped, 5 hairy petals; in clusters
Fruit: oval capsules, 6–9 mm long

Three leaflets growing on a long stalk mark this plant. The foliage looks similar to broad bean leaves, which may be where the "bean" part of the name comes from. • This bitter plant has few traditional uses. Europeans sometimes substituted buck-bean leaves for hops in beer making or mixed the dried, powdered roots with flour in times of famine. **Where found:** standing water; throughout including Cypress Hills, but absent from southern grasslands.

Spreading Dogbane

Apocynum androsaemifolium

Height: 20–70 cm
Leaves: 2–10 cm long, opposite, drooping, smooth edges
Flowers: 4–12 mm wide, pink, bell-shaped, 5 petals, in clusters
Fruit: hanging pods (follicles), 5–15 cm long

Butterflies are attracted to the tiny blossoms of spreading dogbane. The milky white sap is similar to that of milkweeds, which are closely related but in a separate family. • The milky sap of this plant is poisonous and can cause skin blistering, and ingestion has resulted in sickness and death. • Traditionally, mature dogbane stems were soaked in water to remove the coarse outer fibres, then rolled or plaited into cords and used for fishing nets and bow-strings. **Where found:** well-drained, open sites; throughout.

Showy Milkweed

Asclepias speciosa

Height: to 2 m
Leaves: 8–15 cm long, opposite, oval, thick, covered with short hairs
Flowers: 9–12 mm across, pinkish lavender, 5 backswept petals, fragrant, in rounded clusters
Fruit: spiny follicles, 6–10 cm long, in erect clusters

These weedy plants contain glycosides that are toxic to animals and humans, so the insects adapted to feed on them become toxic to predators. They tend to be brightly coloured and conspicuous to advertise their toxicity. Monarch butterfly larvae feed solely on milkweed leaves. They absorb the poisonous glycosides into their bodies, making both larvae and adult butterflies toxic to predators. Several species of bright-orange-and-black milkweed beetles also thrive on milkweeds. **Where found:** open sites such as fields, meadows and roadsides; southern Alberta.

Tall Jacob's-ladder

Polemonium acutiflorum

Height: 40–100 cm
Leaves: compound, divided into 15–27 elliptical leaflets, 1.5–3.5 cm long
Flowers: 8–12 cm wide, blue, 5 hairy petals, bell-shaped, on long stalks, in clusters
Fruit: spindle-shaped capsules

This plant is named for its ladder-like leaves, which resemble Jacob's ladder to heaven in the Bible. Tall Jacob's-ladder grows in moist areas and has blue flowers with hairy petals. • Two other *Polemonium* species grow in the mountains, including showy Jacob's-ladder (*P. pulcherrium*), which inhabits dry, alpine slopes and is distinguished by having 11 to 23 leaflets and blue flowers with yellow bases. **Where found:** marshy ground and wet meadows; mountains north of Banff and northern half of Alberta.

Alpine Forget-me-not

Myosotis alpestris

Height: 4–40 cm
Leaves: up to 5 cm long, oblong, with stiff, whitish hairs
Flowers: 8 mm wide, deep blue with yellow centre, 5 petals, in dense clusters
Fruit: 4 smooth, blackish nutlets

Clusters of diminutive, deep blue alpine forget-me-nots brighten mountain meadows and attract bees and brown-and-orange checkerspot (*Euphydryas* spp.) butterflies. All forget-me-nots found in Alberta are introduced from Eurasia. • The genus name *Myosotis* stems from the Greek *mus,* "mouse," and *otis,* "ear," in reference to the rounded, hairy leaves; *alpestris* means "of the mountains." **Where found:** moist meadows; subalpine and alpine regions.

Narrow-leaved Puccoon

Lithospermum incisum

Height: 10–50 cm
Leaves: 1–5 cm long, slender, with stiff hairs
Flowers: 1–2 cm across, bright yellow, 5 petals, funnel-shaped, in clusters
Fruit: 4 shiny, white nutlets, 3 mm across

Puccoon species have hard, shiny nutlets that were once used as decorative beads. In fact, the genus name *Lithospermum* comes from the Greek words *lithos*, "stone," and *sperma*, "seed." • "Puccoon" is an Algonkian word meaning "plants used for dyeing." Boiling this plant's roots yields a red dye, which was used by First Nations peoples to make face and body paints and to colour fabrics. **Where found:** dry, open sites; southern half of Alberta. **Also known as:** fringed gromwell.

Tall Lungwort

Mertensia paniculata

Height: 30–60 cm
Leaves: 5–15 cm long, elliptical, pointed tips, prominently veined
Flowers: 2.5 cm long, pale blue, tubular, 5 lobes at tip, drooping on hairy stalks, in clusters
Fruit: 4 wrinkled nutlets, 2.5–5 mm long

One of our most striking displays of early spring wildflowers occurs when masses of these blue-flowered plants spring from still-cool soil. They explode into dazzling bursts of rich blue blossoms, and even the most jaded botanist will pause to admire the show. Look quickly, though, because the flowers are ephemeral, wilting quickly to ugly brown detritus and returning to the soil that spawned them. **Where found:** moist or wet woods and bottomlands; throughout except prairies. **Also known as:** northern bluebell.

Blue Giant-hyssop

Agastache foeniculum

Height: 30–100 cm
Leaves: 2–7 cm long, opposite, oval, coarsely toothed, whitish below
Flowers: 6–12 mm long, blue, 5 petals, funnel-shaped, in dense spikes, 2–10 cm long
Fruit: 4 small nutlets

Blue giant-hyssop is an attractive, useful addition to a wildflower garden. This sun-loving plant is easily propagated from seeds, cuttings or root divisions. • The flowerhead can be chewed as a breath-freshener, and the leaves can be used to flavour soups or stews. The leaves may also be brewed into a delicate, anise-flavoured tea, best when brewed weakly. Medicinal teas made from giant-hyssop leaves were traditionally used to treat coughs, colds, chest pains and fevers. **Where found:** deciduous woodlands and well-drained, open sites; prairies of southern Alberta.

Wild Mint

Mentha arvensis

Height: 20–80 cm
Leaves: 2–8 cm long, opposite, lance-shaped, toothed, with a mint-like scent
Flowers: 4–7 mm long, purplish, whitish or pink, 4 petals, tubular, in crowded clusters
Fruit: 4 small, oval nutlets

Delicious, fragrant wild mint is a well-known, edible plant that can be eaten raw or cooked and used to flavour salads, stews, meats, jellies and sweets. Mint makes delicious, fragrant teas, cold drinks and even wine. The active medicinal ingredient, menthol, has been shown to expel gas from and ease the digestive tract—hence the after-dinner mint. Menthol may also relieve coughing and sinus congestion. **Where found:** moist to wet areas, usually near water; throughout but uncommon in the northwest.

Wild Bergamot

Monarda fistulosa

Height: up to 1 m
Leaves: 25–80 mm long, opposite, lance-shaped, hairy, toothed
Flowers: 2–3.5 cm long, pink to lavender, tubular, in round clusters, 3 cm across
Fruit: tiny, shiny nutlets

Wild bergamot's long, tubular, rose to purplish flowers attract hummingbirds, moths and a large variety of butterfly species. This showy, aromatic perennial can easily be grown from seed in gardens, thus bringing a butterfly parade to your yard. • Wild bergamot provides a spice, a potherb and a tea that tastes similar to Earl Grey. Dried leaves were traditionally burned or sprinkled on items to repel insects—rather ironic considering that the living flowers are insect magnets. **Where found:** moist to moderately dry, open sites including old fields, woodland edges and prairies; parkland and prairies.

Common Red Paintbrush

Castilleja miniata

Height: 20–60 cm
Leaves: 5–7 cm long, lance-shaped, prominently veined, 3-lobed tip
Flowers: 2–3 cm long, green with red tips, tubular, hidden by showy, scarlet bracts, in clusters
Fruit: capsules, 9–12 mm long

It is usually easy to recognize a paintbrush but difficult to say which of the 150 to 200 species you have encountered. *Castilleja* is a confusing genus with many flower shapes and colours, and its species often hybridize. • Paintbrushes join roots with nearby plants to steal nutrients, and many depend on their neighbours for sustenance. • Showy, red bracts give these flower clusters their colour. The tubular flowers are greenish with a short, broad lower lip and a long, slender upper lip that is more than half as long as the tube. **Where found:** open, well-drained sites; low elevations to subalpine; southern two-thirds of Alberta.

Butter-and-eggs

Linaria vulgaris

Height: 30–80 cm
Leaves: 2–6 cm long, oval to lance-shaped, clasping the stem
Flowers: 2–3.5 cm long, yellow with orange lip, snapdragon-like, in spikes
Fruit: rounded capsules, 8–12 mm long

Butter-and-eggs is a native of Eurasia that spreads rapidly by both hardy, creeping roots and plentiful seeds (up to 8700 per plant). The cut flowers are quite resilient and last long in the vase. • Most animals avoid this pungent and potentially toxic plant, but large pollinating insects appreciate its abundant flowers. To access nectar, insects must be strong enough to pry apart the "lips" of the snapdragon-like flowers. **Where found:** disturbed sites; parkland and prairies. **Also known as:** common toadflax.

Bracted Lousewort

Pedicularis bracteosa

Height: to 1 m
Leaves: to 15 cm long, elliptical, deeply divided, fern-like
Flowers: 1 cm long, pale yellow (may be tinged with purple), hooded, in spikes
Fruit: dry capsules, 3 mm long

Louseworts depend on special root fungi for nutrient intake and should not be transplanted or disturbed because they will not survive. • It was once thought that if cattle consumed this plant, they would become louse-ridden, hence the name. • Elephant's-head (*P. groenlandica*) grows in similar mountain habitats and has a long, dense cluster of reddish purple flowers. Each flower resembles a miniature elephant's head, with a curved trunk (the flower's upper lip) and flared ears (the flower's lower lip lobes). **Where found:** moist meadows and open forests; montane to alpine zones; mountains of western Alberta.

Twinflower

Linnaea borealis

Height: 3–10 cm, in loose mats with erect stems
Leaves: 1–2 cm long, opposite, evergreen, oval
Flowers: 3–10 cm long, pink, 5 petals, funnel-shaped, in pairs on Y-shaped stems
Fruit: dry nutlets, 2–3 mm long

This trailing, semi-woody, native evergreen forms a ground cover in partially shaded sites. The small, delicate pairs of pink bells are easily overlooked among other plants on the forest floor, but their strong, sweet perfume may draw you to them in the evening. Hooked bristles on the tiny, egg-shaped nutlets catch on the fur, feathers or clothing of passersby, which then carry these inconspicuous hitchhikers to new locations. **Where found:** moist, open or shaded sites; throughout except grasslands.

Common Bladderwort

Utricularia vulgaris

Height: floating aquatic perennial
Leaves: minute, submerged or floating, brownish green, hair-like, with tiny bladders
Flowers: 1–2 cm long, yellow, 2-lipped, on stalks that extend above the water
Fruit: tiny capsules

Like tiny, yellow violets, the flowers of this bizarre aquatic meat-eater jut from the water's surface. Most carnivorous plants trap and eat insects, but aquatic bladderworts digest everything from tiny worms to small crustaceans. Like other carnivorous plants, bladderworts are typically found in cold, acidic, nitrogen-poor environments. These plants get their nitrogen from the invertebrates they digest, so they are able to grow where others cannot survive. • Common bladderwort floats in water or creeps along muddy shores, its tiny bladders festooning the plant's roots and providing the "traps" to capture prey. **Where found:** shallow to deep water of ponds, lakes and marshes; throughout.

Northern Bedstraw

Galium boreale

Height: 20–60 cm
Leaves: 2–6 cm long, narrow, in whorls of 4
Flowers: 4–7 mm across, white, 4 petals, in crowded clusters
Fruit: nutlets, <1.5 mm across, in pairs

Bedstraws are so named because the dried stems were traditionally used to stuff mattresses. • *Galium* species are sometimes called "cleavers" because their bristled fruits "cleave" or adhere to animals and clothing, aiding in seed dispersal. • Bedstraws are related to coffee, and their tiny nutlets can be dried, roasted and ground as a coffee substitute. • Sweet-scented bedstraw (*G. triflorum*), which occurs throughout Alberta, has whorls of 6 broader, bristle-tipped leaves and nutlets covered with long, hooked bristles. **Where found:** open sites; throughout.

Harebell

Campanula rotundifolia

Height: 10–50 cm
Leaves: 1–6 cm long, narrow stem leaves, rounded basal leaves
Flowers: 2 cm long, purple-blue, 5 petals, bell-shaped, in 1–5-flowered clusters
Fruit: capsules, 5–8 mm long

From open woodlands to exposed, rocky slopes, these delicate, nodding bells bob in the breeze on thin, wiry stems. • Small openings at the base of the seed capsules close quickly in damp weather, protecting the seeds from excess moisture. On dry, windy days, the capsules swing widely in the breeze, scattering the seeds. • The species name *rotundifolia* refers to this plant's round, basal leaves. **Where found:** moist to dry, open sites; throughout.

Common Yarrow

Achillea millefolium

Height: 30–90 cm
Leaves: 5–15 cm long, feathery
Flowers: rays 5–12, white to pinkish; disc yellow; in heads 4–5 mm across, in flat-topped clusters
Fruit: flattened achenes

The fern-like leaves of this member of the sunflower family (Asteraceae) are distinctive. Yarrow is often weedy, and both native and introduced populations occur in our region. • This hardy, aromatic perennial has served for thousands of years as a fumigant, insecticide and medicine. The Greek hero Achilles, for whom the genus was named, reportedly used it to help heal his soldiers' wounds. • Yarrow is an attractive ornamental, but beware—its extensive underground stems (rhizomes) can soon invade your garden. **Where found:** dry to moist, open sites; throughout.

Pussytoes, Everlasting

Antennaria racemosa

Height: to 25 cm
Leaves: 1–5 cm long, mainly basal, slender, woolly grey below
Flowers: small, whitish heads, in clusters at stem tips
Fruit: seed-like achenes

The downy flower clusters of this plant resemble the toes of a kitten, hence the name. As the flowers dry, the down-tipped seeds parachute away on the wind. • Pussytoes are widespread across Alberta, and there are about 15 species of these hardy perennials in the province. The blossoms have a pleasant fragrance and keep their shape and colour when dried, making them an excellent choice for dried flower arrangements. **Where found:** roadsides, fields and open sites; throughout.

Heart-leaved Arnica

Arnica cordifolia

Height: 10–60 cm
Leaves: 4–10 cm long, opposite, heart-shaped, hairy
Flowers: rays 10–15 bright yellow; disc yellow; in heads 2.5–6 cm across
Fruit: hairy achenes, 6.5–8 mm long

These cheerful, yellow wildflowers were once used in love charms because of their heart-shaped leaves. The rootstocks and flowers were used in washes and poultices for treating bruises, sprains and swollen feet, but these poisonous plants should not be applied to broken skin. • This single-stemmed perennial produces seed-like fruits with tufts of white, hair-like bristles. **Where found:** mesic to dry forests and meadows; montane to alpine zones; western Alberta and Cypress Hills.

Canada Thistle

Cirsium arvense

Height: 30–150 cm
Leaves: 5–15 cm long, lance-shaped, spiny-toothed
Flowers: rays absent; disc pink-purple; in heads 1.5–2.5 cm across
Fruit: seed-like achenes

This plant was introduced to Canada from Europe in the 17th century, then expanded its range into the United States, where it acquired its common name. Today, this aggressive weed is found in virtually all croplands and pastures. Prickly thistle colonies choke out other plants and reduce crop yields. Colonies grow from deep underground runners that contain tricin, a substance that inhibits the growth of nearby plants. • These plants can be beneficial. The flowers provide a good source of pollen and nectar for honeybees, and humans can eat the shoots and roots. **Where found:** disturbed sites; throughout.

Subalpine Fleabane

Erigeron peregrinus

Height: 10–70 cm
Leaves: 1–20 cm long, highly variable, lance- to spoon-shaped
Flowers: rays numerous, pink, purplish or lavender; disc yellow; in heads 2–6 cm across
Fruit: hairy achenes

Fleabanes are easily confused with asters, but aster flowerheads usually have overlapping rows of involucral bracts with pale, parchment-like bases and green tips. Fleabanes usually have one row of slender bracts with the same texture and colour (not green) throughout. Also, fleabanes generally flower earlier and have narrower, more numerous rays. **Where found:** moist to wet, open areas; all elevations; mountains and foothills.

Great Blanketflower

Gaillardia aristata

Height: 20–70 cm
Leaves: 5–15 cm long, lance-shaped, coarsely toothed
Flowers: rays 10–18, yellow with purplish red at base; disc purplish red; in solitary heads, 3–7 cm across
Fruit: 3-sided achenes with papery scales, about 1 cm long

The flamboyant blossoms of blanketflower might be mistaken for garden escapes, and, in fact, many cultivars have been developed from this beautiful native wildflower. It is hardy, easily grown from seed and does well in dry, sunny gardens. • This perennial has hairy leaves and stems, and the seed-like fruits are densely hairy, tipped with 6 to 10 stiff, white bristles. **Where found:** dry, fairly open sites; southern half of Alberta.

Curly-cup Gumweed

Grindelia squarrosa

Height: 20–60 cm
Leaves: 1–4 cm long, oblong to lance-shaped, clasping stem
Flowers: rays bright yellow; disc yellow; in heads 2–3 cm across surrounded by sticky, backward-curving, green bracts
Fruit: ribbed, seed-like achenes with slender bristles

Curly-cup gumweed, a bushy, aromatic herb, is common along dry roadsides in late summer. This tough plant is drought resistant. • The resin-dotted leaves and flat-topped clusters of sticky flowerheads have sedative, antispasmodic and expectorant qualities, and they have been used traditionally to treat coughing, congestion, asthma and bronchitis. **Where found:** dry, open sites on plains; southern half of Alberta and along the Peace River.

Rhombic-leaved Sunflower

Helianthus pauciflorus ssp. *subrhomboideus*

Height: to 1.2 m
Leaves: to 15 cm long, opposite, diamond-shaped, surfaces rough to bristly
Flowers: rays 15–20, yellow; disc brownish purple; in heads 6–8 cm across
Fruit: slightly hairy, seed-like achenes (sunflower seeds)

This sunflower is named for its rhombic (diamond-shaped) leaves, and the genus name *Helianthus,* "sun flower," refers to the flowerheads that continually face the sun. • The Blackfoot ate sunflower seeds raw or boiled them to release the oil, which was used as a skin and hair lotion. The flowers provided a superior yellow dye, and the seeds were made into black or purple dyes. **Where found:** moist, disturbed sites; southern half of Alberta. **Also known as:** *Helianthus subrhomboideus.*

Narrow-leaved Hawkweed

Hieracium umbellatum

Height: to 1 m
Leaves: 1–8 cm long, lance-shaped, shallowly toothed
Flowers: rays numerous, yellow; disc absent; in heads 2–2.5 cm across, in flat-topped clusters
Fruit: seed-like achenes, 2–3 mm long

Loose clusters of miniature, dandelion-like flowers on long, slender stems identify this common wildflower. The showy flowerheads attract insects, but fertilization is rare, and most offspring are genetically identical to the parent plant. The fruits are cylindrical achenes with tufts of tawny hairs. • Hawkweed's milky sap contains a rubbery latex, and Native peoples chewed the leaves of these plants like gum. **Where found:** moist to wet, open sites; throughout.

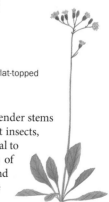

Common Blue Lettuce

Lactuca tatarica var. *pulchella*

Height: to 1 m
Leaves: 5–12 cm long, narrowly lance-shaped (grass-like), with whitish bloom
Flowers: rays blue to purplish, toothed at tip; disc absent; in heads up to 2.5 cm across
Fruit: ridged achenes, 4–7 mm long

Common blue lettuce and other *Lactuca* species may cause skin irritation or poisoning if taken internally. When collected and dried, the milky sap forms the drug known as lactucarium, also called lettuce opium because of its sedative and pain-relieving properties. Used as far back as ancient Egypt, lettuce opium was viewed as a weak, non-addictive alternative to opium. In 1898, it was introduced and standardized as a drug in the U.S. for use in lozenges and syrups for dry coughs, anxiety and other ailments. **Where found:** woods and clearings; widespread throughout. **Also known as:** *L. pulchella*; wild blue lettuce.

Oxeye Daisy

Leucanthemum vulgare

Height: 20–90 cm
Leaves: 4–15 cm long, lance- to spoon-shaped, deeply lobed, becoming smaller up the stem
Flowers: rays 15–35, white; disc yellow; in heads 2.5–5 cm across
Fruit: seed-like achenes with 10 ribs

A favourite among children, this bright white and yellow daisy was introduced from Eurasia 400 years ago and now carpets fields, ditches and abandoned lots across North America. • Despite being common weeds that compete against native plants and crops, daisies are often considered cheerful, welcome additions to gardens. • The shasta daisy (*Chrysanthemum maximum*) is a larger, more robust ornamental variety. **Where found:** open, disturbed areas; throughout. **Also known as:** *C. leucanthemum*.

Pineapple-weed

Matricaria discoidea

Height: 5–40 cm
Leaves: 1–5 cm long, divided into several narrow, thread-like segments
Flowers: rays absent; disc yellow; in cone-shaped heads, 5–9 mm across
Fruit: seed-like achenes, 2-ribbed, often 5-sided

Pineapple-weed is a close relative of wild chamomile (*M. recutita*) and gives off a similar, pineapple-like aroma when crushed. Wild chamomile has similar leaves but white ray flowers with a yellow centre, similar to oxeye daisy. These aromatic plants may be used as air fresheners, insect repellents or as a deodorizing handwash after handling fish. The young flowerheads can be steeped into a soothing tea or eaten raw in salads. • Like closely related ragweed (*Ambrosia* spp.), pineapple-weed causes an allergic reaction in some people. **Where found:** open, disturbed sites; throughout.

Arrow-leaved Coltsfoot

Petasites frigidus spp. *sagittatus*

Height: 10–50 cm
Leaves: 10–30 cm long, basal, variably arrow-shaped, rounded or deeply lobed, grey-green above, woolly below
Flowers: rays and disc white to pinkish; in heads 8 mm across, in dense, rounded clusters
Fruit: seed-like achenes, 2–3 mm long, with a tuft of white, hair-like bristles

The coltsfoots, though very different in appearance, are now considered varieties of one species, *P. frigidus*. • The salt-rich ash of coltsfoot leaves was once widely used as a salt substitute. Dried coltsfoot has been used for hundreds of years to make medicinal teas to relieve coughing and pain from respiratory illnesses. Pregnant women should not eat this plant. **Where found:** moist to wet areas; throughout including Cypress Hills, but absent from prairie regions.

Prairie Coneflower

Ratibida columnifera

Height: 30–70 cm
Leaves: to 10 cm long, hairy, pinnately divided into 5–9 linear to oblong lobes
Flowers: rays 3–7, yellow; disc greyish yellow to purplish brown, in a cone 1–4 cm high; flower heads on long stalks
Fruit: dark grey, seed-like achenes, 2 mm long

The flowers of this plant look like small hats—a ring of yellow florets forms a brim around a tall, cylindrical, brown crown. This distinctive native wildflower is a hardy choice for dry prairie gardens and is popular in habitat restoration. • Once dried, the edible cones are said to taste like corn, but they can be chewy and are best picked when young. An enjoyable tea can be brewed from the leaves. **Where found:** dry, open and disturbed sites; prairies. **Also known as:** red-spike Mexican-hat.

Marsh Ragwort

Senecio congestus

Height: 20–100 cm
Leaves: 5–15 cm long, wavy to deeply lobed edges
Flowers: rays numerous, bright yellow; disc yellow; in heads 1–2 cm across, in flat-topped clusters
Fruit: seed-like achenes tipped with fluffy, white hairs

These hairy plants form yellow rings around prairie ponds. In undisturbed sites, marsh ragwort often occurs singly or in small numbers. • Allergy sufferers beware—this plant produces huge amounts of allergenic pollen. The species name *congestus* refers to the cluster of flowerheads, though, not to congested noses! **Where found:** moist sites and disturbed areas; boreal forest, parkland and Cypress Hills. **Also known as:** woolly-mammoth plant, woolly groundsel.

201

Canada Goldenrod

Solidago canadensis

Height: 30–120 cm
Leaves: 5–10 cm long, lance-shaped, with short hairs
Flowers: rays 10–17, yellow; disc yellow; in heads 3–6 mm across,
in pyramidal clusters
Fruit: hairy, seed-like achenes

Many people blame these bold, pyramid-shaped flower clusters for causing allergies, but the real culprit is probably a less conspicuous plant such as ragweed (*Ambrosia* spp.), which shares the same habitat. Goldenrod pollen is too heavy to be carried by the wind; instead, it is carried by flying insects. • Each seed-like fruit is tipped with a parachute of white hairs. **Where found:** moist, open fields, woods and roadsides; throughout.

Perennial Sow-thistle

Sonchus arvensis

Height: 0.4–2 m
Leaves: 5–40 cm long, lance-shaped, deeply lobed, prickly edges
Flowers: rays numerous, yellow, narrow; disc absent;
in dandelion-like heads, 3–5 cm across
Fruit: achenes, 2.5–3.5 mm across

Tall perennial sow-thistle is something like a dandelion on steroids, growing taller and faster than neighbouring plants. Hardy roots and abundant seeds help it spread rapidly, outcompeting other plants for moisture, nutrients and sunlight. • The young leaves taste similar to lettuce and can be used in salads, along with the edible flowerheads. Older leaves can be cooked as a vegetable. • This plant is devoured by livestock and rabbits and is a host plant for aphids. **Where found:** disturbed sites; throughout except subalpine regions of the mountains.

Lindley's Aster

Symphyotrichum ciliolatum

Height: 20–120 cm
Leaves: 4–12 cm long, lower leaves heart-shaped, stem leaves lance-shaped
Flowers: rays 12–25, purple-blue; disc yellow; in heads 15–30 mm across
Fruit: seed-like achenes with parachute of silky hairs

These cheerful, purplish asters beautify many of our trails, clearings and roadsides. The aster family contains many different species, and Lindley's aster may be identified by the heart-shaped lower stem leaves on long stalks. • Smooth aster (*S. laeve*), found in woodlands, grasslands, ditches and coulees throughout Alberta, has dark purple flowers with yellow centres and oblong, hairless leaves that often clasp the stem. **Where found:** open, disturbed areas and forests; throughout.

Common Dandelion

Taraxacum officinale

Height: 5–50 cm
Leaves: 5–40 cm long, basal, oblong to lance-shaped deeply lobed
Flowers: rays numerous, yellow, narrow; disc absent; in solitary heads, 2–5 cm wide
Fruit: tiny achenes with white, fluffy bristles

Dandelions are probably the most widely recognized forb in our region. • This plant's vitamin-rich leaves and blossoms have been receiving positive press lately. Brought to North America from Eurasia, dandelions were cultivated as food and medicine. Young dandelion leaves and flowerheads are chock full of vitamins and minerals and make nutritious additions to salads. The roots can be ground into a caffeine-free coffee substitute or boiled to make a red dye. **Where found:** disturbed sites; throughout.

Common Goat's-beard

Tragopogon dubius

Height: 0.3–1 m
Leaves: 5–50 cm long, grass-like, clasping stem
Flowers: rays bright yellow, toothed at tip; disc absent; in heads 2.5–6.5 cm across, surrounded by long, pointed, green bracts
Fruit: seed-like achenes with feathery, parachute-like bristles

The yellow flowers of common goat's-beard may be overlooked, but the gigantic, dandelion-like seedheads are hard to miss. Each seed is attached to a downy parachute that floats on the wind, carrying it great distances. • Thick, fleshy goat's-beard roots can be eaten raw, roasted or boiled and are said to taste like parsnips. The dried, roasted roots were also traditionally used as a coffee substitute. **Where found:** open, disturbed sites; throughout.

Ostrich Fern

Matteuccia struthiopteris

Height: 0.5–1.5 m
Leaves: 0.5 cm–1.5 m long, sterile fronds 4–6, plume-like
Spore clusters: on shorter, fertile fronds 20–60 cm long, stiff, dark brown at maturity

Ostrich fern, named for its plume-like fronds, is just one representative of the dozens of fern species that occur in Alberta. • The young, coiled fronds, known as "fiddleheads," are an excellent wild edible and are also sold commercially. They taste a bit like asparagus and are rich in vitamins A and C. When harvesting, no more than 3 tops per plant should be taken because overpicking depletes the rhizome's energy reserves and kills the plant. **Where found:** wet to moist forests, wetlands, riparian areas and roadsides; boreal forest.

Common Horsetail

Equisetum arvense

Height: up to 50 cm
Leaves: small, scale-like
Spore clusters: blue-tipped cones

Most people are familiar with this plant's sterile "horse tail" stems that have many whorls of slender branches, but common horsetail also sprouts unbranched, fertile stems that are often overlooked. These smaller, brownish shoots have blunt cones at their tips and look like slender mushrooms. • Next time you come across a horsetail, feel the stem. Silica crystals cause the rough texture and strengthen the plant. • Nine horsetail species are found in Alberta. **Where found:** moist to wet forests, wetlands and disturbed sites; throughout.

Common Cattail

Typha latifolia

Height: up to 3 m
Leaves: up to 3 m long, up to 2 cm wide, linear
Flowers: tiny, yellowish green, in dense spikes, 8–14 cm long
Fruit: tiny achenes in a fuzzy, brown spike (cattail)

Cattails rim wetlands and line lakeshores and ditches across North America, providing cover for many animals. They are critical for supporting least bitterns, marsh wrens and other wetland birds. • Cattails grow from long rhizomes that were traditionally eaten fresh in spring. Later in the season, when the rhizomes became bitter, they were peeled and roasted, or dried and ground into flour. • Traditionally, the freshly dried seedheads were used to bandage burns and promote healing. **Where found:** shallow, open water; throughout.

Marsh Reedgrass, Bluejoint

Calamagrostis canadensis

Height: 0.6–1.2 m
Leaves: 15–30 cm long, 4–10 mm wide, numerous, drooping
Flowers: spikelets, 2–6 mm long, in a narrow, drooping panicle, 10–20 cm long
Fruit: caryopsis

Marsh reedgrass is an ubiquitous and ecologically important grass, and is common throughout North America. This tussock-forming plant often grows together with sedges in wet meadows. It is an important food for bison and elk, and is sometimes used as forage for livestock. Marsh reedgrass is under research for forage and reclamation purposes because it grows in a wide range of soil conditions and habitats and has a high genetic diversity. **Where found:** moist woods, meadows, lakeshores and wetlands; throughout except dry prairies.

Foxtail Barley

Hordeum jubatum

Height: 30–60 cm
Leaves: 5–15 cm long, 2–9 mm wide, flat, bluish green, rough surface
Flowers: 5–10 cm long, yellow to bronze, in graceful, nodding spikes
Fruit: caryopsis

Fuzzy foxtail barley is a native perennial that grows in bunches from shallow roots. It prefers moist, fertile soils but will thrive under extreme environmental conditions such as drought, flooding or salinity. • The barbed awns are carried away by the wind and catch onto clothing or hook onto passing animals, then work their way inward. The awns can cause serious injury if lodged in the eyes, nose or mouth of dogs or livestock. **Where found:** disturbed sites including sloughs, roadsides and stream edges; throughout.

Wire Rush

Juncus balticus

Height: 20–60 cm tall
Leaves: brown sheaths, 8–15 cm long, at stem base
Flowers: tiny, purplish brown flower clusters seem to grow from 1 side of stem
Fruit: egg-shaped capsules, about 3 mm long

Alberta has almost 25 species of *Juncus* rushes, mostly with stems that are round in cross-section and solid (not hollow like grasses). Wire rush is the most common rush in our province and often grows in dense rows, like the teeth of a large comb. Rushes are extremely important ecologically because they colonize open areas. **Where found:** wetlands, moist to wet openings and forest edges; throughout.

Water Sedge

Carex aquatilis

Height: up to 1 m
Leaves: grass-like, 3–7 mm wide, bluish green
Flowers: terminal spikes of tiny male flowers; lower spikes of tiny female flowers
Fruit: brownish green, egg-shaped achenes, 2–4 mm long

Alberta has more than 120 sedge species, mostly with stems that are triangular in cross-section and solid (not hollow like grasses). Remember that "sedges have edges, and rushes are round." Alberta's sedges range from tall plants (like this one) that can grow to more than 1 m tall, to tiny species no more than 15 cm tall. They occupy terrestrial and aquatic habitats from sea level to alpine. • Sedges provide important habitat and food for aquatic wildlife. **Where found:** wetlands and lakeshores; throughout.

GLOSSARY

A

achene: a seed-like fruit, e.g., sunflower seed

algae: simple photosynthetic aquatic plants lacking true stems, roots, leaves and flowers, and ranging in size from single-celled forms to giant kelp

altricial: animals that are helpless at birth or hatching

annual: a plant that lives for only one year or growing season

aquatic: water frequenting

arboreal: tree frequenting

arthropod: an invertebrate with a hard, segmented exoskeleton and paired, jointed legs (e.g., insects, spiders, crustaceans)

autotrophic: an organism that is able to produce its own food, e.g., by photosynthesis

awn: a stiff, bristle-like projection, especially from the seed of a grass or grain

axil: the point at which a leaf attaches to a stem

B

barbels: fleshy, whisker-like appendages found on some fish

basal leaf: a leaf arising from the base of a plant

benthic: living at or near the bottom of a sea or lake

berry: a fleshy fruit, usually with numerous seeds

bract: a leaf-like structure arising from the base of a flower or inflorescence

bracteole: a small bract borne on a leaf stalk

brood parasite: a bird that parasitizes other bird's nests by laying its eggs and then abandoning them for the parasitized birds to raise, e.g., brown-headed cowbird

bulb: a fleshy underground organ with overlapping, swollen scales, e.g., onion

C

calcareous: soil that has a high level of calcium carbonate, making it very alkaline

calyx: a collective term for the sepals of a flower

cambium: inner layers of tissue that transport nutrients up and down a plant stalk or trunk

canopy: the fairly continuous cover provided by the branches and leaves of adjacent trees

capsule: a dry fruit that splits open to release seeds

carapace: a protective bony shell (e.g., of a turtle) or exoskeleton (e.g., of beetles)

carnivorous: feeding primarily on meat

carrion: decomposing animal matter or carcass

catkin: a spike of small flowers

chelipeds: the clawed first pair of legs, e.g., on a crab

compound leaf: a leaf separated into 2 or more divisions called leaflets

cone: the fruit produced by a coniferous plant, composed of overlapping scales around a central axis

coniferous: cone-bearing; seed (female) and pollen (male) cones are borne on the same tree in different locations.

corm: a swollen underground stem base used by some plants as an organ of propagation; resembles a bulb

crepuscular: active primarily at dusk and dawn

cryptic colouration: a colouration pattern designed to conceal an animal

D

deciduous: a tree whose leaves turn colour and shed annually

defoliate: to drop leaves

disc flower: a small flower in the centre, or disc, of a composite flower (e.g., aster, daisy or sunflower)

diurnal: active primarily during the day

dorsal: the top or back

drupe: a fleshy fruit with a stony pit, e.g., peach, cherry

E

echolocation: navigation by rebounding sound waves off objects to target or avoid them

ecological niche: an ecological role filled by a species

ecoregion: a geographical region distinguished by its geology, climate, biodiversity, elevation and soil composition

ectoparasite: a skin parasite

ectotherm: an animal that regulates its body temperature behaviourally from external sources of heat, i.e., from the sun

endotherm: an animal that regulates its body temperature internally

estivate: a state of inactivity and a slowing of the metabolism to permit survival in extended periods of high temperatures and inadequate water supply

eutrophic: a nutrient-rich body of water with an abundance of algae and a low level of dissolved oxygen

evergreen: having green leaves through winter; not deciduous

exoskeleton: a hard outer encasement that provides protection and points of attachment for muscles

F

flight membrane: a membrane between the fore and hind limbs of bats and some squirrels that allows these animals to glide through the air

follicle: the structure in the skin from which hair or feathers grow; a dry fruit that splits open along a single line on one side when ripe; a cocoon

food web: the elaborate, interconnected feeding relationships of living organisms in an ecosystem

forb: a broad-leaved plant that lacks a permanent woody stem and loses its aboveground growth each year; may be annual, biennial or perennial

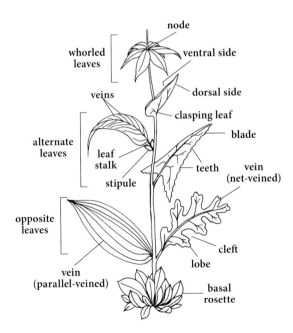

G

gillrakers: long, thin fleshy projections that protect delicate gill tissue from particles in the water

graminoid: a herbaceous plant with narrow leaves growing from the base; includes grasses and grass-like plants such as sedges and rushes

H

habitat: the physical area in which an organism lives

hawking: feeding behaviour in which a bird leaves a perch, snatches its prey in midair and returns to the perch

haw: the small, berry-like fruit of a hawthorn

herbivorous: feeding primarily on vegetation

hibernaculum: a shelter in which an animal, usually a mammal, reptile or insect, chooses to hibernate

hibernation: a state of decreased metabolism and body temperature and slowed heart and respiratory rates to permit survival during long periods of cold temperature and diminished food supply

hip: the berry-like fruit of some plants in the rose family (Rosaceae)

hybrid: the offspring from a cross between parents belonging to different varieties or subspecies, and sometimes between different subspecies or genera

I

incubate: to keep eggs at relatively constant temperature until they hatch

inflorescence: a cluster of flowers on a stalk; may be arranged as a spike, raceme, head, panicle, etc.

insectivorous: feeding primarily on insects

invertebrate: any animal lacking a backbone, e.g., worms, slugs, crayfish, shrimp

involucral bract: one of several bracts that form a whorl below a flower or flower cluster

K

key: a winged fruit, usually of an ash or maple tree; also called a "samara"

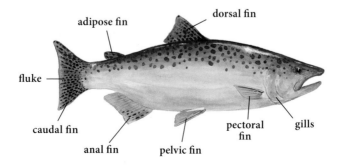

L

larva (pl. larvae): the immature form of an animal that differs from the adult

leaflet: a division of a compound leaf

lenticel: a slightly raised portion of bark where the cells are packed more loosely, allowing for gas exchange with the atmosphere

lobate: having each toe individually webbed

lobe: a projecting part of a leaf or flower, usually rounded

M

mesic: a habitat that is neither very dry nor very wet and has average moisture conditions for a given climate

metabolic rate: the rate of chemical processes in an organism

metamorphosis: the developmental transformation of an animal from a larval stage to a sexually mature adult stage

midden: the pile of cone scales found on territories of tree squirrels, usually under a favourite tree

moult: when an animal sheds old feathers, fur or skin in order to replace them with new growth

montane: the ecological zone located below the subalpine; montane regions generally have cooler temperatures than adjacent lowland regions

myccorhizal fungi/myccorhizae: fungi that has a mutually beneficial relationship with the roots of some seed plants

N

neotropical migrant: a bird that nests in North America but overwinters in the New World tropics

nocturnal: active primarily at night

node: a slightly enlarged section of a stem where leaves or branches originate

nutlet: a small, hard, single-seeded fruit that remains closed

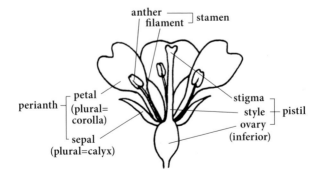

O

omnivorous: feeding on both plants and animals
ovoid: egg-shaped

P

palmate: having leaflets, lobes or veins arranged around a single point, like the fingers on a hand (e.g., maple leaf)
pappus: the modified calyx of composite flowers (e.g., asters or daisies), consisting of awns, scales or bristles at the apex of the achene
parasite: a relationship between two species in which one benefits at the expense of the other
patagium: the skin that forms a flight membrane, e.g., in bats and flying squirrels
pelage: the fur or hair of mammals
perennial: a plant that lives for several years
petal: a member of the inside ring of modified flower leaves, usually brightly coloured or white
petiole: a leaf stalk
phenology: stages of growth as influenced by climate
photosynthesis: the conversion of CO_2 and water into sugars via the energy of the sun
pioneer species: a plant species that is capable of colonizing an otherwise unvegetated area; one of the first species (plant or animal) to take hold in a disturbed area
piscivorous: feeding on fish
pishing: a noise made to attract birds
pistil: the female organ of a flower, usually consisting of an ovary, style and stigma
plastic species: a species that can adapt to a wide range of conditions
plastron: the lower part of a turtle or tortoise shell
poikilothermic: having a body temperature that is the same as the external environment and varying with it
pollen: the tiny grains produced in the anthers and which contain the male reproductive cells
pollen cone: a male cone that produces pollen
polyandry: a mating strategy in which one female mates with several males
pome: a fruit with a core, e.g., apple
precocial: animals that are active at birth or hatching
prehensile: able to grasp
proboscis: the elongated tubular and flexible mouthpart of many insects

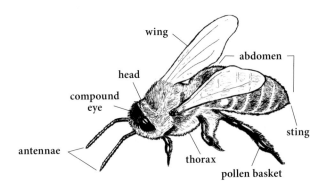

R

ray flower: in a composite flower (e.g., aster, daisy or sunflower), the strap-like outer florets that resemble petals

redd: spawing nest for fish

rhizome: a horizontal underground stem

rictal bristles: the hair-like feathers found around the mouths of some birds

riparian: on the bank of a river or other watercourse

rookery: a colony of nests

runner: a slender stolon or prostrate stem that roots at the nodes or the tip

S

samara: a dry, winged fruit, usually of a maple or ash, with usually only a single seed; also called a "key"

salmonid: a member of the Salmonidae family of fishes; includes trout, char, salmon, whitefish and grayling

schizocarp: a dry fruit that splits into two or more parts at maturity, each part with a single seed

scutes: the individual plates on a turtle's shell

seed cone: a female cone that produces seeds

sepal: the outer, usually green, leaf-like structures that protect the flower bud and are located at the base of an open flower

silicle: a fruit of the mustard family (Brassicaceae) that is two-celled and usually short, wide and often flat

silique: a long, thin fruit with many seeds; characteristic of some members of the mustard family (Brassicaceae)

sorus (pl. sori): a collection of spore-producing structures on the underside of a fern frond

spadix: a fleshy spike made up of many small flowers

spathe: the leaf-like sheath that surrounds a spadix

spur: a pointed projection

stamen: the pollen-bearing organ of a flower

stigma: in a flower, a receptive tip that receives pollen

stolon: a long branch or stem that runs along the ground and often propagates more plants

subnivean: below the surface of the snow

substrate: the surface on which an organism grows; the material that makes up a streambed (e.g., sand or gravel)

suckering: a method of tree and shrub reproduction in which shoots arise from an underground

syrinx: a bird's vocal organ

T

taproot: the main, large root of a plant from which smaller roots arise, e.g., carrot

tendril: a slender, clasping or twining outgrowth from a stem or leaf

tepal: a term used for sepals and petals when there is no clear distinction between the two

terrestrial: land frequenting

torpor: a state of physical inactivity

tragus: a prominent structure of the outer ear of a bat

tubular flower: a type of flower with all or some of the petals fused at the base

tundra: an high-latitude ecological zone at the northernmost limit of plant growth, where plants are reduced to shrubby or mat-like forms

tympanum: eardrum; the hearing organ of a frog

U

ungulate: a hoofed animal

V

ventral: of or on the abdomen (belly)

vermiculations: wavy-patterned markings

vertebrate: an animal with a backbone

vibrissae: bristle-like feathers around the beak of a bird that aid in catching insects

W

whorl: a circle of leaves or flowers around a stem

woolly: bearing long or matted hairs

SELECT REFERENCES

Acorn, John. 1993. *Butterflies of Alberta*. Lone Pine Publishing, Edmonton.

Acorn, John, and Chris Fisher. 1998. *Birds of Alberta*. Lone Pine Publishing, Edmonton.

Acorn, John, and Ian Sheldon. 2000. *Bugs of Alberta*. Lone Pine Publishing, Edmonton.

Bird, C.D., G.J. Hilchie, N.G. Kondla, E.M. Pike, and F.A.H. Sperling. 1995. *Butterflies of Alberta*. Provincial Museum of Alberta, Edmonton.

CARCNET: Canadian Amphibian and Reptile Conservation Network. www.carcnet.ca/english/index.html. Accessed Nov–Dec 2008.

Pattie, Don, and Chris Fisher. 1999. *Mammals of Alberta*. Lone Pine Publishing, Edmonton.

Joynt, Amanda, and Michael Sullivan. 2003. *Fish of Alberta*. Lone Pine Publishing, Edmonton.

Russell, Anthony P., and Aaron M. Bauer. 2001. *The Amphibians and Reptiles of Alberta*. 2nd ed. University of Calgary Press, Calgary.

Sibley, David Allen. 2000. *National Audubon Society: The Sibley Guide to Birds of North America*. Alfred A. Knopf, New York.

Sullivan, Michael G., David L. Probst, and William R. Gould. 2009. *Fish of the Rockies*. Lone Pine Publishing, Edmonton.

Wilson, Don E., and Sue Ruff, eds. 1999. *The Smithsonian Book of North American Mammals*. University of British Columbia Press, Vancouver/Toronto. In association with the Smithsonian Institution and the American Society of Mammalogists.

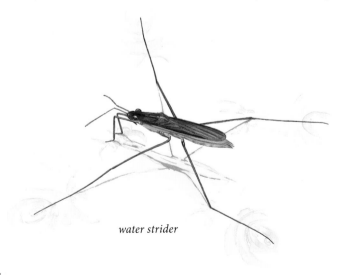

water strider

INDEX

Names and page numbers in **boldface** type refer to primary species.

ABOUT THE AUTHORS

Krista Kagume is a nature writer who has travelled across North America, working as a freelance journalist, cycling-tour guide and deckhand on a commercial fishing vessel. After earning her degree in conservation biology, Krista focused on environmental research and communications. Her work in Alberta and the Northwest Territories has included research on tiny tundra plants, organic farming, breeding birds and one grizzly bear immobilization. She currently lives in a small town outside Edmonton with her adventurous family, who enjoy the outdoors and encourage others to appreciate nature.

Gregory Kennedy has been an active naturalist since he was very young. He is the author of many books on natural history and has also produced film and television shows on environmental issues and indigenous concerns in Southeast Asia, New Guinea, South and Central America, the High Arctic and elsewhere. He has also been involved in numerous research projects around the world ranging from studies in the upper canopy of tropical and temperate rainforests to deepwater marine investigations.